Grieving

FOR

DUMMIES®

Grieving For Dummies®

Cheat Sheet

The Two Fundamental Facts of Grieving

If you're grieving the loss of a loved one, you need to remember these two things as you go through your grieving process:

- ✔ You're not going crazy — losing a loved one just hurts that much!
- ✔ Your grief will end in time.

The Three Basic Tasks of Grieving

Here are the three fundamental tasks of grieving the loss of a loved one:

1. Acknowledge the loss.
2. Experience the grief that the loss produces.
3. Incorporate the loss into the rest of your life.

The Mourner's Bill of Rights

As someone grieving a profound loss, remember that you have the following rights when mourning your loved one:

- ✔ I have the right to grieve the death of my loved one.
- ✔ I have the right to grieve the death on my own time.
- ✔ I have the right to my feelings and upsurges of sorrow.
- ✔ I have the right to grieve even when others think I should be over it.
- ✔ I have the right to remember and talk about my lost loved one at any time.
- ✔ I have the right to demonstrate my feelings of grief in my own way.
- ✔ I have the right to repeat a stage of grieving as many times as I need to.
- ✔ I have the right to phase in and out of a particular stage of grieving as often as I need to.
- ✔ I have the right to attach my own meanings to the loss.
- ✔ I have the right to expect you to empathize with my grieving because some day you'll be in my place.

For Dummies: Bestselling Book Series for Beginners

Grieving For Dummies®

Cheat Sheet

Helping Someone Who's Grieving

If you really want to support a friend or family member in grieving the loss of a loved one, stick to these dos and don'ts:

- Do listen to him as openly as you can.
- Do speak to him from your heart.
- Do tell him how sorry you are.
- Do remind him regularly that he's not going crazy and that one day this pain will end.
- Don't try to take his grief away.
- Don't try to comfort him with platitudes about grief.
- Don't try to hurry his grieving process along to suit your timetable.
- Don't try to persuade him to make changes before he's ready to make them.
- Don't judge him and his ups and downs too harshly.
- Don't give up on him and your friendship.

Typical Responses to a Profound Loss

When you suffer the loss of a loved one, common responses include feeling . . .

- Sorrowful and inconsolable
- Hopeless and despondent
- Angry and frustrated
- Unable to focus and concentrate
- Fearful and withdrawn
- Remorseful and sorry
- Guilty and responsible
- Withdrawn and alienated
- Depressed and lethargic
- Impulsive and highly emotional
- Impassive and unemotional

For Dummies: Bestselling Book Series for Beginners

Grieving FOR DUMMIES®

by Greg Harvey, PhD

Foreword by Carol Schlesinger, LCSW

Wiley Publishing, Inc.

Grieving For Dummies®

Published by
Wiley Publishing, Inc.
111 River St.
Hoboken, NJ 07030-5774
www.wiley.com

WILEY

About the Author

Greg Harvey, the author of a slew of *For Dummies* books running the gamut from *Excel For Dummies* to *The Origins of Tolkien's Middle-Earth For Dummies,* has had a long career of teaching business people the use of IBM PC, Windows, and Macintosh software application programs. From 1983 to 1988, he conducted hands-on computer software training for corporate business users with a variety of training companies. From 1988 to 1992, he taught university classes in Lotus 1-2-3 and Introduction to Database Management Technology (using dBASE) in the Department of Information Systems at Golden Gate University in San Francisco.

In 2000, after starting graduate school, Greg began volunteering at Maitri, a 15-bed AIDS patient care facility located in San Francisco, California. As part of the Masters program, he took courses in Death and Dying and as part of his Doctorate program did his comprehensive exams in Death and Dying in Western and Eastern culture and religion. In 2003, he also received volunteer and group facilitator training at the Center for Attitudinal Healing in Sausalito, California, and began volunteering for their Home and Hospital Visitor program. In 2006, he received his PhD in Comparative Philosophy and Religion with a concentration on Asian Studies from the California Institute of Integral Studies in San Francisco, California.

Greg is currently a member of the American Academy of Bereavement, from which he received Bereavement Facilitator training, and the Association for Death Education and Counseling (ADEC). He is also a patient care volunteer for Maitri AIDS Hospice in San Francisco, Sutter VNA and Hospice in Santa Rosa and a patient care, bereavement, and vigil volunteer at Hospice By The Bay in Marin County and San Francisco.

Dedication

"For such is the way of it: to find and lose, as it seems to those whose boat is on the running stream."

—Legolas to Gimli upon saying farewell to Lothlórien: *The Fellowship of the Ring* by J.R.R. Tolkien

This book is written especially for my life partner, Christopher Aiken, who continually inspires me to live each moment fully.

This book is dedicated to all the people and their families whom I've been privileged to support as a volunteer (and who always to teach me so much about life and love), along with the following fine and outstanding individuals: Helen Rose, Jerry and Jo Ann, Mike and Linda, Susan Dolder, Tara, Shandy, Maggie, Kimma, and Rudy, Carol, Diane, Hilda, Judith, Lynne, Penni, and Sharon.

It's also dedicated to the memory of the following loved ones — both my own and those of many folks who supported this project — lost to us in this life but still found very much alive in our hearts:

Shane W. Gearing, Kenneth H. Harvey, M. Faye Harvey, Clyde B. Harvey, Olive Harvey, Charles (Pop) Pounds, Gertrude Pounds, Walter Harvey, Cornellia Harvey, Herschel Harvey, Edna Harvey, Paul Harvey, Lenora M. Harvey, Fern Grosvernor, Otis Grosvernor, Charles (Jr.) Pounds, Karen Stewardson, Penny, Juno, Nicky, Joshua, Chauncey, Ginger, Kelly, Seung Sahn Nim, Larry Peterson, Philip L. Manly, Hans, George H. Feltman, Mary Catherine Campbell, Margaret Rose O'Neil, Amada Lujan Rubio, Maximo G. Rubio, Marilyn Schlesinger, Dayton Schlesinger, Merlin, Pootey, Sophie, Pokey, Lucky, Scott Dorffman, Vernice Downing, Steve Durkee, Doreen Querido, and Anne Smith.

Author's Acknowledgments

I am deeply indebted to the many folks who helped me complete this project through a combination of inspiration and support as well as a sharing of their insights and experience on death and grieving.

At Wiley Publishing, special thanks to Diane Steele, Grace Davis, Joyce Pepple, Lindsay Sandman Lefevere, Mike Baker, Tim Gallan, Katie Feltman, Elizabeth Rea, and Jennifer Theriot.

At Hospice By The Bay, very special thanks to Mary Taverna, Cheryl Wilkins, Kay McArthur, Ann Bednarczyk, Kathleen Carroll, and Carol Schlesinger.

At the International Institute of Attitudinal Healing, special thanks to Gerald Jampolsky, Jennifer Andrews, Trish Ellis, and Jimmy Peté.

At the American Academy of Bereavement, special thanks to my Bereavement Facilitator trainers, Jackson Rainer, Douglas Gross, Deidre Felton, and Marily Gryte.

In addition, special thanks to all the following people who contributed so much valuable feedback and support for this project: Melinda Bryant, Lynda Smith, Pam Tolbert, Shannon Taylor, Sharon Parr Taylor, Dr. Betty Carmack, Rev. and Dr. Gina Rose Halpern.

Publisher's Acknowledgments

We're proud of this book; please send us your comments through our Dummies online registration form located at www.dummies.com/register/.

Some of the people who helped bring this book to market include the following:

Acquisitions, Editorial, and Media Development

Senior Project Editor: Tim Gallan

Acquisitions Editor: Lindsay Sandman Lefevere

Senior Copy Editor: Elizabeth Rea

Technical Editor: Carol Schlesinger, LCSW

Editorial Manager: Christine Meloy Beck

Editorial Assistants: Erin Calligan Mooney, Joe Niesen, David Lutton, Leeann Harney

Cover Photo: © Ray Kachatorian/ The Image Bank/Getty Images

Cartoons: Rich Tennant (www.the5thwave.com)

Composition Services

Project Coordinator: Jennifer Theriot

Layout and Graphics: Claudia Bell, Carl Byers, Joyce Haughey, Stephanie D. Jumper

Anniversary Logo Design: Richard Pacifico

Proofreaders: Aptara, Todd Lothery

Indexer: Aptara

Publishing and Editorial for Consumer Dummies

Diane Graves Steele, Vice President and Publisher, Consumer Dummies

Joyce Pepple, Acquisitions Director, Consumer Dummies

Kristin A. Cocks, Product Development Director, Consumer Dummies

Michael Spring, Vice President and Publisher, Travel

Kelly Regan, Editorial Director, Travel

Publishing for Technology Dummies

Andy Cummings, Vice President and Publisher, Dummies Technology/General User

Composition Services

Gerry Fahey, Vice President of Production Services

Debbie Stailey, Director of Composition Services

Contents at a Glance

Table of Contents

Foreword

*H*ere you are holding this book, so maybe you're not a dummy after all: What you're starting to realize is that life involves loss. Perhaps you've experienced the death of a loved one, or someone you love has and you want to help. Now what?

Different parts of the world look at this unsettling fact, well, in lots of different ways. But one thing is sure: Loss is here to stay as long as you stick around for this wild ride we call life. So one of the things that is real too is this stuff called grief. Though this fact is far from universally acknowledged, I'm here to tell you that grief is a natural, universal response to loss. You may be holding this book because you're finding it harder than usual to live your life, maybe even feeling like you're going a little (or a lot) crazy. All these other folks are walking around like nothing big has happened, and here you are maybe thinking something really big has happened and you don't know what to do with all the yuck you're feeling — the numbness, shock, overwhelming rage, waves of sobbing, relief, disbelief. Maybe you're not even sure if you can go on or, on a really bad day, whether you even want to. It's *normal!*

As Greg says, illness, accidents, incidents of violence, dying, and death aren't as cool to talk about around the water cooler happy hour as the Super Bowl, *24, American Idol,* stock market ups and downs, the latest electronics, and so forth. Let's face it: Loss and grief just aren't sexy. As a matter of fact, they're taboo, the old clichéd elephant in the room, and there isn't much opportunity for someone like you to learn what to do when you lose someone (or when you want to help someone else who's suffered a loss). You may feel it's like an earthquake in your life, and not only don't you know what to do, you feel ashamed and wonder what's wrong with you if you can't suck it up, get over it, and move on.

Hang in there. This grief thing is doable, and here are a few tips right off: Take it one day at a time (or one hour or one minute or one second), be gentle with yourself by cutting yourself some slack, take as good care of yourself as you can (eat, rest, take a walk around the block, get some respite from the grief), and accept that if ever in your life you need support, it's around a profound loss, so find the strength to ask for some. The Buddha once said that one could travel all around the world and never find anyone more worthy of compassion than oneself. Yeah, that means even you. You'll discover that grief can affect us in a global way: It has emotional, physical, spiritual, mental, and behavioral aspects. You'll also discover that grieving is a process, it takes time, and, oh dear, no one can fix it. You do need to go through it. And no one can tell you how long that will take. One of the most common things I hear is "This is hard and painful and I don't like it; so *when* am I going to feel better?" I wish I could say that you'll feel better on July 2 at 3:30 in the afternoon. Unfortunately, the real answer is that grieving is a nonlinear process and will take however long it takes. The grief is going to shift and get easier, even though right now that seems impossible. This book has lots of information that will help you make sense of this rollercoaster ride you're on.

In our culture, more than a few of us are uncomfortable around grieving people because they remind us that we're mortal, that things change, that loss is inevitable; it might even be catching, and we don't want to believe it can happen to us. For you wonderful people who still want to help someone you love through their grief and feel helpless because you don't know what to do or say, you're not alone. Greg has lots of good ideas and also alerts us to some common clichés that are less than helpful. The best suggestions I can offer are to relax, know you can't fix it, and be the best nonjudgmental listener you can be. We often underestimate the gift of a loving presence: our own.

Loss is a powerful teacher. The more you can be present with what is going on with you, the better off you'll be in the long run. We have a great capacity to learn and grow, to love and be kind. So go ahead, get as comfortable as you can, perhaps put your feet up, and start to read this thoughtful and caring book. May you find comfort and peace.

—Carol Schlesinger, LCSW, Bereavement Services Coordinator

Introduction

*U*nfortunately, grieving the loss of a loved one isn't an optional human activity. Only those who never get the opportunity to love or who die too young are spared this uniquely painful experience. Yet despite its widespread nature, grieving is far from understood and very far from being appreciated in any way in modern society.

For the most part, grieving probably makes us so uncomfortable because it's a concrete reminder of our human mortality and the great fear of death. However, that isn't the sole reason that grieving is so misunderstood that it's barely tolerated and completely underrated; the other big reason for undervaluing grief is that loss of any kind runs completely counter to the major driving force of modern life, which is the idea of gain. People are driven to always be gaining something, whether it's an increase of material possessions, power, and control, or knowledge and skill.

In this book, I attempt to counter this significantly shortsighted attitude toward grieving by presenting it neither as the most tragic process nor the most uplifting one that you can undergo in life. Rather, I see grieving as being somewhere right in the middle of these two extremes.

On the one hand, grieving is truly a tremendously difficult and trying process; it's one that seems to have the power to crush people with its overwhelming emotions. On the other hand, however, grieving is a tremendously transformative process; it's one that seems to have the power to teach people more about appreciating love than they ever thought was possible in life.

My sincere wish is that this little book on grieving is able to shed light on what, up to now, you may have considered a totally mysterious and foreboding process. In the last analysis, grieving is nothing more or less than finding the way that you can come to grips with and abide the permanent separation of a loved one. And in taking this solemn and sacred journey, it's my great hope that you come to a deeper appreciation of the love you shared and, instead of seeing that love as forever lost, you come to an understanding that enables you to keep that love alive in your life all the rest of your days.

About This Book

This book is comprehensive in the sense that it addresses all types of profound loss — specifically defined as the loss of a loved one that results in extended and serious grieving. Therefore, the book doesn't address the grief that comes from suffering any other kinds of loss such as losing your home as a result of some sort of disaster, losing your job, or breaking up with a lover (all of which are traumatic in various ways and produce their own levels of grief).

With one exception, profound loss involves the death of the loved one as the catalyst for the grief and the cause of your grieving. The sole exception is divorce, in which you lose a spouse and grieve the loss without the trauma of your partner's death.

In this book, I approach the process of grieving the loss of a loved one from the following perspectives:

- ✔ Grieving is a natural human response to profound loss — it isn't some sort of mental disorder or other malady that requires curing.
- ✔ People grieve in their own highly individual ways on their own personal timetables.
- ✔ In most cases, grieving does not require any kind of medical intervention, although it can benefit from support from family and friends as well as professional grief counselors and support groups.
- ✔ Grieving can be facilitated through a combination of efforts on the part of the person suffering the loss and outside support.
- ✔ Grieving comes to an end when the person suffering the loss is able to make sense of the loss and incorporate it into the rest of his life.

Foolish Assumptions

This book is written specifically for two kinds of people: those who are in the midst of grieving the loss of a loved one and those who, as close friends, want to support these people in their grieving.

If you're grieving a loss of a loved one, I'll bet some or all of the following assumptions apply to you in your present situation:

- ✔ Your emotions are very volatile and all over the place.
- ✔ You feel pretty alone and hopeless during the worst times.

✔ You're worried that all this emotional upheaval will be more than you can handle.

✔ You're concerned that you'll never see the end of this emotional upheaval.

If you're supporting a close friend who's grieving, I'd venture that some or all of these assumptions apply to you:

✔ You very much want to help your bereaved friend but are very uncertain what you can do in this situation to help.

✔ You're not all that comfortable with death and aren't sure if your discomfort will hinder or prevent you from being an effective source of support.

✔ You're unsure how best to approach someone who's grieving, and you're afraid of saying the wrong thing.

✔ Your experience with grieving your own profound losses is fairly limited or nonexistent.

If you find that some or most (or even all) of my foolish assumptions apply to you as the person grieving or a supporting friend, then I'm sure that you'll find some very helpful information and advice in the chapters of this book. These are the very conjectures that I address throughout *Grieving For Dummies*.

What You're Not to Read

If you're looking for just need-to-know information and want to skip a few text that isn't essential, you can easily ignore any sidebars (the gray shaded boxes) and paragraphs tagged by the Technical Stuff icon. Sidebars contain tangents and anecdotes that aren't germane to the main discussion, and Technical Stuff paragraphs present minutia that not everyone is going to be interested in.

Conventions Used in This Book

The following conventions are religiously followed throughout the text in the hopes that they make the text easier to decipher:

✔ The masculine singular pronoun in all its forms (he, his, and him) is used throughout the text when talking about people in general. (I hate playing the he/she pronoun game.)

✔ Web addresses appear in `monofont`.

✔ New terms appear in *italic* type when first introduced in the text.

✔ Numbered steps and the main parts of bulleted items appear in **boldface** type.

How This Book Is Organized

You can use *Grieving For Dummies* in one of two ways: Pick and choose the topics that look like they pertain to your particular situation and will be of the most help, or read the book from start to finish.

Assuming that you're not all that interested in the subject of grieving and that your time and energy are limited, I suggest that you go with the pick-and-choose method. To help you more quickly locate the topics of interest to you, I summarize the contents of the book's five parts in the following sections.

Part I: Contemplating Grief

Part I contains the nitty-gritty on loss and grief. Chapter 1 introduces the relationship between loss and grief and the factors in modern life that make grieving a little more difficult than it has to be. Chapter 2 presents an investigation on how the manner of death impacts the grieving process. Chapters 3 through 6 and Chapters 8 and 9 cover particular types of losses: parents, spouses and partners, siblings, children, friends, and pets. Chapter 7 deals with the very special topic of how children typically deal with profound loss and how best to support them through their grieving.

Part II: Experiencing Grief

Part II contains practical information on how to deal with the emotional upheaval that grieving tends to bring. Chapter 10 is the grieving person's first-aid kit for dealing with the emotional upsurges and other problems during the initial, acute phase of grieving. Chapter 13, on the other hand, is the first-aid kit for those supporting a grieving friend; it's full of advice on what you can do to help and how to avoid hindering this process at all cost.

Chapter 11 investigates the common stages of grieving as they've been defined by various top-notch experts working in the field of human bereavement. Chapter 12 then deals with the subject of complicated or problematic grieving by investigating the factors that indicate your grieving process is either temporarily stuck in a particular stage or is off track and in some real trouble.

Part III: Healing Grief

Part III contains more practical information about the grieving process and how you can help it along. Chapter 14 takes a long look at ways that you can fully and freely express and release your feelings of grief. Chapter 15 then looks at the physical aspects of grief with an eye toward releasing some of the frustration and sorrow through a wide array of different physical activities. Chapter 16 examines challenges that holidays and anniversaries present to you after suffering the death of a loved one; it contains suggestions on strategies to adopt to help you survive these special and now particularly painful days.

Part IV: Appreciating Grief

Part IV looks at the end of the grieving process and the factors that may help bring it to a successful close. Chapter 17 examines the spiritual side of grief by investigating the ways that major religious and cultural traditions assign meaning to death. Chapter 18 then investigates the vital topic of giving meaning to the loss and becoming reconciled to it so that you can successfully incorporate it into the rest of your life. Chapter 19 concludes this part on appreciating grief with an examination of the many ways that you can commemorate the one you've lost and grieved so that you can keep the love you shared alive in your life.

Part V: The Part of Tens

The Part of Tens is a smorgasbord of practical tidbits for those grieving and those supporting them. Chapter 20 contains my top-ten list of crass clichés and platitudes about grief and grieving. This chapter not only tells you what the clichés are but also why they're so unhelpful to folks grieving a profound loss (even when they're partially or completely true). Chapter 21 contains my top-ten list of things you should do to help support someone you care about who's currently grieving a profound loss. Chapter 22 contains a list of ten online resources that you can consult to get more information about grieving as well as direct support from other people grieving a similar loss. Chapter 23 concludes this part and, indeed, the entire book with ten meditations related to grieving. These are guided contemplations that you can do as a bereaved person to appreciate your loss and alleviate some of the grief associated with it.

Icons Used in This Book

The following four icons are used throughout this book to highlight information worthy of some sort of special attention:

This icon indicates a noteworthy tidbit of information to keep in mind about grieving or grief.

This icon indicates a suggested course of action that may help facilitate your grieving or the support of someone who is grieving.

This icon indicates a course of action you may want to avoid — it may interfere with grieving or make it more difficult.

This icon indicates some nonessential information about grieving or grief that you may find helpful nonetheless.

Where to Go from Here

This book is organized so that you can jump in and start wherever you need to; you really don't need to start at the beginning and work your way through each chapter.

If you're currently in the throes of grieving the loss of a loved one, I suggest that you go directly to Chapter 10, which addresses doing your own grief crisis management. Then look up the chapter in Part I for the particular type of loss you've suffered before finding other chapters that seem pertinent and potentially helpful.

If you're supporting a close friend who's grieving the loss of a loved one, I suggest that you go to Chapter 13, which covers helping someone you care about who's grieving. Then check out Chapter 21 on ten things you can do to support someone else before you go about finding other chapters with information that seems relevant to your friend's particular situation.

Part I
Contemplating Grief

The 5th Wave   By Rich Tennant

"I'm not sure grieving openly is very manly. I sure wouldn't want any of the guys in my crocheting group seeing me do it."

In this part . . .

*B*efore you can do anything about grief, you must
know what you're dealing with. In this part, you find
out about the relationship between loss and grief along with
details on what different kinds of profound losses — from
the death of parents to the loss of pets — mean to people
who have sustained them. In addition, you discover how the
manner of death can impact and complicate the grieving.

Chapter 1

Connecting Grieving with Loss

• •

In This Chapter

▶ Understanding how grieving relates directly to loss

▶ Grieving in a highly competitive society

▶ Debunking death as the ultimate defeat

▶ Making sense of suffering

• •

*B*efore you can find a way to alleviate the pain of grieving, you need to stop for a moment and find out just what grief is and what makes it tick. Our pace of living has become so frenzied that we have less and less time for stopping to investigate anything, let alone something such as grief that doesn't carry the best of reputations. Nevertheless, to have a fighting chance of processing your own grief with a modicum of grace or helping someone you care about process his grief in a like manner, it's imperative that you understand the process known as grieving, particularly the nature of grief, the close association between grief and loss, and the factors in society that complicate the natural response to grief.

A few factors tend to complicate grieving:

✔ The highly competitive nature of modern society, which has an extremely low tolerance for loss and even less patience for grieving

✔ Ignorance about the grief process due in large part to a set of societal norms that stress thinking over feeling and that make the subject of death taboo

✔ Our own inability to find meaning in loss

This chapter looks at all three of these factors along with ways you can mitigate their influence as you and people you care about try to come to terms with grief.

Grieving as a Natural Response to Loss

Here are a few *working* (nonclinical) definitions for three interrelated terms: grief, loss, and grieving. These definitions are designed to give you something to hang your hat on in subsequent discussions about grieving and to show how closely interconnected the terms are.

- ✔ **Grief** refers to the feelings that arise when you suffer a loss in your life.
- ✔ **Loss** refers to a breaking of a bond you've formed with a significant person, place, thing, or idea (including beliefs) in your life.
- ✔ **Grieving** refers to the process of acknowledging the loss, experiencing the grief that the loss produces, and incorporating the loss into the rest of your life.

Grief as an emotional response

Because grief has to do with feelings, it's primarily an emotional response, and emotions, by their very nature, are often quite volatile and unpredictable. The emotions associated with grief, such as anger, sadness, and fear, are ones that we generally consider negative, and as a result, we do everything we can to avoid them (thus my deliberate choice to use the phrase "suffer a loss" rather than the more neutral "experience a loss"). To be blunt, grief, by its very nature, is painful, and the grief that arises from a great loss can often — too often — be excruciating. (As a lovely staff grief counselor at my hospice emphasized in our Bereavement Volunteer training, we often need to affirm with the people we're attending that "Yes, it hurts just that much!")

Loss as it relates to connection

When it comes to the definition of loss, I need to point out a couple of things. First, the bond you have with the person or thing lost is most often the result of a network of associations and relationships formed over time. Most of the time, these associations are positive, but because the bonds are often complex, they can include negative associations as well. Second, because the extent of grief depends upon the strength of the bond you've formed and the degree of significance of the loss, a *profound loss* is necessarily one in which you've developed a strong bond *and* which has high significance for you.

This book deals solely with profound losses of loved ones and the grieving process required to incorporate losses of such a magnitude into one's life.

Grieving as an involved process

The following corollaries regarding the connection of loss to grief and grief to grieving generally hold true:

- ✓ **The stronger the bond you made with the person you lost and the greater the significance that person holds in your life, the more profound your grief over the loss.**

    Although the bond has been broken, the significance of the person you've lost generally remains present in your life. In fact, you may actually find that his significance *increases* after the loss. If you find that the significance of a person fades as soon as or shortly after your relationship with him is over, then you really aren't grieving the loss (you're probably just a little bummed out about the termination of the relationship).

- ✓ **The more profound the grief over the loss, the more involved your grieving process.**

    When I speak about *involved grieving,* I'm talking about a process that usually doesn't adhere to a linear timeline or anything like a recognizable schedule and may never include what's commonly referred to as "closure" (a term that I thoroughly detest but that continues to appear in bereavement literature nonetheless).

    I purposely don't refer to involved grieving as *complex* or *complicated grief* because that's a technical term in the death, dying, and grieving profession (which goes by the $10 name *thanatology,* from the Greek for the study of death and dying). As a clinical term, complicated grief refers to a grieving process that gets really stuck in some way because of a deep inability to acknowledge, experience, or integrate the loss. An example of complicated grief is a mother who keeps the room of the child she lost 25 years ago exactly the way it was at the time of the death. Chances are good that this mom's having an extremely hard time acknowledging and incorporating the loss and maybe even experiencing the pain of the loss. Most often, complicated grief requires and benefits from psychological counseling. (I discuss seeking psychological help in Chapter 14.) The good news is that most people, even when their grieving is really messy and they get a little stuck in some aspect of it, aren't really experiencing complicated grief (it just feels that way at the time).

When it comes to the definition of grieving, the three tasks that I single out as being integral parts of this process are

1. **Acknowledge the loss.**

    This task can run the gamut from accepting the awful truth of it to finally facing up to its lasting impact on your life.

2. **Experience the grief the loss produces.**

This task can run the gamut from suffering the wave of emotions it brings up to contemplating its influence on your life.

3. **Incorporate the loss into the remainder of your life.**

   This task can run the gamut from simply surviving the grief produced by the loss to fully integrating the loss into your everyday life (something that professional grief counselors sometimes refer to as "creating a new normal").

Keep in mind that for some of the most profound losses, the grieving may never come to a complete end. Although you may finish acknowledging the loss for the most part and may seldom suffer the pain it engenders, you may continue to be involved in the intricate dance of fully incorporating the loss in your life all the rest of your days.

Grieving as a Totally Personal Process

Zen Buddhism has a story (and I apologize in advance for its rather off-color nature, but Zen does tend to deal with the concrete and, at times, is intentionally quite graphic) about a master whose student asks him about how to go about getting enlightened (presumably when both are side by side at whatever serves as the monastery latrine). The student is then completely surprised when his master responds to his question by starting to urinate and then saying, "Such a small thing, but only I can do it for myself." Grieving may not fall into the category of such a small thing (but then neither does becoming enlightened), but it's right in there among those things that you can do only for yourself (although not necessarily all by your lonesome).

The point is that no one else can spare you the pain that accompanies the grief your loss engenders no matter how desperately that person wants to alleviate your suffering. In fact, even if it were somehow possible to fix somebody else's grief, it's entirely debatable whether or not this would be a good idea. And the reason for this stance has absolutely nothing to do with some hackneyed cliché about how "that which does not kill you makes you strong" or some notion about grieving as a noble growth process that enriches the soul — don't worry, you'll never hear such things from me.

Although it may be tempting when I'm on the floor doubled up by the intense pain of my grief, I'd tell you not to try to fix my grief from a profound loss because in trying to fix my grief, you inadvertently negate my loss by devaluing the bond I had with the person I've lost. Consequently, you discount his significance in my life.

Can you share another's grief?

The question sometimes arises as to whether or not another person who shares your loss can share in your grief. Given the way I define grief as a personal response to loss (even a commonly shared one), my answer is a definite "No." Of course, people grieve together when they're a family facing the loss of a family member or when they come together to mourn a regional or national tragedy, but each person is grieving in his own way, albeit in response to a shared loss.

 If you're a parent suffering a family loss that affects your children, you may well feel that it's a natural part of your parental duties to protect your children from the pain of their grief over this loss. Although witnessing their pain may add notably to your own grief, it's really important that your children be allowed to do their own grieving. See Chapter 7 for information on how profound losses can affect children and suggestions of how you can go about helping your children through this difficult and trying period without also impeding their own grieving.

Some factors that influence grieving

Although each of us must do our own grieving, this doesn't mean that we all do it in a completely different manner. Grief is certainly idiosyncratic inasmuch as each loss is personal and the grief it produces surely varies with the strength of the bond to the person lost and his significance in one's life. Nevertheless, for the vast majority of people, the process of grieving profound losses shares some common characteristics (as discussed in Part II) that span gender, generations, and even cultural differences to a certain extent.

Certain factors affect the way in which you grieve a profound loss in your life, including:

- How naturally outgoing or introspective you tend to be
- How easily you express your feelings
- How well integrated you are into a circle of friends, your family, and the local community
- How confident you are
- How secure your worldview is

Many social scientists would consider the first items in this list to be gender based, pointing out that, traditionally, most societies attempt to socialize their men to be more outgoing to fulfill their roles as the protectors and breadwinners and their women to be more introspective to fulfill their roles as the nurturers and caregivers. As a result of this overt attempt to socialize men and women differently, on the whole, women tend to be able to express their feelings more easily than men.

Whether or not you accept this gender-based viewpoint, you need to keep in mind that many different traditional gender roles currently are being challenged in societies all over the globe; more and more, the time-honored roles allotted to men and women are being interchanged. In addition, even where people accept and follow conventional gender roles, the actual degree to which a man or woman is extroverted or introverted and able or unable to openly express his or her feelings is still quite personal. (See the "What to do when feelings aren't your forte" section, later in this chapter, for a few suggestions on approaching grief for folks who tend to hold their emotions inside and in check.)

It's pretty easy to understand how the last three factors in the list — how well integrated you are into your society, how self-confident you are, and how secure you are in your worldview — can mitigate your grieving by offering you indispensable external and internal support throughout your time of need. Be aware, however, that a loss that occurs in one of these areas or fundamentally disrupts one of them can greatly intensify your grieving process and make it more involved. For example:

- Losing the person who functions as primary head of your immediate family, such as your mother or father, could well result in an inability of the remaining family members to act as a cohesive unit that's mutually supporting, thus making this loss all the more difficult to integrate into your life.

- Suffering a catastrophic physical loss, such as the loss of your eyesight or your limbs, could well negatively impact your self-confidence in ways that ensure your grieving will be more complex and involved.

- Suffering an inexplicably tragic loss, such as the loss of a child, could well shatter your worldview by undermining your belief in God, thus making a tremendously arduous grieving process all the more grueling because you don't have the support and solace of your accustomed religious beliefs.

Everyone has a right to his or her grief

Each of us has a *right* to our grief because the bond that we cultivated and shared with the person now lost to us is entirely worthy of grieving. I believe quite firmly that, should you somehow be prevented from grieving or choose not to grieve a profound loss in your life, you run a much greater risk of becoming embittered by that loss. Obviously, the disenchantment that necessarily accompanies such bitterness benefits no one in the long run, even if bypassing the grief appears more convenient in the short term.

I recognize that grief isn't convenient for us or for those around us (I have a great deal more to say on this point; see the section "Grief as a nuisance," later in this chapter). I also understand that grief is often seen as quite scary because it runs counter to all notions (or are they delusions?) of control. But I also realize that grieving is a basic part of being human, and, like it or not, you need to engage in the process for as long as it takes. In my view, we all owe that much to the people we've lost as well to our own well-being. (You can come out of hiding now. I've gotten down off my soapbox.)

Dealing with Loss in a Highly Competitive World

Grieving is hard enough on its own without the complication of a society that has very little patience or time for loss of any kind. Given the emphasis — some may say overemphasis — on winning and achieving success in all aspects of modern society, it's no wonder that loss carries such a poor reputation.

Loss is an inescapable part of life. When it's relegated to such a low status in society, the grief that necessarily accompanies it also is consigned to that netherworld. As a result, when untoward circumstances hand you a profound loss that places you squarely in the grips of grieving, you're burdened not only with the pain of the grief itself but also with the onus that society places on loss.

The impact of competition on grief

"Winners never quit, and quitters never win." How many of these kinds of platitudes about "the thrill of victory and the agony of defeat" can you name? It seems that there's no end to such banalities when it comes to loss, which, after all is said and done, is just another four-letter word in today's society.

It's one thing to use winning as a motivating force for achieving goals and dreams; it's quite another to make it into the be-all and end-all of life. The spirit of winning at all costs seems to permeate all aspects of society — school, sports, business, love, war, and, last and always least, politics. In this highly competitive environment, loss becomes a fate worse than death (if you pardon my pun).

It's really not our fault that we're so inept at dealing with grief (both our own and that of people we care about). After all, we live in a secular society that's highly adept at training us how to acquire and refine the cognitive skills needed to become successful in a highly competitive society. We receive no instruction on how to suffer defeat gracefully, cooperate fully with one another, and express and release our feelings.

With no role models for grieving available, people have a very difficult (if not impossible) time judging whether or not the cascade of extreme feelings — ranging from anger to depression to despondency — they experience is normal. I can't map out in advance all the feelings that a grieving person will experience during his grief process, but when the people close to you who are also grieving the same loss appear to have none of the same feelings that you do, you may question whether or not your grief has unhinged you.

It may not surprise you that one of the most common questions that grief counselors are asked initially by the people they see is "Am I going crazy?" The answer is a quick and unequivocal "No." Although you may never guess it by the outward appearance of a typical grieving person, the sky-high level and all-over-the-map range of emotions that most people experience after a profound loss is entirely normal.

Few people have an adequate sense of what grief typically looks and feels like, and most don't comprehend that grieving profound losses isn't an optional part of living (like getting married and having children) but rather is a sure bet for which it's never too soon to be prepared.

Although we mostly associate an exaggerated emphasis on winning with the realms of achieving power and acquiring material goods, I've also seen it rear its ugly head in spiritual communities where winning is equated with attaining enlightenment or achieving some sort of sainthood. Unfortunately, competition is alive and well and thriving in the both the secular and sacred worlds.

The impact on grieving of negative attitudes toward loss

The idea that loss is somehow deserved negatively impacts your acceptance of grief by making grief often appear as something shameful; it insinuates that the loss that generates this grief somehow reflects badly on you. In its most extreme form, this viewpoint gives rise to the not-so-subtle suggestion that the loss is somehow the result of your own doing, justified by some sort of failing on your part or on the part of the loved one you've lost.

The worst example of this addlebrained thinking occurs in religious circles when seemingly well-meaning people or religious leaders indicate that losses from disease, natural disasters, or untimely death are divine punishment for sinful activities (see my discussion of the biblical Book of Job in the section "When bad things happen to good people," later in this chapter, for the classic example of this type of thinking in religious literature) or the comeuppance of bad karma from this or a previous life.

A similar sentiment is expressed when people insinuate that a chronic disease such as cancer has to be the ill person's fault in some way, either as the result of an unhealthy lifestyle or activity or negative attitude or thinking. Such people regard any and all protestations to the contrary as suspect and continue to ignore the contributions of environmental and hereditary factors (over which we exercise little or no control) to the person's condition.

Maintaining these narrow and unconstructive viewpoints simply may be attempts by otherwise well-meaning people to make sense of suffering in the world and to shield themselves against loss (assuming that they have and continue to lead blameless lives). Holding such perspectives, however, is fraught with danger because the day may dawn (heaven forbid) when the doctor hands one of these people a severe diagnosis, a natural disaster visits his neighborhood, or someone in his family suddenly dies out of turn. This person's not only left bereft with his grief but also is forced to deal with the very uncomfortable notion that either his beliefs regarding divine punishment and bad karma turned out to be really unproductive safeguards or he has some serious explaining to do about his own past behavior!

Grief as a nuisance

The highly competitive nature of modern society can also negatively impact you by turning your grieving process into a veritable nuisance, for which very few people have adequate patience. (If thus far you've been so blessed that you haven't suffered a profound loss, you haven't had the extreme displeasure of meeting up with this kind of impatience.)

All too soon (for you, at least), you may find that dear friends and seemingly caring family members are done with your grief and therefore expect you to be done with it as well. In subtle and some not-so-subtle ways, they start suggesting that it's time for you to move on by taking whatever course would seemingly assuage the pain of your particular loss, such as starting to date again, visiting the animal shelter, considering trying to conceive again, or adopting.

Friends and family no longer have time to hear your stories about the loss and the one you're grieving, and they no longer have patience for what they consider to be your intense mood swings, your overly developed sensibilities, and your need to wallow (their words, not mine) in your feelings. They may even start avoiding you, and, if you're really unfortunate, they may go so far as to temporarily or, in some extreme cases, permanently break off their relationships with you.

For the most part, these people mean well. They sincerely want to see you get through your grief with as little pain as possible (just as long as you do it according to their timetable). Unfortunately, they're usually operating from ignorance about the nature of the grieving process. For the most part, people have no idea that grieving a profound loss is necessarily and quite normally a lengthy process. For example, some studies suggest that five years is the *average* time for grieving a profound loss such as the death of a spouse and that grieving the death of a child may take even longer.

Each person grieves slightly differently. It doesn't matter whether your grieving process takes longer or shorter than what's considered average or the norm for your type of loss — the important thing is that you're able to take the opportunity to grieve as completely as you need to.

Even when the people around you are aware from their own losses that grief has no quick fix and tends to want to take its own sweet time, they still may want you to get through your grief in short order. If they were forced to abbreviate their grieving, they naturally figure that if they could do it, you can do it, too. The only trouble is that they may only think that they've grieved. The necessities of life coupled with society's pressure to move on as quickly as possible can easily conspire to interrupt a person's natural grieving cycle. It's entirely possible that they got through their grieving in such crack time because they abandoned the process midstream. In this situation, your grieving is particularly problematic because it may trigger their unfinished grieving processes, giving them all the more incentive to get you over your grief as quickly as possible.

You may find that your grieving process unnerves some of the people you're close to in your life (especially if you're rather expressive with your feelings). You may find yourself in the uncomfortable role of a pariah within your circle of friends or family. Most of the time, this change occurs because your loss and grief threatens the other folks' naïve notions about how life works (or should work). Your grief also may trigger unresolved grief over losses in another person's life (thus, it just cuts too close). If you see this kind of change happening, you have very little choice but to seek out people who stand outside of your circle and who can be with you without triggering their own issues with grief (see Chapter 14 for suggestions on how to locate such people).

Winning and losing: Two faces of the same coin

"Heads you win, and tails you lose" is a common saying. I particularly like it because it points outs very clearly and concretely that the winning (joy) and losing (grief) are just two sides of the very same coin. This image underscores how these two pairs of opposites are necessarily and completely conjoined (unless you can somehow conceive of a one-sided coin).

These pairs of opposites are *correlative,* which means that when you're facing the side of the coin with loss and grief staring you in the face, you can be sure that the flip side of gain and joy are there as well, just waiting for the moment when you turn the coin over.

This point is sort of obvious but can't be stated too often: Just as with other pairs, such as life and death, good and evil, truth and falsehood, or beauty and ugliness, you don't have one member of the pair without the other. Both parts of the pair arise together and mutually support each other, even in cases where one item usually precedes the other. For example, you have to gain something before you can lose it, and you experience the joy of a relationship before you experience the grief over losing it.

Unfortunately, in their narrowest forms, some Western religious and philosophical systems greatly downplay the reciprocity of these pairs by overemphasizing the more desirable member of the couple (gain, joy, light, good, beauty, and so forth) at the expense of the other. A few even argue that you actually can have the more desirable one without the less desirable other. These one-sided views give rise to a sort of utopian thinking in which the goal is the eradication of the less desirable member of the pair. This black-and-white view of the world leaves little or no room for the orphaned member of the pair (loss, grief, death, darkness, and the like).

Such one-sided thinking leads directly to the unrealistic expectation of many people that they can live lives absent of the less desirable member of the pair or, at the very minimum, should lead lives that emphasize, examine, and strive for only its polar opposite. Most of us have grown up with and accepted this worldview without question, but clearly it makes grieving all the more difficult by associating grief's direct cause (loss) with the side of the coin that we rather naïvely believe we can do without.

How Fear of Loss and Death Impact Grieving

Most people harbor a certain amount of fear and loathing for one or more of life's more distasteful aspects, what I like to refer to collectively as *Life's Big Downers.* For some, the physical and mental decline from illness and disability are top items on the list of Life's Big Downers. For others, the physical and mental deterioration associated with growing old is high on the list. For still others, the physical and mental displacement that can come from joblessness, homelessness, and even expatriation is the big-ticket item on the list. And for almost every single person, the physical and mental dissolution coupled with death claims the number-one spot.

In this section, I look at how the natural loathing associated with physical and mental decline, disability, and displacement, along with the ever-present fear of death, complicates grieving. First, I look at three of Life's Big Downers — decline, disability, and displacement — and how they can impact grieving. Then I turn to death, the granddaddy of downers, and attempt to determine how this fear really makes it difficult to be open to grieving (especially when the people around you are grieving, too).

Loathing decline, disability, and displacement

Each morning, I get up and repeat to myself the maxim "panta rhei," which translates as "everything flows" or "all is in flux" (my loose translation is "there's only flowing"). This adage is attributed to one of the world's first Western philosophers, an ancient Greek fellow by the name of Heraclitus.

The message at the heart of the panta rhei axiom isn't simply that change is ongoing and therefore inevitable (a truism if there ever was one) but that change is all there is! This idea of eternal changing poses a definite problem when the type of change you have to look forward to is one that involves a declining, disabling, and displacing of the resources you've worked so hard to obtain or the faculties that you've taken for granted.

Yet, unfortunately, this is exactly the type of change that potentially faces all of us who are fortunate enough to live on into our golden years. It's possible for some people to turn their fear and loathing of the decline associated with aging into an intangible loss that they actually grieve. For example, for some folks in our society, becoming elderly seems to be a fate worse than death. These people react so strongly to the natural aging process that they invest untold sums on ultimately ineffective antiaging products and even go so far as to suffer the risks of unwarranted plastic surgery and the pain of recovery.

The fear of mental and physical decline, disability, and displacement that hides in us can readily complicate our grieving of a profound loss. The lack of control over emotions and mental focus in grieving mimics the lack of control we associate with and fear in these debilitations. In us and in the people who care about us, this connection easily triggers the fear that the emotional and mental disruption and debilitation we're experiencing due to this profound loss will somehow become a permanent part of our being, like a physical disability from accident or disease.

Rest assured that the extreme emotional upheaval and serious lack of mental focus that you so easily experience at the outset of grieving a profound loss are definitely temporary and will eventually wane. That's not to suggest that you won't ever find yourself suddenly riding that old emotional roller coaster again after integrating the loss into your life or spacing out about the loss after actively grieving it (these experiences can and do happen at what often seem like the most unlikely times). However, ultimately, you'll no longer be at the mercy of wildly fluctuating feelings and will have your previous level of mental focus and concentration back.

Dealing with the fear of death

No human fear is more deep seated while at the same time less heeded than the Big Kahuna, the fear of death. We all *know* that death is our ultimate end, yet we live our lives as though we're going to stick around forever. How so? We make the greatest efforts during the entire course of our lives to cultivate wealth and influence, both of which we're destined to leave behind in the hands of others. Strangely enough, very few of us make an equal effort to cultivate spiritual growth and love, legacies that may just have a fighting chance of surviving the grave and accompanying us to the other side.

This discrepancy between fear and how we live our lives offers some explanation of why, on the whole, we don't deal well with death. We like to fool ourselves into believing that, despite teachings to the contrary in all the great spiritual traditions, our efforts to "have it all" have no debilitating effects on the quality of our souls. We tend to play the role of Scarlett O'Hara when it comes to confronting our inevitable death, reacting in the spirit of "Oh fiddle-dee-dee, I'll think about it tomorrow!"

The process of grieving is aggravated by the simple fact that it takes place in a death-denying society. Because most of our grieving is over the death of loved ones, it can trigger our own fear of death as well as that fear in the people around us. People we come in contact with during our initial stages of acute grieving are often strikingly short with us (and in some rare cases, they actually become angry with us) because our grief sets off their own fear of death.

Because your grieving can so easily remind others of their mortality and trigger their fear of death, when seeking out someone to help you through your grieving process — even a professional who isn't specifically trained as a grief counselor — you need to make sure that this person is comfortable with the subject of death. The best way to find out, of course, is to ask how he feels about death. If this proves too awkward, you should note carefully how he responds to you when you speak about death. If you feel that he doesn't fully engage with you, or if he attempts to change the subject, you know that he has issues with mortality that more than likely will adversely affect your ability to grieve openly around him.

Developing a personal definition of birth and death

I once had the pleasure of attending a lecture by Maezumi Roshi, the founder and head of the Los Angeles Zen Center, and experiencing his deep and extraordinary energy. Later, I read one of his books in which he challenges the reader to confront his own death by coming up with his own personal words and definition for it. We use so many euphemisms for death, such as *passed away, late, departed,* and *deceased,* that this exercise is a good one for everybody to do.

TIP

One technique for dealing with debilitating fears

The fear of physical or mental decline can be more debilitating than the actual disability itself. You can deal with such fears by adapting the three tasks of grieving that I outline in the section "Grieving as a Natural Response to Loss":

1. **Acknowledge the fear to yourself and to others if you can get them to listen.**

2. **Experience the fear rather than try to suppress and escape it.**

   For example, feel the closeness of breath and shivers down your spine if that's the way your body responds to the fear. This is definitely the most difficult task of the three.

3. **Assimilate the fear by finding ways in which to incorporate it into your life.**

   One way I assimilate my fear of becoming mentally and physically disabled is by taking stock of the caregivers and hospice workers whom I've had the privilege of knowing and working with. This reflection gives me some measure of confidence that if I become enfeebled, some sweet soul will treat me with the same respect and care that I've known these people to give.

Although Maezumi Roshi was never my personal teacher, I decided to take up his challenge and create my own personal definition for death. This is something that you may want to do as well. If so, I suggest you start by contemplating the meaning of your life in light of your mortality.

The definition I came up with is the result of not only my Zen training and graduate school learning but also my direct experience with death both on a personal level and as a patient-care volunteer with a hospice. It's also heavily influenced by the fact that many of my fellow hospice workers liken themselves to acting as midwives for the dying.

My definition for death is *being born into the world of unity* (a world which takes a whole bunch of different names, including the Kingdom of Heaven, World to Come, Paradise, World of the Spirit, Nirvana, Moksha, One Mind, Infinity, and even nothingness). Conversely, my definition of birth is *being born into the world of diversity*.

I find the image of both birth and death as entrances into vastly different experiences of a single reality to be quite helpful. It reminds me that although we live in a world of multiplicity, these many facets are, in fact, simply the face of unity. Likewise, the definitions enable me to approach my own demise as a complete integration with this unity and another way of experiencing it rather than as a complete dead end (pardon the pun).

Also, keeping this image of birth and death as entrances clearly in mind is helpful in my hospice work because I'm reminded that, just as some births into this world are easier than others (my mom would have readily told you that my birth as a breech baby was a great deal more difficult than my brother's), some deaths — as births into another phase of the world — are as well. And as with being born into this world, the most important aspect about dying isn't whether or not you go into the next world headfirst (at peace and willingly) or feet first (kicking and screaming) but whether or not you're properly supported throughout this great transition.

Putting the fear of death to good use

In Buddhism, death is to be appreciated as a very good friend (albeit one that we certainly want to keep at a distance and definitely don't want to bring home to dinner) because it reminds us that our time as human beings is brief and limited and thereby goads us into doing spiritual practice while we're still able.

That's the theory at least, and I've found it to be a sound one. Unfortunately, this idea just happens to run directly counter to the values that modern society esteems and pushes so relentlessly (especially in the able hands of the advertising and entertainment industries). In the modern age, dying is most often hidden away, placed squarely in the hands of healthcare and then funeral professionals. In their expert hands, death becomes sanitized, associated with institutions outside the home, and removed from our direct consciousness. As a result, it's now not that uncommon for young people to have no direct experience with the death of a loved one, having never directly experienced any person's dying or been with a person's body after death.

This personal unfamiliarity with death within a society that actively encourages its disregard makes death very unreal for most people, to say the least. Couple this lack of firsthand experience with the entertainment industry's highly stylized and often totally unrealistic depiction of death and dying, and you have a prescription for an extremely distorted view of one's mortality.

Instead of seeing death as the most natural thing in the world (the one single experience that every person can count on having), death takes on an unreal air and often becomes macabre. Instead of acting as an incentive to fully experience every aspect of life, death becomes the ultimate enemy. Because it's currently impossible to defeat, death must be held in contempt when it's not totally overlooked.

Viewing death as the enemy does everybody a disservice because it so easily steers us toward spending our lives achieving goals that seem hollow and empty in light of its certainty. This viewpoint also complicates our relationship to grieving and so hinders our ability to fully honor those we loved who are so worthy of our grief. Thus, it exaggerates our natural apprehension over our own mortality, thereby compromising our ability to live fully and realistically and inhibiting our ability to help others we care about with their grieving.

Meditation to lessen the fear of death

When my own fear of death overtakes me, I do the following meditation. I suggest that you try it, too, if you find yourself overwhelmed by your fear.

1. Sit for a second and imagine your state before you were born. Examine the feelings, if any, that you associate with that period before exiting your mother's womb, before being a part of time and change.

2. Breathe for a moment or two, examining and gently holding those feelings or lack of feelings.

3. Contrast the tranquility or neutrality of the feelings connected to the state before you were born with the agitated feelings connected to your fear of death.

4. Silently repeat this thought to yourself: "If being dead is anything like not yet being born, then I need not fear my death because I can experience the type of composure that death will bring me by contemplating my state before birth."

By coming to grips to with our mortality, we're not only better prepared to deal with the deaths of others and help them through their grief but much more apt to live our lives fully engaged. In this way, although never our "best" friend, death is a very useful one.

We're All Bozos on the Grief Bus

When it comes to grieving, we are, to quote Wavy Gravy, "all bozos on this bus." Of the many reasons for our inexperience and discomfort with grief, first and foremost is our overall ignorance and fear of death (as discussed in the preceding section). To complicate matters, there exists a strong cultural bias, at least in the United States, against the overt display of grief. Many people, especially men, aren't comfortable showing their emotions (especially crying), and even those who are comfortable expressing their emotions do so only behind closed doors.

The result is that we live in a society that doesn't really know what grief is or how it normally unfolds. We don't comprehend that it's entirely natural and healthy to grieve and, most important, that the grief resulting from a profound loss isn't something that you can get out of your system in just a few months, let alone a few weeks.

What to do when feelings aren't your forte

The grieving process is perhaps most difficult for those folks who have trouble openly expressing their feelings. Men, in particular, are traditionally socialized to be stoic thinkers who ideally remain impervious to pain and sorrow (and necessarily out of touch with the particular feelings of sorrow that grieving stirs up). Even today, boys often are taught that showing grief (especially by crying) is unmanly and a terrible sign of weakness. When young men internalize this idea, their grieving is made more difficult by an understandable inability to express the strong feelings that naturally arise.

Although most women generally aren't socialized to suppress emotions and normally have an easier time expressing their feelings, this isn't always the case. Studies by professionals in the grief field indicate that women who don't freely express their feelings and who work more from their heads than their hearts have the most difficult time of any group in processing their grief. The reason may be because the traditionally socialized men and women around them misinterpret their manner of grieving (without the expected emotional expression) as not grieving at all.

Regardless of gender, if you happen to be someone who isn't particularly comfortable getting in touch with your feelings, you have to be particularly patient with yourself when grieving a profound loss. You may find that the intensity of your feelings overwhelms your normal capacity to suck them in and sit on them. You also may discover that the grief brought up by your current loss triggers past grief that remains unincorporated into your life.

Although the resurfacing of unresolved grief can add to your current grief work, it also may be a golden opportunity that you can't afford to pass up. Not only can you possibly mend past and present grief by dealing with your current pain, but also you can discover ways to handle and honor your powerful emotions without automatically suppressing them. This work, however, may be too much to attempt on your own and may require the help and guidance of a professional grief counselor (see Chapter 14 for information on seeking out professional help).

Making a place for cooperation in the world of competition

Throughout this chapter, I underscore how a society that stresses competition and winning as the be-all and end-all of life makes the already unpleasant task of grieving all the more difficult. In our world of arduous and relentless competition, we need a lot more cooperation, or mutual support, when it comes to grieving.

Bringing death and dying back into the home

A steady and growing movement is afoot to bring dying and death back into the home, where it typically was almost a quarter century ago. The hospice movement makes every attempt to enable a person to die in the comfort of his own home surrounded by family and friends if that's the dying person's wish. In addition to dying at home, there's a growing movement to bring wakes back into the home for those who find funeral homes too impersonal or too expensive.

For more information on hospice services, visit the Hospice Patients Alliance at `www.hospice patients.org` and the Hospice Web at `www.hospiceweb.com`. For information about home funerals, visit the Final Passages Web site at `www.finalpassages.org` and the Sacred Crossings Web site at `www.sacredcrossings.com`.

Cooperation not only opens up a natural space for loss but offers new ways of supporting each other in grief. Recently, I had the good fortune of attending a workshop entitled "The Healing Power of Grief," presented by Sobonfu Somé, a truly lovely woman from the small west African nation of Burkina Faso. Somé introduced participants to the Dagara people's communal grief ritual.

Participating in this culture's public and shared grief ritual was a powerful experience that showed me the value of collective grief and reinforced the efficacy of mutual support. The cooperative nature of this rite removed any notion of competition over whose grief was greater. It also underscored the universality of grief among a group of people of different ages and very different life experiences. And while I don't advocate grafting the communal grief ritual of the Dagara culture onto our society, I do think that it's a good lesson in the effectiveness of mutual support and the need for it when it comes to individual grieving (to say nothing of public mourning).

Here are three separate yet interconnected steps toward being able to offer mutual support to one another in times of grief:

1. **Become more realistic about death.**

   Even if you aren't able to become friends with death, at the very least, you can be acquaintances instead of total strangers (with the understanding that this is one acquaintance you're going to get to know really intimately at some, hopefully distant, point in your life). This first step is necessary because you can't make a very big place for grief (in your own or somebody else's life) if you can't stand to be reminded of your mortality.

2. **Make it crystal clear to yourself that grief is not optional in life.**

   You can't get through life without experiencing profound loss (in most cases, multiple losses often compound one another). When it dawns on us that we're all in the same boat (a leaky old tub named the SS *Good Grief*), we're much more likely to cut each other some much needed slack when it comes to grieving.

3. **Promote the understanding that grieving is nothing extraordinary (in the sense of being weird or abnormal).**

Grief is a totally natural response to loss and, in the vast majority of cases, represents an attempt to restore health to a temporarily wounded system. However, although natural and shared by all, it's also an individual response and, as such, follows its own course and takes its own sweet time.

Armed with a degree of comfort with death and a clear understanding that grief is a common and normal human condition, we can all mutually comfort and better support one another through our inevitable turns with grief. (And that just happens to be the goal of this book!)

Searching for Meaning in the Midst of Sorrow

A common misconception is that people of faith and religious practice are steeled by their beliefs against the pain of loss and therefore suffer less in their grieving. The idea is that the larger worldview offered by faith enables them to put meaning to the loss, and this meaning somehow alleviates the pain. I'm sorry to burst anybody's bubble, but I strongly disagree with this analysis.

Religious faith and practice can facilitate a person's grieving not by lessening the intensity of the person's grief but rather by better enabling him to incorporate the loss into his life by offering a much greater context in which to place it. This broader framework is what gives the loss meaning. In the tech-speak of the grief professional, the person's religious faith better enables him to *reframe* the loss. However, reframing doesn't absolve the person from suffering the pain of the loss because the new framework only provides a means for absorbing the loss after the person tackles the hard work of acknowledging it and feeling the grief it generates.

Grief can try a person's faith and even best it. Some people find their losses to be so heavy and incomprehensible that they not only question their faith but actually abandon it — occasionally only for the duration of the grieving but sometimes for good. For those who aren't particularly religious or who have fallen away from a particular religious tradition, the lack of a comprehensible meaning behind a profound loss can either reinforce their separation from religion or set in motion a new round of existential questioning that ultimately brings them to accept and participate in a new system of belief.

Making some sense of suffering

Goodness knows that when grieving hits us squarely in the gut, the human defense mechanism kicks in. We're convinced that we wouldn't be in nearly as much pain if we could just make some sense of the crazy world that produced this unfortunate loss. I resist this notion because I see grieving primarily as a response to the loss of a relationship with a loved one and not as a response to the cause of that loss. From this point of view, there's no reason to grieve any less. For example, suppose you lose a beloved parent by the natural death of ripe old age (may we all be so blessed). Surely you can say that there's a good reason for the loss — your parent's body could no longer renew itself and keep on functioning. Even with that reasonable explanation, however, you can't expect not to grieve your loss fully.

Unfortunately, this logic doesn't cut both ways. If you suffer an incomprehensible loss that's totally unjustifiable because it so easily could have been avoided, you suffer not only the pain of the loss but also the fact that the loss was so needless. For example, if you lose a dear friend in a car accident caused by someone under the influence of drugs or alcohol, you're devastated by both the loss of your friend and the fact that his death was so unnecessary. In such a situation, you have to deal with your righteous anger as well as the pain of the grieving (and this is a case in which the grieving can be complicated — in the clinical sense — and thus requires the help of professional counseling).

The real problem of spending time and energy trying to make sense of a profound loss is that it doesn't change the outcome. No matter what theory you come up with to explain a loss, the explanation doesn't bring the person back or excuse you from grieving the loss.

Sometimes, I get the feeling that people fixate on understanding the reason for the loss because, in their inexperience with grief, they think this is a necessary part of grieving. Other times, I get the feeling that people fixate on the reason for the loss rather than the loss itself because they hope against hope that doing this releases them from having to feel the pain of the loss.

Although it may seem as though I'm pooh-poohing seeking out a reason for suffering in this world, I'm really not. Making sense of a profound loss, if you feel compelled to do so, is one of the last tasks that you should assume in the grief process. In other words, it doesn't take the highest priority when you're first thrust into grieving a profound loss. Rather, making sense of the loss is a natural fit with the third task, incorporating the loss into the remainder of your life (see "Grieving as an involved process," earlier in this chapter). In this stage, finding meaning can enable you to stay connected to the one you've lost and can guide you in reconnecting with the wider world around you.

We can't pretend to know the real answer to the question of why bad things happen to good people (and I'm not sure that it's part of our job as human beings to have this understanding). We do, however, always run the risk of sabotaging our grieving by obscuring the question of how best to grieve with the question of why we have to grieve.

To the enlightened person, investigating why bad things happen to good people is nowhere near as vital as investigating how best to alleviate the suffering that arises from the bad situation.

When bad things happen to good people

From time immemorial, people have questioned why bad things happen to good people. And for the longest time, some well-meaning people have put forward the same tired answer that bad things don't happen to good people, they happen exclusively to bad people who often are deluded into thinking that they're good.

Oh, for the patience of Job!

The Book of Job in the Bible is one of the most famous Western examples of a search for an answer to the question of why bad things happen to good people. In brief, it's the story of a righteous man named Job (rhymes with globe) whose faith in God is sorely tried — first by the loss of his wife and children, along with his cattle and servants (both counted as wealth in those days), and later by the loss of his own health.

God authorizes this test of Job's faith after Satan (who else would be so bold?) openly questions Job's motivation for remaining upright in the sight of the Lord. Satan suggests that if God were to remove the many blessings He has bestowed on Job, Job will "certainly curse Thee to Thy face" (Job 1:11).

After Satan destroys all that Job has (including his good health), Job continues to protest that he has done nothing to deserve this fate. Job's (so-called) friends insist that he must have performed some iniquity to have caused God to punish him with all his profound losses.

This argument over whether or not Job is really a good man to whom some really crummy things have happened takes up most of the book. Job, however, is nothing if not persistent in his own defense and doesn't stop protesting his innocence to his friends and heaven itself. God finally has enough of Job's protestations and confronts him directly by, in essence, asking him who he thinks he is to question God's motives. Job finally pipes down and says, "I had heard of Thee by hearsay, but now my eye has seen Thee. That is why I sink down and repent in dust and ashes" (Job 42:4–6).

In terms of how to make some sense of seemingly undeserved suffering, the Book of Job argues strongly and consistently against the commonly held notion that bad things only happen to bad people. It offers no clear answer to the persistent question "Why does God allow evil in the world?" other than the severe view that pain like that suffered by Job is visited on people simply as a test of faith.

Better, I think, to adopt Job's final position wherein instead of being content to hear about the divine through hearsay, you establish a direct relationship with the divine that enables you to see it directly with your own eyes. Then, as with Job, you can sink down (relax) and repent (in the sense of atoning by being truly in harmony with the divine) in your dust and ashes (your very mortal body).

By the way, in case you're the slightest bit interested, the Book of Job has a perfectly acceptable Hollywood ending. After Job repents, God takes Job's friends to task for arguing the false theory that bad things don't happen to good people and for falsely accusing Job of unrighteousness. He then has them offer Job cattle for forgiveness. After Job forgives his erstwhile friends, God fully rehabilitates Job, recompensing him double what was taken from him. Job lives happily ever after to the ripe old age of 140 years and sees four generations of children and grandchildren grow up (fade to black).

Karma as cosmic comeuppance

Karma as the Buddhist law of cause and effect is often touted as the reason that bad things *appear* to happen to good people. Accordingly, the people who now appear to be so good and innocent were once bad people (in one or more of their past lives), and although it appears (especially to the untrained eye) that they're now needlessly suffering, they are, in fact, just reaping the bitter harvest that they sowed in the past. It just took an awful long time for conditions to be right for their bad deeds to spring up like weeds and grab hold of them.

So as a result of some very subtle thinking, we're right back where we started with the idea that bad things in fact don't happen to good people. In this Eastern version, they just sometimes take their own sweet time in catching up to the wicked and punishing them — so much time, in fact, that they end up punishing the good. I don't know about you, but this theory does me no more good than that of Job's dear friends.

The Zen school of Buddhism teaches that cause and effect constitute a single process. Even when one can't know exactly the reasons for the loss he suffers, he does know the consequential grief with great precision. Accordingly, it can be through the experience of grieving the loss that one rediscovers that what matters isn't primarily what happens to him but how he responds to that experience.

Chapter 2

Relating Grief to the Manner of Death

*W*hen you lose a loved one, it's important to understand the loss from the viewpoint of the type of relationship you have with the deceased. But you can't overlook the importance of the way in which your loved one dies. The manner of death influences your grief and grieving process as well.

This chapter takes a detailed look at the various kinds of losses ranging from slow and fully anticipated deaths to sudden and quite violent deaths. The chapter surveys these modes of death without any particular regard to your relationship to the deceased. It does this on the assumption that the particular stresses associated with each kind of death add to the overall grief work that you need to do.

The chapter begins with an examination of death caused by illness or natural debilitation (better known as old age). These causes of death result in some type of prolonged dying process that ultimately ends in an anticipated and, depending upon how protracted the dying process is, a longed-for death. As part of this investigation, I look at the phenomenon known as *anticipatory grief* (the grief you experience before the death of a loved whose passing is highly anticipated) and its relationship to the other stresses of caregiving. Next, the chapter looks at the impact of losing a loved one through some sort of *dementia* (a progressive decline in cognitive brain function) that robs you of your loved one sometimes long before his physical death; this condition often is seen in people with Alzheimer's disease and sometimes in folks with advanced Parkinson's disease.

The chapter then moves on to look at the impact of experiencing the sudden loss of a loved one through natural causes or violent death as well as the heartbreak and trauma of losing a loved one as the result of suicide. This special type of death is particularly difficult to handle given the widespread social and religious censure of the taking of one's life and loved ones' guilt and regret at not being able to prevent it.

The chapter concludes with suggestions for other resources that you can consult to get more help dealing with the particular kinds of loss covered in this chapter. These resources include books and Web sites with information and online communities as well as a listing of community resources you can contact directly.

The Impact of an Anticipated Loss

With anticipatory grief, you're grieving what you've already lost and what you're in the process of losing in the present as well as what you fear losing in the future. And in so doing, you're caught in the impossible position of having to find ways to grieve all these losses without relinquishing any attachment to your loved one at the same time.

The psychological impact of an anticipated loss of a loved one depends upon a number of factors, of which the following are normally the most important:

- ✔ The pace of the disease or disability and the amount of time you have left with your loved one prior to his death

- ✔ The amount of pain and suffering that your loved one has to endure in this period of declining health

- ✔ The degree of mental alertness, recognition, and cognition that your loved one maintains during the period of declining health prior to death

- ✔ Your loved one's ability to communicate with you

- ✔ Whether you're primarily responsible for making healthcare decisions on behalf of your loved one or you share this responsibility with other family members

- ✔ Whether you can provide care for your loved at home or he must be cared for in a skilled-nursing facility or other long-term care facility

- ✔ Whether you're the primary caregiver for your loved one and whether you're relieved from time to time by other caregivers, either professional or volunteer

In reviewing this list of factors, it's quite obvious that the two biggest issues are the amount of time you have left to spend with your loved one and the quality of life that you and your loved one enjoy during this time.

If your loved one is suffering from a particularly aggressive form of a fatal disease or disability, your time together may be quite limited. In this situation, there's also a good chance that he will endure some degree of pain, and medication, as well as the speed of the decline, may well impair his mental alertness and recognition.

If your loved one is suffering from a fatal disease or disability that normally has a slow and somewhat steady decline, you can be pretty sure that your time together won't be limited. You can also count on having to deal with the stress of more healthcare- and caregiving-related issues than usually accompany other causes of death.

What is less clear with an anticipated loss is the amount of pain and mental decline that your loved one will suffer.

- ✔ With some conditions, such as dying naturally from old age, pain may be almost nonexistent, and mental alertness may remain high until the very end.

- ✔ With other conditions, such as Alzheimer's disease, pain may not be much of an issue, but mental faculties may suffer a notable decline in the later stages.

- ✔ With some conditions, such as Parkinson's disease, the main challenge may have less to with pain and mental decline and more to do with the ability of your loved one to communicate with you about his condition and needs.

   In their advanced stages, many long-term diseases and disabilities make it extremely difficult for your loved one to speak loudly enough or clearly enough to be understood. Some conditions may make it impossible for your loved one to speak at all.

The stress of trying to ensure comfort and quality of life for your loved one takes its toll both physically and emotionally. You must get relief from others (family members, professional caregivers, or volunteers) whenever and wherever you can. Handing over responsibilities — even temporarily — enables you to decompress so that you don't fall apart and can be with your loved one for the long haul.

Using the time you have left

One worthwhile aspect of experiencing an anticipated loss of a loved one from a disease or disability is that you usually have sufficient time to tie up any loose ends, make amends by forgiving any real or supposed injuries, review your relationship together, and say your goodbyes.

Although an anticipated loss usually affords you the opportunity to get all these ducks in a row, unfortunately, this time is seldom used in this manner. Instead, you may find yourself far too busy with caregiving and helping your loved one maintain a brave face in his desperate attempt to stave off the inevitable to ever bring up such discussions.

Whenever the fight against death is relentless and unremitting to the very end, a real tragedy can ensue. By the time everyone on the team (sufferer, loved ones, family, and doctors) finally agrees that nothing can or should be done to fight the disease, it's often too late to have important, heart-to-heart discussions. By that time, your loved one may be too weak, medicated, pain-ridden, and close to the end to maintain the alertness and focus needed to engage in these kinds of discussions.

Instead of receiving the reassurances that you need to hear from your loved one before he dies, you may have to settle for reassuring him of your love and forgiveness. Too often, however, when death is imminent or your loved one has slipped into a coma, you don't even get the satisfaction of knowing that your loved one has heard your words and understood what you're saying.

Even if your loved one is unconscious or very near death, go ahead and express your love and let him know how much he'll be missed and how much your relationship with him has meant to you. Although you won't know for sure that he has heard and understood your words (although I believe that those close to death do hear and understand on some level), at least you don't have to live with any regret about not having told him these feelings before he died.

Preparing for the end with the help of hospice services

One way to get some help and alleviate some of the stresses associated with an anticipated loss is to make use of the hospice services in your local community (see the sidebar "About hospice and its basic services"). The aim of hospice is to help your loved one die in dignity and comfort. Hospice services are geared to ensuring that your loved one is as pain free, alert, and active as possible until the very end of his life.

If you register with a local hospice organization (as opposed to placing your loved one in a live-in hospice facility), the hospice team assigned to your family may arrange for your loved one to be cared for and die at home. The team also can provide you with pain medication and needed medical supplies. In some cases, the social worker on the team can help secure specially needed medical equipment as well as deal with all the paperwork and bureaucracy associated with private health insurance as well as Medicare or Medicaid.

The hospice team can also support you by providing you with visits from the following individuals:

- ✔ An interfaith chaplain who can offer spiritual care
- ✔ A home health aid volunteer who can bathe your loved one
- ✔ A patient-care volunteer or a paid caregiver to give you some respite and enable you to do needed errands
- ✔ A complementary-care volunteer who can give your loved one a massage or some other form of body work appropriate to his particular physical condition

As your loved one's condition declines and he nears death, many hospice organizations have trained vigil volunteers who will sit with your loved one for periods when you or other members of the family can't be there. This service is particularly helpful if your loved one is dying in a skilled-nursing facility and the family lives at some distance and hasn't yet assembled at the bedside. In this circumstance, you have the comfort of knowing that someone is attending to your loved one; you don't have to worry that he will die alone before a member of the family can get there.

Hospice services don't end with the death of your loved one. Hospices offer many grief services, usually in the form of trained bereavement counselors and, in some cases, bereavement volunteers who can help through one-on-one support as well as a variety of grief support groups (see Chapter 14 for more on these support services).

The one little problem with any hospice service is getting your dying loved one registered on its rolls in enough time to make good use of its end-of-life services. Too many times, the people who are ill, their doctors, and their families don't stop to consider hospice as an appropriate option (as opposed to aggressively fighting the disease) until the sufferers are literally at death's door (or at least sitting on its stoop). Then, instead of months of great end-of-life care, your loved one receives only a week or two's worth, which, while it is sufficient time to assemble the hospice team and develop the plan of care, deprives you of the very important support that hospice can offer you over time.

About hospice and its basic services

Most hospice services are delivered in one of two forms: dedicated hospice organizations or dedicated hospice facilities. Both are designed to provide end-of-life and *palliative care* (care designed solely to alleviate mental and physical discomfort) for people with terminal diseases or disabilities. The following are their primary differences:

✔ **Hospice organizations:** Care usually is provided to your loved one in the home, although certain hospice organizations offer their services to people who are living in nursing homes and other types of long-term care facilities.

✔ **Hospice facilities:** Your loved one is admitted to the facility, where he lives and receives around-the-clock professional care.

To qualify for the these hospice services, your loved one's primary physician must recommend him for the program on the understanding that his medical condition is steadily declining and that he's most likely near the end of his life (usually with a prognosis of six months or less to live). The physician also must confirm that your loved one's no longer seeking active treatment to reverse or cure his disease or condition but instead is ready to receive only palliative care to manage pain.

When your loved one qualifies for hospice services, the following occurs:

1. **A core hospice team comprised of a hospice nurse and social worker under the management of hospice's medical director assembles.**

2. **Optional members, such as a chaplain, home health aid, and patient-care volunteer, may augment the core team as desired by the patient and his family. Occasionally, a bereavement counselor may be brought in for help in dealing with anticipatory grief.**

3. **The core hospice team draws up a plan of care for the patient and his family that includes regular visits by the nurse and the social worker in the home or skilled-nursing facility.**

4. **The core team reviews the patient's status with the medical director and other professional hospice staff on a regular basis for the rest of the time the patient is in hospice.**

When the anticipated loss becomes a blessing

With some diseases and disabilities, your loved one may linger a long time in a state where the quality of his life is nominal before dying. Depending upon how minimal his quality of life is and how much suffering he had to endure before his passing, it's entirely possible that initially you may feel relieved rather than grieved when he finally dies.

Being relieved that a loved one is no longer suffering or suspended in some state between life and death is an entirely natural reaction for which you should feel no guilt. Just remember that the feelings of relief will be followed in short order with feelings of loss and grief. Although a great burden on your heart is lifted when someone you love finally is no longer suffering or caught in a vegetative state, you're not relieved of the burden of grieving his loss. Even if you longed for the loss because of the dire circumstances, the relationship is nonetheless broken with death, and you still need to honor it and the bond you had with your lost loved one by accepting and experiencing your grief.

Dealing with anticipatory grief and the stresses of caregiving

Anticipatory grief is the name given to the angst and sorrow that accompanies the knowledge that your loved one almost certainly is going to die from whatever disease or debilitating condition he's suffering. The watchword of anticipatory grief is angst: You fear the loss that you know is coming more than you actually grieve it.

Anticipatory grief often is accompanied by outbursts of sorrow and rage followed by bouts of depression. Because this type of grief is intertwined with fear, you find it particularly draining, especially when you're dealing with the other stresses associated with being a caregiver for your dying loved one.

Many people mistakenly believe that, in suffering anticipatory grief, they lessen the grief that they'll experience when death finally comes. Unfortunately, this is not so. Don't expect the grief that you feel and the grieving process that you have to undergo when your loved one finally passes away to be any less even if you've suffered a ton of anticipatory grief.

Some grief professionals debate whether or not anticipatory grief can be separated from the other stresses you undergo as a caregiver. It's well documented that being a caregiver for a loved one who's dying is extremely stressful for any number of the following reasons:

- ✔ Burnout from trying to do all the caregiving on your own without the help of others or from having to be the caregiver for more than one loved one (as in trying to care for both your aged or ailing parents at the same time)

- ✔ Feelings of extreme isolation when the caregiving seems to take over every aspect of your life

- ✔ Resentment toward the loved one for needing the care, frustration with the medical or insurance bureaucracy, and/or anger toward other family members for not helping with caregiving

> ✔ Guilt that you aren't able provide to better care for your loved one, for finally having to put him in a nursing home, and/or for not being able to save his life
>
> ✔ Difficulty watching the health and vitality of someone you love decline
>
> ✔ Helplessness in the face of the anticipated loss and the overwhelming and growing demands of being the caregiver for an increasingly incapacitated loved one

Don't ignore the feelings of angst and stress associated with anticipatory grief and with caregiving for a loved one. Instead, find ways to express and validate your feelings. Seek the help of family or grief counselors, social workers, or psychologists in order to keep yourself going. If you're a primary caregiver, you also may need to get some help with the caregiving from other family members, community services, or a hospice team. Although you may feel as though you have to "keep it together" in order to be an effective caregiver, you may actually be less effective if you don't deal with the psychological tolls from the stresses related to caregiving.

Dealing with a loss from dementia

Dementia refers not to the name of a particular disease but rather to a number of neurological disorders that arise from various types of diseases, most notably Alzheimer's disease. Most of the symptoms associated with dementia involve the loss of cognitive function (especially memory loss), although personality and behavioral changes are also common and can include extreme agitation, delusions, and sometimes even hallucinations.

When a loved one suffers from a form of dementia that involves progressive memory loss (as with some forms of Alzheimer's disease), you may have the tremendously sad experience of feeling as though you've lost your loved one before he actually dies. The anticipatory grief associated with this type of situation can be quite overwhelming, especially if you're also a primary caregiver for your loved one.

Even when dementia doesn't involve memory loss, the challenges of caring for someone suffering various types of dementia can be quite daunting. It's particularly trying to watch a loved one become extremely agitated, especially if he can't communicate the reason and you have no idea of what to do to help. Some families also find it particularly difficult to experience their loved one's becoming delusional, often by relating true events out of sequence.

Caregiving for a loved one suffering from advanced stages of Alzheimer's can be especially tough because he may develop a strong inclination to wander whenever he gets the chance. This urge puts an extra burden on you in terms of watching him and, in extreme cases, putting him under some sort of restraint.

Whenever a loved one suffers a loss of mental capacity or memory, or shows signs of being delusional, it feels as though the person you love is disappearing before your very eyes, especially if, earlier in life, he strongly identified with his mental prowess and achievements (for example, a professional, educator, or entrepreneur). Many people feel as though their cognitive abilities are essential elements of their personalities and identities, without which they might as well be dead.

The anticipatory grief associated with caring for someone with dementia is enormous. As with grief from other anticipated losses, you need to be mindful of the stress that this situation brings and take any steps you can to prevent caregiver burnout. This can include getting outside help so that you can take regular breaks as well as seeking counseling from a professional grief counselor so that you can fully express your feelings.

Grieving a Sudden Loss

Because you can't predict the sudden loss of a loved one ahead of time, you can't prepare yourself, and the loss almost always comes as an enormous shock to you and other bereft family members and friends.

The bottom line of suffering the sudden loss of a loved one is that you never get a chance to say goodbye. This missed opportunity, plus the shock of the unexpected death, can make grieving a sudden loss particularly difficult. For suggestions on how to deal with regret stemming from the inability to say goodbye to your loved one before his death, see Chapter 14.

A sudden loss can result from any number of causes. The three general causes responsible for almost all sudden deaths are

- **Medical conditions** such as a stroke, brain aneurism, or fatal heart attack
- **Accidents** that can be man-made, as in the case of a car crash or a bridge collapse, or natural, as in the case of a hurricane or an earthquake
- **Assaults** including physical attacks in a whole array of circumstances: domestic violence, gang warfare, military war, shootings, robberies, and terrorist attacks, for example

Blaming yourself for not preventing the death

When dealing with the death of a loved one due to a medical condition, accident, or assault, it's not unusual for a surviving loved one to assume some personal responsibility for the death. Yet in the case of some sudden deaths, survivors consider the death almost completely random and simply a case of very bad luck or simply being in the wrong place at the wrong time. Here are some examples of both scenarios:

- ✔ Your loved one is diagnosed with heart disease yet continues to smoke like a chimney, refuses to exercise, and continues to eat a diet high in the bad LDL cholesterol. He heightens his risk of dying from heart disease and may even bear some responsibility if he actually suffers a fatal heart attack.

- ✔ Your loved one is going to a grocery store to pick up a few things and must drive over a bridge to get there. This bridge is old, but it doesn't carry any warning signs, and your loved one travels over it regularly. Without any warning, the bridge buckles and collapses, and your loved one dies in the ensuing crash of his car. Undoubtedly, the death is considered a freak accident. No one blames your loved one for taking an unnecessary risk in crossing the bridge and thereby causing his own demise.

The interesting thing in terms of grief over sudden loss, however, is that bereaved loved ones can find ways to feel guilty and somewhat responsible for a death regardless of the circumstance. For example, in the case of the heart attack, you may blame yourself for not being more persistent in pressuring your loved one to stop smoking, go to the gym, eat his greens, and take his cholesterol medicine.

Even in the case of the bridge accident, you may find a way to blame yourself, even if it's more of a reach. You may feel guilty that you suggested that your loved one go to the store that's over the bridge for the things he needed. You may even go so far as to blame yourself for not having picked up the things he needed during the day so he wouldn't have had to venture out that fateful night!

The fact is that bereaved people who have suffered the sudden loss of a loved one more often than not feel compelled to second-guess their responsibility and take on some of the blame for the death, regardless of whether the circumstances of the death actually warrant such feelings. This need to question what you possibly could have done to prevent the loss is therefore quite natural. Assuming blame only becomes a problem if you start to fixate on your responsibility in the death and can't get beyond it to grieve the loss of your loved one. (See Chapter 14 for suggestions on ways to deal with feelings of responsibility.)

Blaming someone else for causing the death

In some instances, blaming yourself for what you consider your part in the death of a loved one gives way to placing the blame on someone else. You may blame someone else regardless of whether the loss is the result of a medical condition or an accident, although blaming others is much more common in the case of death from an assault.

Holding other people responsible

When you hold someone else responsible for a death caused by a medical condition, you're likely to look to someone in the medical profession — the attending physician, nurses, or some other medical staff. Sometimes, however, the fault falls on the medical insurer or even the medical facility.

In the case of an accidental death not related to a natural disaster, you may blame the people you feel are responsible for the incident either directly or indirectly. For example, in the case of a car accident, you surely blame the other driver, especially if it's proved that he's clearly at fault. In the case of a bridge collapse, however, you'd have no one to blame directly; you may look to the people indirectly associated with the bridge mishap, such as the engineers who may not have properly designed the structure or the county officials who failed to ensure proper upkeep of the bridge.

Blaming God when no one else is to blame

In the case of an accidental death in a natural disaster, normally you can find no one to blame (and this fact alone can be quite frustrating). Sometimes, such losses give rise to a crisis in faith, especially if you believe that God personally intervenes in human history. In such a case, you may even go so far as to blame the Almighty for not intervening and preventing the disaster that caused your loss.

However, as I point out in Chapter 1 in my discussion of the biblical story of Job, this kind of thinking makes for a very slippery slope. It's all too easy for others of faith holding a similar concept of the Almighty to turn the tables on you: They can just as easily assert that the natural disaster was God's will and was therefore visited on your loved one and all who perished with him as some sort of rightful retribution or punishment for some iniquities.

Blaming the responsible party

Deaths resulting from a physical assault of some kind almost always require finding and laying blame on the responsible party. In fact, this is the one area where a great deal of time and energy goes into not only identifying the guilty party but also bringing him to justice.

Finding the guilty party and seeing him brought to justice is often a necessary first step in grieving the death of your loved one. This is the one time when the concept of *closure* may well apply. Discovering exactly what happened to your loved one and how and sometimes why he died, although extremely painful and maybe even traumatic (see Chapter 12 for more on trauma), may be your only access to grieving the death of your loved one. Until the facts surrounding the death are clearly resolved, you'll have a tremendously difficult time moving through the normal stages of grieving (which I cover in Chapter 11).

Identifying the person or persons responsible for the death of a loved one and establishing the facts surrounding the death are undoubtedly key elements in getting closure for many bereaved families. It's open to question, however, whether seeing justice done to the perpetrator(s) is also a necessary element.

For certain bereaved families, seeing justice done is important. The problem, however, is that the family's concept of what constitutes justice in the case may differ widely from that of the justice system itself. Moreover, there seems to be a fine line between justice and retribution, and when the family crosses this line, they may become consumed with the need to settle the score. This quest for vengeance often has a corrosive effect on the family's ability to move on into successfully grieving the loss.

The real problem with retribution, as summed up in the old biblical "eye for an eye" philosophy, is that it doesn't restore sight to the semiblinded victim. Instead, it only succeeds in making yet another person somewhat sightless. And although this type of retribution may represent justice in its most basic form, it's devoid of the caring qualities that you need in order to heal the loss of a loved one. Worse, retribution offers no guarantee that you'll be released from fixating on the wrong done to you and your loved one, which can make it nearly impossible to grieve the loss. Only forgiveness can offer you this type of assurance (see Chapter 14).

If you feel the need to lay blame on the persons or circumstances responsible for the death of your loved one, be very careful that your drive doesn't displace your need to grieve the loss. Especially when the loss is fresh and particularly painful, it's easy to become fixated on the liability issue rather than the loss itself. Although you definitely need to work through all the feelings you have surrounding responsibility, doing so isn't a substitute for grieving your lost loved one but rather a way to access the grief work you still need to do. (Turn to Chapter 12 for more on troubled grieving.)

Grieving a Death by Suicide

Suicide produces a very special and complex type of loss. It's a death in which you definitely know who the responsible party is, although you still may not know all the circumstances that led up to it. Death by suicide can be either of the following:

- ✔ An anticipated loss that you desperately tried to prevent, fighting long and hard side by side with your loved one
- ✔ A sudden loss that didn't come with the traditional warning signs, as well as one that you naively thought your loved one had put far behind him

Making matters even more difficult is the fact that suicide is one of those rare types of losses that's almost universally disapproved of by traditional religions and society at large. As a result, the people left behind often feel shame along with the inevitable guilt. The typical bereaved family deals with a triple whammy of pain: dishonor and recrimination heaped on top of the grief of the loss.

Experiencing the suicide of a loved one

Although suicide is deemed an unnecessary death, all suicides are not equal. Consider the case of an old man racked with the progressive pain and disability of a terminal illness who ends his own life. Consider the case of a young, healthy, and extremely bright teenage girl racked with depression and self-doubt who ends her own life.

Although religions and society at large may see no qualitative difference between these two examples, judging both to be cases of senseless and needless deaths, most people wouldn't see them as quite the same. More important, the bereaved families of the two people probably wouldn't grieve the deaths in quite the same way.

In the case of the old man with the terminal illness who commits suicide, his family may have a sense of understanding. Moreover, they may even harbor a sense of relief, seeing that their loved one is no longer in physical pain or suffering psychological distress over his deteriorating physical condition and increasing debility.

In the case of the teenage girl suffering from deep depression who commits suicide, the family may not understand at all why this had to happen. They may harbor a real sense of guilt over not having been able to prevent the death, as well as real feelings that this loss is as senseless as it is tragic.

Many times, the members of a family bereft of a loved one lost to suicide have a great deal of anger over the situation. They may direct their anger at themselves for not having been able to decipher the warning signs and prevent the death. They also may direct anger toward the lost loved one for not reaching out to someone to get help, for going through with the suicide, and for putting the entire family through a preventable nightmare. Altogether, survivors can experience a combination of hurt feelings that can include rejection and abandonment, along with a profound shattering of their self-esteem.

Dealing with guilt and second-guessing

Families grieving the suicide of a loved one usually aren't dealing with the relatively straightforward and mild type of "woulda, coulda, shoulda" second-guessing that seems to routinely accompany the other types of losses. Instead, these families are much more apt to be plagued by a deep sense of responsibility and remorse for not having prevented the act.

This deep sense of guilt of bereaved family members is fueled in no small part by the idea that the death was totally unnecessary. And as a result, the loss not only could have been avoided but, in fact, should have been avoided.

The feeling that you should have been able to prevent the suicide is, in turn, fueled by the understanding that the people who commit suicide generally give warning signs before committing the act (see the sidebar "Classic warning signs of suicide"). However, it's also true that even if you recognize the signs (and most people do) and try to get your loved one the help he needs, there's no guarantee that you can save him and ultimately prevent his death.

Some people who commit suicide never show the classic signs before completing the act. You may find your loved one more withdrawn and down than usual, but you may not get any indication that he's in serious trouble and about to end it all.

Dealing with shame

Unfortunately, the unyielding condemnation of suicide by major religions such as Judaism, Christianity, and Islam and the secular societies that they influence makes many people grieving the suicide of a loved one feel a real sense of shame over the death. Some religions go so far as to deny the victim of suicide traditional burial rites (Judaism), while others teach that suicide is a major sin that may preclude the victim's ultimate salvation (some sects of Christianity and Islam).

The belief that suicide is such a major and unforgivable sin is rooted in the notion that God is the source of all life, and as such, all life is sacred and not to be taken in vain. To me, it's highly ironic how easily religions can justify the taking of others' lives (when they're deemed enemies of the faith or the state) and be forgiving of those killings while remaining so unrelenting in their condemnation of taking one's own life.

The big difference between someone who contemplates and someone who acts is that the former doesn't lose all hope in the future and is able to pull back and recover his normal, balanced sense of life before it's too late.

My take on suicide is that no one actually commits the act while in his right mind. The person who does may be out of his right mind for any number of reasons — chemical imbalance, genetic propensity, child abuse, chronic depression, and who knows what else — but he's out of his normal way of thinking nonetheless. Therefore, I can't believe that anyone who actually commits suicide is culpable for his own murder in the same way as someone who takes another person's life premeditatively. And, as a result, I think that the person who commits suicide actually is much easier to forgive.

Classic warning signs of suicide

The classic warning signs of suicide include the following behaviors:

- Previous suicide attempts

- Talking about suicide

- Making statements about feeling hopeless or about how life is no longer worth living

- Preoccupation with death

- Suddenly putting one's business and/or personal affairs in order

- Suddenly giving away one's possessions

- Overindulging in drugs or alcohol

- Suddenly becoming much happier after being depressed for a time

Note that some of these classic signs, including talking about suicide, making statements about life no longer being worth living, and overindulging in drugs or alcohol, are also common signs of grieving the death of a loved one. Keep this in mind when dealing with someone who's grieving: These signs may be nothing more than normal grieving, but they also may indicate that the bereaved person is seriously contemplating suicide.

Dealing with the public and religious disapproval of suicide can be very tough indeed. Try to keep in mind that this disapproval stems from a deep respect for life that in no way demeans or denies the many worthwhile qualities in your loved one that you now miss so intensely. As much as possible, keep your focus on your loved one, the relationship you shared, and the grief that you now feel, and let any criticism by others about the manner of death be their concern and not yours.

Resources to Help You Deal with Different Kinds of Death

There are many resources to turn to for help dealing with the different kinds of death (anticipated, sudden, and suicide) discussed in this chapter. I begin with a short list of the Web addresses and hotline phone numbers for three main nonprofit foundations that can answer your questions regarding hospice, Alzheimer's disease, and suicide:

- **Hospice Foundation of America** at www.hospicefoundation.org: This Web site contains basic information on hospice services along with tools and articles on grief and loss. This site also contains a message board where you can share your story with others as well as a link to the Hospice Directory Web site, where you can locate a hospice organization operating in your local area.

- **National Alzheimer's Association** at www.alz.org or call the 24-hour help line at 1-800-272-3900: Call the 24-hour help line to receive information about Alzheimer's disease and the latest research; caregiving for someone with Alzheimer's; and legal, financial, and living-arrangement decisions, as well as referrals to local programs and services. The site also contains a link to a CareFinder page that helps you locate qualified professional caregivers in your area.

- **National Suicide Prevention Lifeline** at www.suicideprevention lifeline.org or call the 24-hour crisis line at 1-800-273-TALK (1-800-273-8255): Call the crisis line if you or someone you love is seriously contemplating suicide or in the midst of an emergency that could possibly result in suicide. The crisis line routes callers to the closest local suicide crisis center for immediate assistance and guidance. Visit the Web site for information about the warning signs of suicide and how you can get involved in suicide prevention.

Books

The books on sudden death, caregiving, and suicide are numerous (especially on caregiving and suicide). I've boiled down this rather extensive book list to the following favorites:

- ✔ *I Wasn't Ready to Say Goodbye: Surviving, Coping, and Healing after the Sudden Death of a Loved One* by Brook Noel and Pamela D. Blair (Champion Press Ltd.): This is a comprehensive book on grieving the sudden death of a loved one. The authors cover the emotional and physical aspects of grieving a sudden loss, the Kübler-Ross stages of grieving, ways to overcome blocks to grieving, and suggestions for relating your story to others. This book covers losses of a wide range of people, including parents, partners, children, siblings, and friends.

- ✔ *Caregiving: The Spiritual Journey of Love, Loss, and Renewal* by Beth Witrogen McLeod (Wiley): This is both a very practical book on being the caregiver for a loved one and an inspirational work. McLeod covers topics that range from a definition of what family caregiving is to caregiving as a rite of passage. The author includes basic action steps that you can follow in addition to the text that's intended to inform and motivate and encourage you at every turn in your caregiving journey.

- ✔ *The Fearless Caregiver: How to Get the Best Care for Your Loved Ones and Still Have a Life of Your Own* by Gary Barg (Capitol Books): In this book, you get great practical information on being an effective caregiver for a loved one. In addition, it contains vital information on ways that you can take care of yourself and avoid the all-too-common burnout that so many caregivers suffer.

- ✔ *The Comfort of Home: A Complete Guide for Caregivers* by Maria M. Meyer and Paula Derr (Care Trust Publications): This illustrated book is a basic and practical guide to providing care for a loved one at home. It's divided into three parts: "Getting Ready," with information on what it takes to do caregiving at home, how to get in-home help, dealing with financial matters, and procuring the necessary equipment and supplies; "Day by Day," with information on how to plan daily activities as well as deal with emergencies and avoid burnout; and "Additional Resources," with a glossary and bibliography along with a list of common abbreviations used in the healthcare profession and medical specialists whom you may want to consult.

- ✔ *No Time to Say Goodbye: Surviving the Suicide of a Loved One* by Carla Fine (Main Street Books): In 1989, the author's husband took his own life after being deeply depressed over the deaths of his parents. This practical and inspiring book on surviving the suicide of a loved one written from the perspective of a suicide survivor is at the same time both sensitive and informative.

✔ **Sanity & Grace: A Journey of Suicide, Survival, and Strength** by Judy Collins (Penguin): In 1992, folk singer Judy Collin's son Clark committed suicide. This book contains a moving account of a mother's attempt to make sense of and come to grips with her adult son's death by his own hand. Most of the chapters begin with personal journal entries covering the period from 1997 to 2001 that the author then uses to discuss particular challenges associated with surviving the suicide of a loved one.

If you're a fan of the *For Dummies* series (as I'm sure you are judging by the fact that you're reading this book!), be sure to check out Dr. Rachelle Zukerman's *Eldercare For Dummies* (Wiley) for good, solid information about caregiving and *Alzheimer's For Dummies* by Patricia Smith, Mary M. Kenan, et al. (Wiley) for tons of invaluable information about dealing with the care and treatment of this disease.

Online resources

Online resources for this chapter include three categories of Web sites: those that support family and professional caregivers, those that help survivors of a violent death or homicide, and those that help prevent suicide and support the survivors of suicide. In these categories, I recommend that you visit the following:

✔ **Today's Caregiver Magazine** at www.caregiver.com: Gary Barg, the author of *The Fearless Caregiver* (see the preceding list of books) is the editor-in-chief of *Today's Caregiver* magazine. In addition to giving you information about the magazine and its articles and enabling you to obtain a subscription or buy back issues, this site contains informational links. You can link to information on particular ailments such as Alzheimer's and schizophrenia and on particular challenges for caregivers such as mobility and long-term care. You also find a page with links to regional resources to help support your caregiving.

✔ **National Alliance for Caregiving** at www.caregiving.org: This site is designed for both family caregivers and professionals. It contains useful information on Medicare resources (including the Medicare prescription drug benefit) along with caregiving tips.

✔ **Family Caregiving 101** at www.familycaregiving101.org: This site devoted to family caregivers contains basic information on the skills and resources needed to provide effective care for a loved one. You also get valuable information on how to navigate the healthcare maze and assist a family caregiver.

✔ **Teen Life: Suicide** at `dmoz.org/kids_and_teens/teen_life/suicide`: This Web page contains links to a whole array of articles about teenagers and suicide. Online articles run the gamut from "Adolescent Suicide in the School Setting" to "Youth Suicide Prevention Programs."

✔ **Violent Death Bereavement Society** at `www.vdbs.org`: Although this Web site primarily offers training and support to professionals and agencies helping survivors who are grieving a loss through a violent death, it also contains valuable links to other Web sites that survivors of violent death or homicide can use themselves.

✔ **Stop a Suicide, Today!** at `www.stopasuicide.org`: This site clues you in to the warning signs of suicide, how to help a friend who's contemplating suicide, quick facts on suicide, and suicide and its relationship to mental illness. It has a page for survivors of suicide with links to information on coping with the loss and getting support.

✔ **Suicide.org: Suicide Prevention, Awareness, and Support** at `www.suicide.org`: This is one of the most comprehensive Web sites ever put together on suicide prevention and support. You can find links to information on almost every conceivable condition that can contribute to suicide, such as depression, bipolar disorder, PTSD (post-traumatic stress disorder), postpartum depression, domestic violence, rape, and divorce. This site also contains lots of information and links to support the survivors of suicide.

Chapter 3

The Loss of Parents

*I*t's entirely fitting to begin the investigation into common types of profound losses and the kind of grief they produce by looking closely at the loss of parents and the significant effects of this type of loss. The loss of parents is one of the most common types of loss that anyone is likely to experience in his life.

Surprisingly, it's also a loss whose effects many people underestimate. This may well be because most people (fortunately) don't lose their parents until they're adults, often with children of their own. As a result, they assume that they're of an age to be more prepared for such a loss. Unfortunately, whatever the age, the loss of a connection to one's matrix can rank among the most powerful and life-altering experiences, setting in motion a number of momentous changes.

This chapter, therefore, begins with an exploration of the nature of the relationship with your parents that's severed upon their departure and the onset of feeling orphaned. The chapter concludes with an investigation into the impact that this break in generations may bring, depending upon your age, the manner of the loss, and the relative health of the relationship at the time the loss occurs. It also looks at the challenges of dealing with and helping a surviving parent before listing resources you can turn to get to more information and help on dealing with this very challenging type of loss.

Looking at Parental Roles

At their best, parents provide us with a whole lot more than just their DNA. They play a number of vital roles that you can divide into two basic categories:

- **Nurturing,** which includes all the ways parents protect, provide, and rear their children, fostering in them a sense of security and well-being. In their roles as nurturers, parents provide a roof over your head, food in your belly, and shoes on your feet. They also tend to your wounds, both physical and emotional, wipe the tears from your eyes, and get you back on your feet after suffering setbacks, both real and imagined, as well as watch over your development.

- **Maturing,** which includes all the ways parents teach, encourage, and challenge their children, fostering in them a sense of responsibility and independence. In their roles as maturers, parents teach you to walk and talk and even play with you. They also scold you when you do wrong and guide you in rectifying your less-than-stellar deeds. They act as role models after whom you can mold your character, as well as coaches who encourage you to take responsibility for your actions and challenge the assumptions, both inflated and understated, that you hold about yourself.

Your parents tend to perform more nurturing roles when you're an infant and young child and more helpless; they perform more maturing roles when you're an older child and teenager and less helpless. But it's also true that they continue to play these roles in some measure throughout your entire life, even after you've left the nest and are living on your own.

Even after they no longer pay your rent, put the food on your table, and keep clothes on your back, you still know that your parents are there if you get in a jam, and they would again provide some of these things should you really need them. And although they may no longer be able to prescribe the consequences you endure as a result of your actions, chances are good (almost too good) that they still give you advice, both asked for and unsolicited, on what course of action you should take, and they continue to care what you do and what happens to you all your life.

When parents don't excel at nurturing and maturing, this lack of good parenting greatly impacts your grieving their loss. The death of such parents can heighten your awareness of what you didn't get and will never receive from them. See "Dealing with the death of an absent or abusive parent" later in this chapter for more on this subject.

TECHNICAL STUFF

Bereft and bereaved

The word "bereft" is actually an alternative form of the past tense of the verb "bereave" (bereaved). Bereave comes from the Old English verb "bereafian" meaning "to be robbed or plundered." Although bereavement has come to describe the state of being that's brought on by the loss of a loved one through death, you may want to keep in mind its original meaning of being robbed, as this may be exactly how you feel.

Feeling orphaned at any age

The concept of being orphaned carries two meanings: being deprived of one's parents and being deprived of some protection and advantage. The first definition is normally applied to children who lose their parents, on account of the parents' death or inability to care for them, and who then grow up in the care of others. The second definition for being orphaned is one that I think applies to all who lose parents at whatever age and in whatever circumstances.

When you lose your parents as a young child, you're most likely to feel bereft of the basic security and well-being that otherwise may have been yours. When you lose your parents as an adult, you're less likely to feel bereft of basic security and well-being, although you may well miss terribly your parents' guidance and feedback (even if you didn't always listen to their advice).

Reversing roles with aging parents

If you're fortunate enough to see your parents into their golden years, you may experience some role reversal as you and your siblings become care-givers for your parents. Just as in earlier days your parents provided you with shelter and protected you from harm, now you're called upon to provide them these things. Depending upon the state of your parents' health, you may also be called upon to provide them with the necessary encouragement and challenges to foster in them a sense of self-reliance and some semblance of independence.

This form of parenting your own parents often marks the beginning of a gen-erational changing of the guard, a process in which the younger generation of the family assumes the roles of the older one. It also can mark the decisive end of your own extended childhood, especially if you don't have your own children and therefore aren't parents in your own right.

Because so few people, even those blessed with tons of relatives, can tap into nonstop support from extended family, providing adequate care for ailing and aging parents can be one of the most challenging and difficult tasks you face before their actual passing. The situation becomes all the more challenging when the care must be provided by paid caregivers or can't be given in the home, meaning that a trustworthy and affordable skilled-nursing facility must be found.

The stress of being a caregiver and dealing with anticipatory grief is an important subject.

The Loss of Grandparents as One's Initial Experience with Grief

For many, the death of a grandparent marks a person's very first experience with grief in the immediate family. It may also be one's very first up-close and personal experience with death.

While the impact of the death may fall mostly on your mom if the grandparent was one of her parents and on your dad if the grandparent was one of his parents, the loss can be expected to affect the entire nuclear family.

If you're fairly young when your grandparent dies, the way your immediate family deals with the death and the way the parent who lost his or her parent grieves the loss can greatly influence both your views toward death and your understanding of grief.

In my case, my maternal grandfather was the first person in my immediate family to die. His death occurred when I was about 10 years old. I didn't know him very well because my maternal grandparents had divorced when I was a baby and my family visited him only occasionally. His funeral was the first one I attended, and it had a great impact on me even though I wasn't particularly sad at my grandfather's passing given that I didn't know him all that well. After the funeral, I noticed that my mother was rather quiet and introspective for about a week and thereafter seemed to be unaffected.

My second experience with death and grief in the family came with the passing of my maternal grandmother some years later. After divorcing my grandfather, she had moved to Pasadena, giving real meaning to the Beach Boys' hit "The Little Old Lady From Pasadena," but visited my family back in Chicago regularly for extended periods. As a result, I became very close to her as she cared for me when I was a young child. When my grandmother became critically ill, my mother and aunt went to California, where they stayed until my grandmother died and was buried.

After returning home from the funeral, my mother responded to her mother's death more or less as she had to her father's. Although somewhat more openly emotional this time, her depression seemed to last no more than a week. My emotional response to this death, however, was not so measured. This was my first experience with grief, and I was amazed and confused by my feelings. Also, because my feelings of sadness seemed to be so much stronger than my mother's, I figured that there must be something wrong with me for taking the death so hard (after all, my mother had just lost her mother and was able to cope with the loss so much better than I was).

These initial experiences with death in the loss of my maternal grandparents and my family's response (including my own) to them were quite misleading. I took away the mistaken impression that the death of one's parents, provided that it occurred in the natural course of time when they were seniors and the children grown, was not that big of a deal. It was something that you could get over in a relatively short time and that had no lasting effects.

I didn't discover how misguided this assumption was until I lost my own parents many years later — my dad when I was just about to turn 40 and my mom a decade later.

Exploring the Impact of Losing Parents

The impact of the death of your parents shouldn't be minimized. The actual extent of the grief it produces for you depends upon a great many factors, which can include:

- ✔ Your age at the time of your parent's death
- ✔ Your gender and that of your parent
- ✔ The intimacy of your relationship with your parent
- ✔ The number of brothers and sisters you have and your birth order

These factors can combine to magnify the loss and extend the grief. For example, if you're a girl who loses her mother when you're young and you're also the eldest of several siblings, you may not only find yourself dealing with the loss of your mother's advice and guidance as you grow up but also continually struggling with your own attempts to mother your younger siblings. If you're a boy who's an only child and who loses your dad, with whom you've had a persistently strained relationship as an adult, you may find yourself dealing not only with the feelings of being orphaned and alone but also with all the unresolved issues between you and your father.

Experiencing the death of a parent as a child

Experiencing the death of a parent is traumatic at any age, but it's particularly harrowing for young children. With the death of a parent, young children are deprived not only of the guidance and love that that parent would have provided as the children grew up but also the sense of security that the parent's ongoing presence in the home would have bestowed. More often than not, the child feels terribly vulnerable, especially when the death is accompanied by a relocation of the family.

Because one of the two people the child counted on being with him and supporting him (in all aspects) until adulthood is now gone, it's not at all unusual for the child to cling to the surviving parent. The child can easily become quite concerned with this parent's health, afraid that, should the parent fail to take care of himself or herself, the child will be without anyone to support him and be truly orphaned.

Although they may never fully go away, these feelings of vulnerability are often alleviated to some extent by the grieving process, especially if the child's able to share this process with his surviving parent and siblings. In situations where the surviving parent has great difficulty grieving the loss of his or her spouse and continuing to function as a parent, it's not unusual for the child to try to step in and care for the parent. This role reversal, of course, puts an undue and unfair burden on the child, while running the risk of stifling the child's ability to grieve the loss. In families with many siblings, the oldest child may also try to care for and parent the younger children in an attempt to lighten the load on the surviving parent.

Grief can manifest itself in many different ways in children, some of which are physical and others psychological. Also, guilt over the death is quite common, especially in younger children. See Chapter 7 for details on the ways in which children deal with grief and suggestions of ways to help them through their grief.

Integrating the grief as you mature

The grief that accompanies the loss of a parent as a child (as opposed to such a loss as an adult) is made more complex by the fact that the child has to integrate this loss into his life as part of growing up and becoming an adult. As the child reaches different plateaus in his life and experiences the rites of passage that mark the transition from childhood to adulthood (such as graduations, communion, bar mitzvah, getting a driver's license, and proms), he does so without the parent. In the face of the parent's absence, more often than not, the event becomes another opportunity to revisit the grief and another challenge to integrate it into the child's life.

The events that a child doesn't get to share with the lost parent don't stop with adulthood. As the child moves through adulthood, several salient events are opportunities to revisit the grief. Chief among them are marriage (especially for girls who've lost their dads and have to ask someone else to give them away during the ceremony) and the births of grandchildren.

Reaching the age of your deceased parent

Perhaps the most salient milestone for a person who's lost a parent as a child is reaching the same age that the parent was when she or he died. For many people who've experienced parental loss as a child, this birthday is the most poignant they've ever experienced. It often touches off a whole new round of longing for and reminiscing over the lost parent, but, more importantly, it also initiates intense soul-searching about the future.

The introspection that accompanies reaching the age of the deceased parent seems to be particularly true for people who are the same gender as the parent who died. In this case, many report genuine surprise that they've lived as long as their deceased parents. Some report even doubting they'll live beyond the age at which the parent passed away and feeling apprehension over their own imminent death. Even when this fear isn't present, they still wonder about their futures and take the anniversary as an occasion for taking stock of their lives and questioning the direction of the next stage of their lives.

If you lost a parent as a child and are now reaching the age at which he or she died, you may want to make this an exceptional birthday celebration in which you honor your deceased parent and his or her accomplishments alongside your own. You can use this special occasion to take stock of your life up to now and decide whether or not its direction needs some fine-tuning.

Experiencing the death of a parent as an adult

When your parent dies when you're an adult — especially one who's pretty well established and has at least reached middle age — and your parent is a senior, many people assume that the grief that accompanies the loss will not be all that devastating and life altering. While it's true that adults who lose their parents don't face the same challenges as children, especially when it comes to security and guidance in growing up, this doesn't mean that they get a free ride.

For many people, the death of a parent is the most devastating loss they experience in their lives, unless and until they experience the death of a spouse or partner. Moreover, the extent of the grief attached to the loss often comes as a surprise even for people who are very close to their parents and part of a very close-knit family.

In addition to the shock over the depth of the grief, many are also dumbfounded by the many ways in which the loss of a parent as an adult affects their own self-image as well as their relations with their spouses and other family members. For some reason, the assumption is that because you're an adult who's relatively well established in life, the passing of a parent will not (or should not) have anywhere near the same kind of devastating effect that it sometimes does.

The end of childhood

You may have long regarded yourself as an adult, functionally independent of your parents, and you may even be a parent of your own children. Nevertheless, it's not until the day that the first parent passes away that you feel that your childhood has come to an abrupt and final end.

With that loss, you come to appreciate that the mantle of adulthood has now really fallen squarely on your shoulders. This understanding can dawn in a couple of ways:

- ✔ It can come with the understanding that you (and your siblings) must now assume full responsibility for the surviving parent.
- ✔ It can come with the comprehension that your generation is in the process of moving up a notch and is now not only the "responsible" one but the next in line to face the Grim Reaper.

Following the loss of the second parent, some people — especially only children (otherwise known as *singletons*) and lastborns — can experience feelings of both being lost and liberated at the same time. They feel lost because they're now truly orphaned, and, in the case of singletons, they really have no one in the immediate nuclear family upon whom to rely. They feel liberated because for the first time they're truly in a position to make all their own decisions independent of any parental assessment. (Of course, this feeling of liberation also can be quite intimidating if the adult child continued to be rather dependent upon his parents until their demise.)

It's not unusual for adults who've lost a parent with whom they shared freely and were particularly close to experience feelings of uncertainty along with the usual feelings of sadness. This uncertainty, however, is quite unlike the kind experienced by a child who's lost a parent; it stems from missing a trusted confidant and guide rather than from losing a protector and benefactor.

In my own case, I continue to miss consulting with my dad over big decisions in my life. As an adult, I came to rely upon my discussions with him over matters that I considered particularly crucial. These discussions helped me clarify the issue at hand as well as get some advice from someone not only who knew me very well but also who I had no doubt always had my best interests at heart. After he died, I didn't have anyone whom I could count on in quite the same manner (even among close friends whose advice I trusted). Over time and as part of grieving his death, I realized that I learned to internalize my father's advice; by thinking through what my dad may have counseled me when I faced a tough decision in my life, I had developed a way of keeping him alive for me and keeping in communication with him.

Many adults report that, after the death of their parents, they finally come to appreciate all that their parents did for them and meant to them. They also report that they undergo a process of soul-searching and a kind of identity crisis, at the end of which they finally feel that they've really grown up and are finally ready to completely assume adult responsibilities. Part of this soul-searching can mean coming to terms with the fact that they've lost the possibility of getting what they felt deprived of and wanted so badly in the relationship.

Changes to your relationships within the family

It pretty much goes without saying that the death of a parent is very disruptive to the immediate nuclear family (that is, you, the surviving parent, and your siblings), even when all surviving children are grown and living independently. The shock of the death tests the family system, emphasizing both its strengths and weaknesses:

- ✔ In a close-knit family, the death can bring the immediate family closer together than it's ever been before.

- ✔ In a family prone to some level of dysfunction, the death of a parent can expose existing fractures and reignite old rivalries, sometimes between the surviving children and the surviving parent but more often between siblings. These outbreaks of tension can arise during the funeral as well as later on in the course of trying to aid the surviving parent in settling the deceased parent's estate and dealing with the pain of the loss of his or her partner (see "Helping the Surviving Parent," later in this chapter).

✔ In the best of situations, the death actually spurs estranged siblings to reconcile and helps to mend fences between those siblings who've grown apart after leaving home.

✔ In the worst of situations, the death can provoke old jealousies and drive new wedges between siblings who haven't been on the best terms since childhood.

✔ If the deceased parent acted as a power broker or peacemaker among the adult children, his or her absence may lead to a certain amount of sibling infighting as the family system attempts to reestablish equilibrium and one or more of the survivors attempt to fill this role. As part of this process, the surviving children may get caught up in critiquing their relationship to the deceased parent ("I was always Dad's favorite") as well as in engaging in a blame game regarding their siblings ("You were never there for her").

During this time, it's especially important to guard against ganging up on a particular sibling, especially if he or she has been particularly absent in the parent's life or has been tagged a "black sheep." This kind of scapegoating isn't destructive to the family system but is very counterproductive when it comes to your own grieving process.

Changes to your relationships with your spouse

In addition to affecting changes in your relationships with your siblings, suffering the death of a parent as an adult may also lead you to experience a change in your relationship with your own spouse or partner. Many adults who've lost a parent to whom they were close then turn to their spouses not only for comfort in their grief but also for the approval that used to come from that parent (even if the adult child didn't particularly crave this kind of endorsement when the parent was alive). Of course, this greater emotional dependence upon your spouse or partner can cut both ways: It can either bring you closer to your partner or drive a wedge between you.

If, after losing a parent, you find yourself needing your spouse's praise almost as much if not more than his or her empathy, you may want to consider the role that your deceased parent played in cultivating your self-esteem. If the lost parent was vital in this process, discuss this situation with your partner and let him or her know what may be happening. That way, you have more of a chance of getting your emotional needs met and less of a chance of alienating your partner in the bargain.

Losing a parent through divorce

Divorce may not bring with it the finality that the death of a parent does, but for many children, divorce produces a sense of loss that must be grieved in very much the same manner. For most children of divorce, the breakup of the family only disrupts the influence of one of the parents (more likely than not, the father). In some instances, however, the divorce ends the parent's inter-action in the child's life, effectively ending his influence and, for all intents and purposes, rendering him deceased. The only mitigating factor with a loss of a parent through divorce rather than death is the fact that because the parent isn't physically deceased, the possibility of reconciliation and reunion is always possible.

Grieving the loss of a parent as a result of divorce is often made more difficult by the fact that divorce is frequently accompanied by a level of animosity and recriminations that, thankfully, rarely attends a parent's death. Often the child of divorce doesn't feel safe expressing his sorrow and acknowledging his grief in such an environment. The child also may feel compelled to take the side of the parent with whom he stays to show his loyalty and as a way of helping that parent through her pain.

Keep in mind that children, especially young children, are prone to blame themselves in some way for the breakup of the family just as they're inclined to find blame for the death of a parent (see Chapter 7). This aspect of guilt can be a form of questioning the parent's love for the child as well as a mech-anism for explaining the situation. Regardless, it adds another layer to the grieving process and must be dealt with before moving on to dealing with the sadness over the loss.

Dealing with the death of an absent or abusive parent

One of the most difficult parental losses to grieve is one in which the deceased parent was primarily absent from your life or, even worse, abusive in some manner. Both situations bring their own extra difficulties to grieving, although the feelings that they evoke are very different.

In terms of a parent who's been mostly or totally absent from your life, if you never had a chance to know that parent, let alone come to depend on and love him or her, it's impossible to really grieve the loss. You never got the proper chance to develop a deep connection with the parent, and therefore you can't expect his or her death to represent a profound loss for you (as would the death of the parent who did stay in your life).

This doesn't mean that you don't feel any sadness or remorse in regard to the death, however. You may well find yourself extremely sad and going through all the stages associated with the normal grieving for a parent. In this case, though, it's likely that you're grieving the parent's absence from your life more than his or her death. The loss in this case isn't the bond with the parent but the lack of the bond. All the feelings of remorse and shame that you associate with the abandonment are likely to surface and become among the primary things you have to deal with in order to process the grief you feel.

In terms of a parent who has been psychologically, physically, or sexually abusive, the death may actually represent a relief rather than any kind of great sadness. This personal sense of relief may be accompanied by a larger sense of cosmic or divine justice.

This sense of relief can too easily turn into feelings of guilt. These feelings of guilt may play directly into any misplaced feelings of responsibility that the abused child harbors regarding the abuse, compounding the abuse and complicating the grieving.

Other family members can make grieving an abusive parent all the more difficult if the family never properly or openly acknowledges the abuse. The family may underrate or even totally deny the abuse so as to protect the public legacy of the deceased parent. This denial leads to even more pain for the child or children who suffered the abuse to process as part of their grieving.

As TV's Dr. Phil is so wont to remind us all, the person who was made to suffer abuse is never responsible for that abuse. That dishonor rests entirely upon the shoulders of the abuser. It's important to remember this little truism if you're someone dealing with the death of an abusive parent so as not to be tempted to take on some of the accountability for the abuse, especially if the rest of the family is in deep denial.

Like children of absent parents, the children of abusive parents may end up grieving not so much the deceased parent as the lack of love and nurturing in life. In addition to mourning this loss of love, the children undoubtedly also grieve the loss of innocence and trust that they suffered as a direct result of parental abuse.

Because grieving an abusive parent is sure to stir up your emotions surrounding the abuse, this is one of the few times when you may be better off putting aside the grieving until after you have a chance to process your feelings about the abuse. Consider seeking counseling from someone who specializes in recovering from child abuse before you join a grief support group or seek out a grief counselor.

Helping the Surviving Parent

In addition to grieving your own loss of a parent, you may find yourself in the position of having to help your surviving parent cope with the loss of his or her spouse (see Chapter 4). You also may have to help settle your deceased parent's estate, help your surviving parent manage the financial affairs (especially if the parent relied entirely on his or her spouse to take care of these matters), and even relocate the parent to a more appropriate living situation.

In some cases, you may even have to go so far as to provide care for the surviving parent, especially in the case of an older parent who's ailing or frail at the time of the spouse's death. This care may take the form of having the surviving parent come to live with you or finding affordable and trustworthy housing where your parent can receive professional care.

Helping your surviving parent cope with the loss

Although you typically look to your parents as your guides through the difficult situations in life, this is one case where, assuming you're an adult, you may be called upon to take the lead. The surviving parent is often in no shape to guide you and is in need of all the help you can give. This can be especially true of older parents for whom the intimacy and long duration of the relationship make it nearly impossible for the surviving parent to conceive of life without his or her spouse. (This was true for my parents, who had just celebrated their 59th wedding anniversary when my father died.)

The best thing you can do in such a situation is support your surviving parent in his grief as a person who has lost his partner in life while you honor your own grief as a child who has lost a parent. Many times, providing support simply means staying in close touch with your parent and offering to listen. Other times, it may mean reminiscing about your lost loved one and actively mourning his or her passing.

The most important thing, however, is to stay as present as possible with your parent's grief while at the same time acknowledging your own. Because you're both mourning a great loss, you should be able to express and exchange feelings and remembrances about your lost loved one relatively freely. You know better than most your parent's comfort level when it comes to expressing his or her feelings, so share as much as feels right, and don't pressure for more interaction in grief.

Suffice it say, grieving a parent is not the time for recriminations and fact-finding missions. No matter how great your need is to explore a topic involving the deceased parent, leave it alone if you know very well that your surviving parent is uncomfortable with the topic. There's a time later in the grieving process when you're actively incorporating the loss into your lives when it's not only appropriate but often helpful to share and explore the less saint-like aspects of the deceased.

When the loss is fresh and the grief acute, share the endearing stories and memories that highlight what your lost loved one means to you and just what you're missing and mourning. When you're dealing with a parent for whom the loss is just too raw and for whom such reminisces bring too much pain, find a relative or a mutual friend with whom to share these memories. You can still support your surviving parent by just sitting with him or her and being there in silence.

Helping the surviving parent manage affairs

One of the most effective ways to help your surviving parent is to help him or her manage financial and practical affairs — from helping to make the funeral arrangements and arrange for the disposition of the deceased's personal effects to balancing the checkbook and paying the monthly bills.

The degree of management help that a parent needs and can benefit from depends upon several factors:

- **Parent's age and health:** An 80-year-old parent in failing health will need more assistance than a 60-year-old parent in excellent health.

- **Parent's gender and roles in the home:** A mother who has never worked a day outside of the house and who relied on her husband to take care of all the financial affairs will require a lot more assistance than a father who worked in an office until the day he retired. So too, a father who never cooked a meal in his life will require more guidance and help in the kitchen than a father who was close to being a gourmet chef.

- **Parent's personality and level of self-assurance:** A gregarious parent with tons of friends in the community and who tackles every challenge with gusto will need less help than a shy, retiring parent who goes into new experiences kicking and screaming.

This section is about *helping* your surviving parent manage his or her financial affairs, not managing the affairs for the parent. It's very important that you take on no more than necessary. A parent's sense of independence and self-sufficiency is always an important element in his or her survival and can ultimately go a long way in helping him or her successfully grieve the loss.

Providing care for the surviving parent

With elderly parents, it may be the case that, after the death of one parent, the surviving one is no longer capable of living on his or her own. This is especially true when the parent who dies acted as a caregiver for the surviving parent. In this situation, you face a choice between providing the care for the surviving parent in your own home or that of one of your siblings or finding a facility that can provide professional care.

Your decision on how to provide necessary care for the surviving parent is primarily based on economic and logistical factors. Senior housing, independent-living centers, and skilled-nursing facilities may well be beyond the family's means. On the other hand, your home or those of any siblings willing to take in Mom or Dad may not be large enough or properly equipped for your parent to live in comfortably. For example, a second-floor bedroom may be out of the question depending on your parent's mobility.

Caring for the surviving parent in your own home

Becoming your parent's caregiver can be more rewarding than you ever anticipated, bringing you and the other members of your family (especially your children) closer to your parent than ever before. Even so, caregiving may be something that you'd love to do to repay your parent but realistically is beyond your ability to provide.

Even if your home has room for your surviving parent and a layout that accommodates his or her needs, you still have to look long and hard at your willingness and ability to become your parent's caregiver. Depending upon the health and temperament of your parent after the loss, the state of your relationship with the parent, and your own state of affairs, this undertaking can be a whole lot more challenging than you ever expected.

You have to consider all angles of a caregiving situation in order to be able to decide what's best not only for your parent but also for you and the others in your household. You definitely need to consult with the other members of your immediate family, including your spouse or partner and your own children. Remember that everyone's life will be affected by this decision, so everyone needs to be on the same page. Also, be sure that your mom or dad isn't feeling as though she or he will be a burden on the household and is genuinely okay with the new living situation.

Finding appropriate independent housing for a surviving parent

Many people have a justified abhorrence of nursing homes and recoil from the thought of ever putting their parents in one. As a hospice patient-care volunteer, I've had the opportunity to visit many of the local skilled-nursing and independent-living facilities in my area, some of which are ritzier than others and, more important, better staffed. I've found in every case that the staff-to-patient ratio is much more important to the residents' well-being than the quality of the physical facilities and planned activities, although sometimes these two things go hand in hand.

When trying to locate suitable independent housing for a surviving parent, you first need to consider whether or not your parent can live in an independent-living center or requires a skilled-nursing facility. Here's a brief description of each:

- ✔ **Independent-living centers for seniors** usually provide apartment-type living with access to shared meals in a common dining area, transportation to and from doctor's appointments, planned activities, and some sort of professional and building security on the site.

- ✔ **Skilled-nursing facilities** provide completely assisted living with around-the-clock professional care usually in rooms equipped with two beds. Meals are served in a common dining room for residents who are independent enough to make use of it and at the bedside of those residents who are not. Also, there are scads of planned activities for those who want and are able to participate.

When locating suitable independent housing for your parent, do a background check on the facility, get information about the security it provides, and inquire about the staff-to-patient ratio it maintains. In addition, you should talk with other residents (or families who are visiting residents) about their experiences with the facility and its staff.

Resources for Healing the Loss of a Parent

If you find that my coverage in this chapter of the loss of parents and the kind of grief that can result has raised more questions, you're fortunate that many other resources are available to answer your questions and get you connected to the right people. This section presents resources — books and Web sites — on losing a parent with which I'm personally familiar.

Books

I recommend two books on the loss of parents:

✔ *Losing Your Parents, Finding Your Self: The Defining Turning Point of Adult Life* by Victoria Secunda (Hyperion): This book is based on the responses to a survey on parental loss by 94 respondents. Secunda carefully examines the aftermath of losing parents in terms of one's self-image and career as well as one's relationship with others, including siblings and partners.

I highly recommend this book for adults who have lost their parents and now find themselves searching for new identities or struggling to finally grow up.

✔ *Never the Same: Coming to Terms with the Death of a Parent* by Donna Schuurman (St. Martin's Press): Donna Schuurman is the executive director of the Dougy Center for Grieving Children & Families in Portland, Oregon (one of the recommended online resources in the following section), which helps both adults and young people through the process of grieving their parents' passing. The great thing about this book is that it's designed somewhat as a workbook: Each chapter's full of questions and blank note pages for the reader to write his or her responses.

Online resources

You can consult many online resources for help in coping with the loss of a parent either as a child or an adult.

The following online resources provide you both general and specialized information on losing a parent:

✔ **Death of a Parent** at www.griefhealing.com/deathparent.htm: This page contains links to a whole bunch of individual articles on particular parental losses, such as "Father Loss," "Healing Mother Loss in Early Childhood," and "Helping Yourself Heal When a Parent Dies."

- ✔ **Dougy Center** at www.dougy.org: This home page for the Dougy Center for Grieving Children & Families Web site contains information and links for supporting children, teens, and adults through the grieving process.

- ✔ **When a Parent Dies** at www.hospicenet.org/html/parent.html: This page from Hospice Net gives pointers on how to inform children about the death of a parent and support them in their grieving.

- ✔ **Grief and Children of Military Personnel** at www.griefandrenewal.com/article35.htm: This article contains specific information about what the children of military personnel go through when a parent dies.

- ✔ **Death of a Parent during Adulthood** at www.supportofficer.org/grief/parent.htm: This article from the book *No Time for Goodbyes* by Janice Harris Lord (Compassion Press) contains suggestions for healing from a sudden or traumatic death of a parent.

- ✔ **KinderStart: Death and Grief Management** at www.kinderstart.com/familydynamics/deathandgriefmanagement.html: This page is full of links to other Web pages that specialize in coping with all kinds of grieving, including many dedicated to a child's loss of a parent.

- ✔ **Children and Separation/Divorce: Helping Your Child Cope** at www.helpguide.org/mental/children_divorce.htm: This page contains information, suggestions, and links on helping your children face and cope with the loss of a parent through divorce or separation.

Chapter 4

The Loss of Spouses and Partners

*I*f finding a partner with whom you can share your days is one of life's greatest rewards, then losing a partner with whom you shared your years surely has to be one of its greatest sorrows. Whether through divorce or death, the loss of a partner or spouse has major emotional consequences.

The chapter begins with an examination of both the spiritual and practical aspects of sharing your life with that special someone. It then moves on to an evaluation of the many psychological, practical, and social challenges involved in enduring the loss of one's best friend who coincidently happens to be a key breadwinner or parent.

The chapter concludes with the challenge of recovering love and companionship in one's life after the loss of a spouse or partner. To help you with this important process, you get a list of additional resources for healing the loss of a spouse or partner.

Note: The term "spouse" usually refers to just a husband or wife in an officially authorized marriage, and "partner" usually refers to a significant other of either gender in some other type of less official relationship. For purposes of this chapter, however, I use these two terms interchangeably.

Love, Companionship, and Partnership

Nothing quite compares to the feelings of joy and fulfillment that come from finding true love. This is all the more true when that love leads to a long-term relationship with someone who becomes your best and most intimate friend. Understandably for many people, finding this kind of love and establishing this kind of special relationship ranks as one of life's most important goals.

True love, however, is only one part of the total equation. Most couples who are able to establish a long-term relationship find that the companionship and partnership become every bit as important as the romance. Over time, the friendship and trust you build with your partner can become the defining aspects of the relationship.

Romantic partnerships often fulfill many different needs in people's lives; the most obvious are financial, social, and sexual. And who does what in meeting these needs goes a long way toward determining the types of roles that both you and your partner play in the relationship. When you lose your partner and the relationship dissolves, these needs remain, and the roles you were so used to playing are thrown up for grabs.

Losing a love, especially a true, long-standing love, either through a breakup or death is one of the most heart-rending experiences in life. In fact, for many, the first taste of profound grief comes as the result of losing a loved one not through death but rather through a breakup. And the feelings of helplessness, despondency, and suffering naturally experienced at the breakup of a loving relationship are magnified many times with the death of someone with whom one intimately shares one's life.

The Impact of Losing Your Spouse

Your spouse is your rock, and when you lose him or her, you probably feel as though you've lost the very foundation of your life. In the loss, you're bereft of your closest friend with whom you undoubtedly shared the most intimate and important aspects of your life. Therefore, this type of loss is quite devastating on many levels.

In some ways, losing your partner, especially when you've been with that person for a long time, is like losing a twin brother or sister (see Chapter 5 for specifics on losing a sibling who's a twin). As the years roll on and you share more and more experiences together, you and your spouse think and act more like a single unit and less like two individuals; you're able to finish each other's sentences and often anticipate each other's wants and needs without a single word being spoken. In the end, people may even mistake you and your spouse for brother and sister when they first meet you.

The loss of this kind of cohesiveness is difficult beyond measure. Instead of feeling like you've lost a person you love deeply, it may feel more as though you've lost a part of yourself. In fact, in mourning the loss of a long-time spouse, you may mourn not only the lost loved one but also the severing of the greater self of which your spouse was such a vital part.

This section explores the emotional impact of losing your partner in one of two ways: as the result of a breakup or divorce and as the result of death. Divorce and death both represent profound losses that bring about their own types of grief and their own ways of grieving.

Experiencing loss through divorce

When most people think of grieving a spouse, they naturally think of the grief that comes from the death of one of the partners. In fact, given the high percentage of marriages that end in divorce, you're more likely to suffer the grief of a breakup than the grief that comes from the death of a spouse.

The impact of anger

The emotional impact of losing a partner through divorce differs from losing one through death mostly in the amount of upfront anger involved. Although some divorces are completely amicable, they usually include a great deal of disappointment, frustration, and regret. These angry emotions may have been present some time before the actual separation as well as being present in abundance during the divorce proceedings.

Along with disappointment with the failure of the relationship, many people also experience sadder emotions normally associated with grieving the loss of a loved one; these emotions can include depressed feelings of isolation and deep sorrow over the loss.

Anger is often the overriding emotion during divorce, and you may need to use the energy of your anger to get you through all the practical and legal aspects of your divorce. If anger dominates, however, keep in mind that you need to deal with it and ultimately dispense with it before you can complete your grieving this loss (see Chapter 14 for suggestions on how to process your feelings).

The stages of grief still apply

Grieving the loss from divorce often includes many of the classic Kübler-Ross stages of grieving a loss through death (see Chapter 11 for details on the stages of grief). You may find yourself easily bouncing between any and all of the following stages in any order:

- ✔ **Denial:** You're convinced that this isn't really the end of the relationship and that you and your estranged spouse will someday reconcile.

- ✔ **Anger:** You're totally unable to get beyond your feelings of disappointment and hurt over the breakup of the relationship.

- ✔ **Bargaining:** You're ready to offer anything for the opportunity to give the relationship another go.

- ✔ **Depression:** You're convinced that you'll never get over the hurt and sadness caused by the breakup.

- ✔ **Acceptance:** You see the end of the relationship as the best thing for you and your erstwhile partner in the long run, and you feel ready to move on and try to make it on your own.

Perhaps the most significant difference between mourning the loss of a partner through divorce and through death is that, in divorce, you can (and often have to) still deal with the person after the event. Although you still have to mourn the loss of the romantic relationship and all you shared on that level, you retain the possibility of continuing a physical relationship with that person even if it's on an entirely different level. When a partner dies, however, the only way to continue the relationship is on some sort of spiritual level.

Experiencing loss through the death of your partner

When you lose your spouse through death, you obviously get no say-so in the matter. This lack of control and utter helplessness is in strong contrast to the loss of a spouse through divorce, which, though it may be unavoidable, is still an act of will rather than a loss of control over one's destiny.

Lack of control is the salient factor in the profound loss of any loved one. In the death of a spouse, however, you face the loss of someone you specifically chose to be with and whom fate saw fit to take from you.

Feelings of anxiety

Besides deep sorrow and regret, you also may feel a great deal of anxiety related to the new sense of insecurity created by the loss. Often the vulnerability that you feel upon the death of a spouse relates directly to the roles that your partner played in the relationship, particularly the following:

- ✔ Primary breadwinner for your family
- ✔ Primary caregiver for you and your children
- ✔ Primary decision-maker within your relationship
- ✔ Primary catalyst for personal growth and change within your relationship

Because the two of you formed a team, the lack of the other essential member and the roles that he or she played is sure to be keenly felt. This absence adds an extra challenge in terms of grieving the loss: Not only must you grieve the loss of your dearest friend but also you must stretch yourself in assuming new, untried roles associated with taking care of yourself and the rest of your immediate family.

You suddenly may be called upon to step into and fill unfamiliar roles that you're apprehensive about. This pressure to assume new roles couldn't come at a worse time than precisely at the moment you feel most alone and vulnerable. To help you get through this trying situation, recall the way your partner handled the roles that you must now assume. Keep in mind that you had a pro after whom you can model your new behaviors.

Health concerns

Another major concern after the death of a spouse is the health and survival of the remaining partner. Although considered anecdotal, many spouses, especially seniors, don't live long after the death of their partners. Some people refer to this phenomenon as dying of a broken heart, whereas others consider it the result of giving up in the face of what seems to be the insurmountable task of living apart from the person who so long completed the surviving spouse.

If you're a caregiver for an elderly surviving partner who's recently lost his or her long-time companion, you need to be particularly vigilant about that person's physical and mental health. Look for any signs of resignation or deep depression, and listen for serious talk of not wanting to go on living. If you notice these conditions, you may want to seek the advice and help of a professional grief counselor (see Chapter 14). The health and even the continued existence of this person may depend upon getting help so that he or she sees that even this terrible grief is survivable.

The Practical and Spiritual Aspects of Partner Loss

The loss of a spouse has both practical and spiritual aspects. This section includes a review of the more common challenges that you may face as you grieve the loss. Most of the practical challenges fall into one of three major categories: financial, social, and sensual.

The most significant spiritual challenge that anyone who loses a spouse faces is how to function on his or her own. After being part and parcel of a team for such a long time, you may find the notion of living on your own incomprehensible and the very idea of ever falling in love again and building an entirely new romantic relationship completely absurd.

Managing the financial impact

Given the economic realities of modern life, very few couples can afford to have only a single breadwinner. Therefore, in many households, both partners must work in order to make ends meet and ensure the economic health of the family.

The loss of income previously provided by the deceased partner can put an extra strain on the bereaved surviving partner. Even if your late spouse didn't work outside the home but instead provided primary care for your children, the loss has a financial impact if you must resort to day care or some other paid childcare in order to continue working outside the home.

Financial challenges are compounded if you weren't the one usually in charge of tracking and managing household finances. It's not all that unusual to find a surviving partner who rarely, if ever, paid the monthly bills or juggled the household finances. For such a person, assuming sole responsibility for finances is an extra burden in grieving the loss, not to mention a real test of his or her mettle.

For some people, taking over control of the household finances, while quite challenging (especially when the person's concentration and mental sharpness suffer from the stress of the grief), provides a much needed escape from grieving. For others, this new responsibility proves to be too much, at least during the initial phase of grieving. If you find yourself overwhelmed by financial tasks, turn to other family members or close friends to help by organizing the financial records, assessing the financial health of the household, and even getting the bills ready to pay. Many times, the boost from this initial financial help is all that you need in order to take on your new financial role.

The financial impact of the death of a spouse is greatly complicated when, at the time of death, the partners weren't legally married or protected by some kind of state-certified domestic partnership or other legal agreement such as a living trust. People who live together as partners and who share finances in a relationship that isn't legally sanctioned or protected in some way need to understand that they put the surviving partner at great financial risk in the event of one of their deaths. Under this sad state of affairs, combined assets such as joint checking and savings accounts become immediately frozen and therefore completely unavailable to the surviving partner. This turn of events can have disastrous effects if the money is needed in order to pay monthly bills and provide for the family's other daily necessities (as it almost always is).

To minimize these types of financial hardships, couples must do some estate planning before anything happens to either one of them. At a bare minimum, married couples should have individual wills that dictate how any assets not held in common are to be apportioned. Couples who aren't legally married need to have a revocable living trust in place that indicates the beneficiaries of all shared assets. Note that even married couples can benefit from setting up a living trust because it enables the surviving spouse to settle financial affairs without the additional expense and complication of Probate Court. For more ideas on how to protect your partner financially, see *Estate Planning For Dummies* by N. Brian Caverly and Jordan S. Simon (Wiley). For help on creating a will or living trust, visit the Legal Documentation Service Web site at `www.legalzoom.com` or visit the Estate Plan Center Web site at `www.avoid estatetaxes.com`.

Disenfranchised partner grief

Partner grief is made much more difficult in cases where members of either or both families refuse to accept the relationship and recognize it as legitimate. The lack of acceptance can range from a steadfast refusal to acknowledge your partner and the true nature of his or her relationship to you all the way to a total repudiation of your partner and condemnation of the relationship you share.

When this lack of acceptance comes from your partner's immediate family and is combined with a lack of the legal protection afforded by marriage or some sort of state-sanctioned domestic partnership, you may experience terrible problems upon the loss of your partner. Under these circumstances, these rather unwelcoming next of kin are the only ones with the legal right to make decisions about your partner's medical care and funeral arrangements.

Also, in the absence of a will, these people are the only ones whom the courts recognize as having an interest in your partner's finances and remaining material goods. In short, you may be left with nothing and not be allowed to make any decisions concerning your deceased partner.

To avoid this kind of disastrous situation from ever becoming a reality (even when you're both on good terms with each other's immediate families), you and your partner need to have each of the following things in place:

- ✔ **Wills** that clearly indicate each of your wishes upon your deaths

- ✔ **Power of attorney** for each other that gives you and your partner control over the other's finances when either one of you is incapacitated

- ✔ **Medical power of attorney** for each other that gives you each the power to make critical medical decisions when either one of you is incapacitated

- ✔ **Living trust** that determines the apportioning of your partner's estate and keeps you out of Probate Court

For help with any of these kinds of legal forms, visit the Legal Documentation Service Web site at www.legalzoom.com.

Even when control of your partner's estate isn't an issue, not having your own family's acceptance of your relationship often makes grieving your partner's passing much more arduous. Many times, disapproving family members may not actively support you in grieving the loss and even may go so far as to discourage you from expressing any of your feelings of grief around them. Without this support, you can feel even more isolated and depressed about the loss than you normally would. When you don't have your family's support, you need to seek out people (friends or a grief counselor or support group; see Chapter 14) who can honor your relationship and who recognize the seriousness of your loss.

Dealing with the social solitude

As the old Three Dog Night song says, "One is the loneliest number that you'll ever do." This message really rings true when it comes to dealing with the social aspects of losing a partner. Suddenly, you find yourself to be a party of one rather than part of a couple; so many of the social situations in which you were completely comfortable before you now find to be quite awkward.

Many people who are part of a couple rarely interact socially as individuals except with a select group of friends. When they're widowed, they then become the proverbial third wheel in these social situations. This feeling of being out of place not only discourages future social interaction with other couples but also tends to act as a vivid reminder of the bereaved partner's new alone status.

For many surviving spouses, undertaking any activity that they almost always would have done as a couple is difficult to contemplate, let alone undertake. Nothing brings home the sense of social solitude associated with the loss of a partner like the first time you do an activity alone that you normally did as a couple, such as go to a restaurant for dinner or take in a movie. This solo experience either reinforces the loneliness that you're feeling or marks a new stage in the grieving process in which you get ready to find and define a new individual identity outside of the old relationship.

Coping with the sensual isolation

Intimacy, both physical and emotional, is the watchword of a romantic partnership. In losing your partner, you're immediately and permanently bereft of the comfort and well-being that both types of intimacy bring you.

Touch is a fundamental and vital part of the romantic relationship. With the loss of your spouse, not only do you suffer from loss of being able to touch your partner but you suffer from no longer being touched by him or her.

Longing for the touch of your beloved is only one part of the story; you also suffer from not being able to express your affection. For some bereaved widows and widowers, this shutdown of physical closeness and touch leads to an emotional shutdown that naturally creates more distance between them and their friends and family. The distance reinforces the sense of isolation that's already an inescapable part of this type of grief and, in the end, makes grieving the loss of their spouses even more difficult.

When you're feeling deprived of touch, there's not a lot you can do on your own to mitigate the situation. The best thing you can do is to seek out touch from other family members and from those friends with whom you're comfortable being physical on this level.

When you're supporting someone who's grieving the loss of a partner, the best thing you can is to make sure that you touch him repeatedly during each visit, not just when you first greet him and finally take your leave (assuming, of course, that you check with him beforehand to make sure that this touching is welcome). Perhaps put your arm around him or hold his hand at times as you converse — whatever's appropriate to your particular relationship with the person. Although it's no substitute for what he's lost, your touch can go a long way in helping the person through sensual deprivation and help keep him connected on both the physical and emotional levels.

Learning how to be on your own

Even more difficult than the practical challenges that you face after losing a spouse is the spiritual challenge of learning to live once again as an individual — what you might call "making it on your own."

After losing my own partner of nearly 20 years, I maintain that one spouse does not outlive the other. By that I mean that such a large part of each person's identity is invested in the couple of which they are a part that, when the couple ceases to be, not only is the deceased partner lost, but a large part of the surviving partner's sense of self is lost as well.

As a result, the surviving partner faces the ultimate challenge of redefining himself as an individual whose identity doesn't depend upon his better half. This challenge is daunting for all but the best of us and often complicates and extends the grieving process.

Part of what can complicate this task is the mistaken notion that, in becoming someone who can live on your own, you debase the memory of the partner you're grieving by somehow discrediting the relationship that you shared together. Many times people hold onto their old identities for fear that it's the only way to keep alive the memories of what they shared with their partners.

Another part of the challenge of redefining yourself stems from simply not knowing how to act and be an independent person after being an integral part of a couple. Remember that it takes time to find your own way and rebuild your self-assurance. Sometimes, assuming the roles that your partner used to fulfill in the relationship is the first step in becoming your own person. In seeing yourself successfully take over and manage the tasks required by these new roles, you gain a new confidence in yourself that can help you see where you want to go and ultimately who you want to be.

Successfully becoming your own person again sometimes runs a parallel course to your stages of grieving the loss (see Chapter 11). As you're able to express more of your grief and accept the loss, you may find that you're increasingly ready to make decisions about your own future. In turn, you're able to take on new responsibilities that help to identify the new, independent person you'll be when you finally integrate this loss into the rest of your life.

Keeping Your Love Alive

After the loss of your spouse, it's quite natural to feel as though you'll never find love again and be a part of another long-term romantic relationship. Moreover, you may even feel as though you never again want to invest yourself in such an arrangement.

After all, you now know firsthand just how tremendously tough it is to survive the loss of a beloved partner. And although you know it's possible to get through terrible grief and come out on the other side, the memory of the pain involved in the process is so deep and real that you really can't conceive of ever making yourself vulnerable to that kind of suffering again.

In time, as your grieving comes to an end, you'll start recalling more and more of the sweetness of what you shared with your partner. As part of incorporating the loss into the rest of your life, you'll remember the good in the relationship, and the stark memory of the pain of the grieving will begin to soften. As part of defining yourself as a new, independent person, you may begrudge the loneliness and long again for something akin to the warmth and security you knew in the relationship you shared with your deceased love.

Remaining true to your lost partner

The first hurdle you face in even contemplating falling in love again is figuring out how to love again while remaining true to the memory of your lost partner. The essential challenge is how to keep the love you had with your deceased partner alive while leaving yourself open to the possibility of another relationship.

At first, it can't help but feel like a huge betrayal to consider loving anyone else but your deceased spouse. By the way, this feeling of infidelity usually isn't mitigated much by any discussions you may have had with your spouse before his death about remarriage (you know, the old "If anything ever happens to me, promise me that you'll marry again" argument). Although it may be somewhat reassuring to know that your deceased spouse didn't want you to remain forever celibate, this knowledge still won't guide you in deciding how to be true to his memory and still find love again.

In my humble opinion, you can't move on without first figuring out a way to be confident that falling in love again and building a new relationship with someone else will not threaten your memory of your deceased spouse. To accomplish this, I recommend that you incorporate his memory into your new life. One very effective way to do this is by thoroughly reviewing all the positive qualities that your partner brought into your life and finding ways to emulate those qualities and make them a part of you and your new relationship (see Chapter 18 for more on this subject).

Finding love again

No matter how many years intervene, finding love again after grieving the loss of a deceased partner isn't as easy as it may first sound. Assuming that you've dealt successfully with the problem of how to keep the love from your earlier relationship alive and even bring it into a new relationship, you still have the challenge of rebuilding your trust in these kinds of romantic relationships.

Gathering the courage to commit

After the hard work of grieving a long-time partner, it's not all that easy to reestablish your trust in romantic relationships. After all, you now know beyond a shadow of a doubt that investing yourself in such a relationship is risky. There's no guarantee that you won't ever have to face such grief again, and even more important, you understand that none can be given. True love is no longer a defense against death, and hard grief is the price that love exacts.

The only way around this predicament is to have faith in the new person you've become. You know how much you hurt when you grieved your partner's death, but you also know that you survived it — and came through it with the desire to give another go. That's not only a tribute to the strength of the love you had with your deceased partner but also a testament to your resiliency.

Avoiding comparisons

The other potential snag in building a new romance can come from comparing the relationship you build with your new partner to the relationship you had with your deceased partner. It's all too easy to romanticize your old relationship and canonize your deceased spouse. From this rather skewed perspective, your new romance, not to mention your new partner, doesn't stand a chance when things aren't going exactly as you expected or wanted.

The best way to avoid counterproductive comparisons is to remind yourself that each person is totally exceptional and irreplaceable. Take to heart that your deceased partner was one of a kind, as are you. Together you built a matchless relationship. You carry part of this unique character into the new relationship but can expect only to create something new and nonrepeatable.

Keeping in mind that you're no longer the same person you were and your new love is without comparison can go a long way toward keeping you open and preventing you from wallowing in comparisons between your old love and your old relationship.

Resources for Healing Partner Loss

If you're grieving the loss of your life partner, you can turn to a great number of print and online resources for helpful advice and valuable information. Books on this topic run the gamut from the very practical all the way to moving narratives designed to inspire as well as inform you.

Online resources include a variety of informational pages as well as online communities. These online communities enable you to reach out and communicate with other people who are dealing with the same kinds of losses.

Books

The books on grieving the loss of a spouse are a diverse lot. They include very practical workbooks and guides as well as inspirational case histories and narratives. The top books on grieving the loss of a spouse on my list include:

- *Finding Your Way after Your Spouse Dies* by Marta Felber (Ave Maria Press): This book consists of a series of short vignettes about grieving the loss of a spouse that cover such topics as creating your own "comfort place," greeting the day, ignoring certain messages, assuming control, and seeking additional help. Many topics include short prayers and scriptural passages to which you may refer.

- *Surviving the Death of Your Spouse: A Step-by-Step Workbook* by Deborah S. Levinson (New Harbinger Publications): This workbook looks at grieving a spouse as a journey divided into three stages: treading water, pseudoequilibrium, and renewal and resolution. Each chapter contains question-and-answer sections that enable you to reflect on the feelings that arise and the desires that you have as you work through each stage.

- *Life Is For the Living: Recovering and Rebuilding after Spousal Loss* by Gil Blum (Timed Resources Inc.): This book on grieving spousal loss comes out of the author's own experience with the death of his wife and finding new love. It's full of practical advice on how to meet new people and get back into the dating scene after your grieving is over.

✔ ***Widow to Widow: Thoughtful, Practical Ideas for Rebuilding Your Life*** by Genevieve Davis Ginsburg (Da Capo Press): This book by a therapist who was widowed is chockfull of practical advice for women of all ages who lose their husbands. Topics include learning to travel and eat alone as well as creating new routines for surviving holidays and anniversaries.

✔ ***The Widow's Resource*** by Julie A. Calligaro (Women's Source Books): The subtitle of this book written by a probate and trust attorney is *How to Solve the Financial and Legal Problems That Occur Within the First Six to Nine Months of Your Husband's Death,* and that just about says it all. It's full of practical information for widows, including applying for insurance and Social Security benefits as well as dealing with taxes and probate. The book includes sample forms and letters with simple instructions.

✔ ***The Year of Magical Thinking*** by Joan Didion (Vintage): Hailed as a classic memoir about grief and loss, Joan Didion writes about her personal experience the first year after the death of her husband, when she also had to deal with the serious illness of her only child (a daughter who was in a coma at the time of her father's death). This memoir is an honest and raw look at sudden loss and the grief that it brings.

✔ ***The Loss of a Life Partner*** by Carolyn Ambler Walter (Columbia University Press): In this book, Walter examines the grieving process for nonmarried people who lose their partners, including those in mixed and same-sex male and female relationships. The book includes narratives by surviving spouses that chronicle their experiences and challenges in grieving their losses.

✔ ***Gay Widowers: Life after the Death of a Partner*** by Michael Shernoff (Haworth Press): This book on grieving the death of a gay male life partner consists of a series of essays by various gay widowers. They chronicle their own experiences and challenges in grieving the deaths of their spouses and then finding and creating new identities as widowers.

✔ ***Lesbian Widows: Invisible Grief*** by Vicky Whipple (Harrington Park Press): This book on grieving the death of a female life partner consists of a series of case histories about lesbian widows facing the challenges of recovering from the loss of their partners and living without them.

Online resources

The online resources for grieving the loss of a life partner include some really good and informative essays targeted at particular groups. They also include some very good online communities designed specifically for those who are grieving the loss of a spouse and who need to share their feelings with people who really understand what they're going through. My list of online sites to check out includes the following:

- **Helping Older Adults Who Are Grieving** at www.uhseast.com/ 135484.cfm: This Web page contains information on helping seniors who are grieving from the loss of their spouses. The information includes how grief is different for seniors as well as advice on helping a senior grieve a loss.

- **The Divorce Grieving Process** at www.divorcetransitions.com/ articles/grief.htm: This article on grieving a divorce is tied to the Kübler-Ross Five Stages of Grief. The page also includes links to other valuable articles, including "Dealing with Shock and Guilt in a Divorce," "How to Use Journaling in Divorce Survival and Recovery," and "Divorce Counseling for Closure."

- **On Being Alone: A Guide for the Newly Widowed** at www.aarp.org/ families/grief_loss/a2004-11-15-newlywidowed.html: This article from AARP gives you things to remember at the outset of grieving the loss of your spouse. In addition to this article, the AARP Web site has links to other invaluable and detailed information on the financial and legal steps to take after the death.

- **When a Spouse Dies: Dealing With Loss and Grief** at www.ahealthy me.com/topic/srloss: This article is directed at people who were caregivers for their spouses prior to their loved one's death.

- **Widows and Widowers International** at www.wwinternational.net: This Web site enables people who are grieving the loss of their spouses to communicate and comfort one another. It contains a chat room where you can share with others who are in a similar situation and a bulletin board where you can post messages.

- **Fellowship of Young Christian Widows-Widowers** at www.foycwidows-widowers.com: This site is dedicated to Christians who have lost their spouses. It contains many postings from widows and widowers, an e-mail list for contacting others who are grieving a similar loss, and a memory page with suggestions on how to keep your spouse's memory alive.

- **Young Widows or Widowers** at www.ywow.org: This Web site for Young Widows or Widowers, a nonprofit organization in Virginia, contains information on how to start a local chapter of this organization as well as excellent links to resources and services related to spousal loss.

- **Gold Star Wives of America** at www.goldstarwives.org: The Gold Star Wives of America is a nonprofit organization chartered by the U.S. Congress for people whose spouses died while on active duty in the U.S. Armed Forces or who died from a service-related disability. This site contains information on local chapters of this organization as well as recent news and legislation that affects survivor benefits.

✔ **Widownet** at www.widownet.org: This site has loads of information for widows and widowers. It includes several insightful articles as well as links to chat rooms, e-mail lists, and bulletin boards. You can also access a book list containing personal recommendations.

✔ **Gay Widowers: Grieving in Relation to Trauma and Social Supports** at www.thebody.com/shernoff/widower/widower.html: This Web page is part of The Body: The Complete HIV/AIDS Resource Web site. The article on this page is geared specifically to gay widowers (that is, gay men who have lost their partners); it includes the general dynamics of being a gay widower and issues specific to gay widowers as well as how to move through grief.

✔ **ReMarrieds.Net** at www.remarrieds.net: This Web site is dedicated to those who have lost spouses and then created new partnerships. It addresses the special issues that you face when putting together new households and relationships after profound loss. Note that you must join this community in order to have access to its message boards, and membership is dependent upon approval from the administrators of the site.

Chapter 5

The Loss of Siblings

Sibling loss is marked by the loss of a brother or sister and the grieving that the surviving siblings undergo as a result. Some grief professionals refer to the grief from this type of loss as *disenfranchised grief,* by which they mean that the grief of the surviving siblings is commonly overlooked or undervalued by society at large and sometimes even by the other family members suffering the loss. At the opposite end of the spectrum from surviving siblings experiencing disenfranchised grief are bereaved siblings who fail to appreciate the magnitude of their grief, especially if they lost their brothers or sisters when they were young children.

In an attempt to validate this kind of loss, the chapter begins by evaluating the types of relationships that brothers and sisters establish, including a look at sibling rivalry as well as the incredible closeness that brothers and sisters can establish.

From there, the chapter moves on to examine the impact of losing a sibling — either when you're a child or when you're an adult. I also explore the special phenomenon of losing a twin brother or sister. This chapter concludes with suggestions on how parents and surviving siblings can help each through their grief. I also provide you with lists of both print and online resources that you can use to help deal with and heal sibling grief.

The Pain and Pleasure of Siblings

Anyone who isn't an only child knows both the pain and pleasure that come with growing up with brothers and sisters. Having siblings to contend with for your parents' affection and time and to compete with over everything from food, clothes, and toys to the family car can be both extremely frustrating and extremely exhilarating.

The three salient factors operating in the dynamics of sibling relationships are:

- **Birth order:** Often determines which sibling leads and assumes a more parental role in regard to the other kids and which sibling follows
- **Sibling rivalry:** The degree of rivalry that exists in the family as brothers and sisters compete with each other for parental affection and family resources
- **Sibling solidarity:** The degree of closeness that grows and exists between particular pairs of siblings, especially twins

The following sections examine each of these three factors in more detail before taking a look at the impact that they can have in dealing with loss of a brother or sister and healing the grief that ensues.

Sibling birth order

Strangely enough, even among siblings who are twins and therefore by definition share the same birthday, birth order is very important; it's often a bone of contention for the younger sibling and acts as some sort of badge of honor for the older sibling. More often than not, people refer to their brothers not just as "my brother" but as "my older brother" or "my kid brother" and sisters not as "my sister" but as "my older sister" or "my kid sister."

The rank that traditionally follows the birth order is often a key factor in the roles that brothers and sisters play in each other's lives and the type of bonding that goes on between them. Many child psychologists and behaviorists associate the following roles with the three major ranks in sibling birth order:

- **Firstborn:** The eldest child who once had the experience of being an only child and then had to share the limelight with other siblings. Firstborn children are said to be more competitive, more independent, and sometimes more intelligent.
- **Middle child:** The child who has never had the parents' undivided attention and therefore has never known the limelight of being an only child. They're said to be more even-tempered, more pioneering, and sometimes perfectionists.
- **Lastborn:** The child who's the baby of the family and is often the most spoiled and pampered. Youngest children are said to be more outgoing, more charming, and sometimes more manipulative.

Naturally, these characterizations of the firstborn, middle, and lastborn children in a family are probably just as often wide of the mark as they are spot on. About the only generalization I think is justifiable is that siblings remain very aware of their birth order and jockey for family resources using every advantage that their rank in the family affords them.

Sibling rivalry

Undoubtedly the most famous aspect of having brothers and sisters is the almost incessant and ongoing competitiveness known as sibling rivalry. Although some sibling rivalry involves real aggression, sibling rivalry is not to be confused with sibling abuse, in which one sibling victimizes another.

Most sibling rivalry revolves around competing for the parents' attention (which becomes more and more limited the more siblings there are) and sometimes other limited physical family resources such as food, clothes, and toys that must distributed and shared.

Studies have shown that brother pairs within the immediate family are the most rivalrous siblings, with sets of male twins being the most competitive of all. Pairs of sisters within the immediate family, however, tend to be the least rivalrous and the most bonded.

Provided that the competitiveness isn't encouraged by the parents, sibling rivalry tends to diminish over time so that most adult siblings outgrow it. Sometimes, however, it lives on into adulthood and is fueled by resentments over real or imagined wrongs that occurred when the siblings were growing up.

Oddly enough, although sibling rivalry can drive a wedge between particular pairs of brothers and sisters, this competitiveness just as well can strengthen the bonds between adult siblings. The lasting effects of sibling rivalry depend upon many factors, including the spread in years between the particular pair of siblings (the more years in between, the less likely it is that the rivalry will have a healing effect in adulthood).

Sibling solidarity

Just as rivalry may exist between siblings in a family, close bonds may exist between pairs of siblings. Sometimes, these bonds are forged in childhood and remain strong (despite the occurrence of intermittent tiffs and spats) throughout the siblings' lives. For example, my mother and her only sister bonded in this way when they were girls and remained physically and emotionally close to each other their entire lives.

Solidarity between siblings usually involves pairs of sisters or, to a somewhat lesser extent, pairs of brothers in the immediate family. It also can involve a mixed pair of a brother and sister, although this scenario usually happens when they're the only two children or they're bonded together by some extraordinary circumstances such as a family tragedy or illness.

The factors that make for this kind of special bonding between pairs of siblings are diverse. The most important are probably

- ✔ Age difference
- ✔ How well the natural personalities of the two siblings mesh
- ✔ Shared family experiences

Most really close pairs of brothers and sisters are usually close in age, with not more than a difference of five years between them. Although their personalities can differ (for example, one sibling may be a really gregarious person and the other more reserved), they normally need either to complement one another or meld well together. The big exception to this rule is identical twins: They may have personalities that aren't normally complementary, but the twins still may be very close for a number of other reasons both genetic and experiential.

Shared experiences also may create strong, enduring bonds between a pair of siblings. These mutual experiences can run the gamut from those that arise from shared interests to those that involve one sibling protecting or acting as a parent toward the other. Whatever their nature, reciprocated experiences serve to create rich memories and deep feelings of loyalty that help to cement the bond between the pair of siblings, a bond that often lasts their entire lives.

Exploring the Impact of Losing a Sibling

The relationships between brothers and sisters can be intricate and multifaceted. Therefore, it should come as no surprise that the grief that comes from their deaths is complex. Factors such as the birth order of the deceased sibling, the degree of sibling rivalry that existed and its residual effects, and the degree of closeness with the deceased sibling all come into play.

In addition, as with the deaths of other loved ones, the time in your life when you suffer your loss contributes significantly to its impact on your life. It matters a great deal whether you're a child still living under your parents' roof when one of your siblings dies or you're an adult living on your own and, perhaps, raising your own family.

When you lose a sibling as a child, you're left to wonder what it would have been like to grow up with your lost brother or sister as well as what type of person he or she would have grown up to be. When you lose a sibling as an adult, you're left with vivid memories of your childhood together as well as with a sense of regret that you're unable to continue that relationship in adulthood.

Experiencing the death of a sibling as a child

As I point out in Chapter 7 on children and grief, children grieve differently from adults, and how they understand death and are able express their grief depends directly upon their development (which most often is a function of their ages).

Special challenges

When you lose a sibling as a child, you're confronted with all the same challenges of comprehending the meaning of the loss and expressing your grief as you are with any other kind of loss, such as that of a grandparent, parent, or other close relative or friend. In addition, however, the loss of a sibling in the immediate family often brings with it the following special challenges to a surviving sibling:

- Concern that someone else in the immediate family will now die, either one of the parents or, many times, the grieving sibling

- Guilt over the death, especially if the deceased sibling had been ill for some time and the surviving sibling was particularly jealous of all the attention he received before death

- Resentfulness toward the deceased sibling and/or the parents if the surviving sibling thinks (almost always mistakenly) that the parents would have preferred him to die rather than the deceased brother or sister. This idea often comes from hearing the parents say something like "Why did dear little Suzy have to die?"; the child incorrectly interprets this to mean "Why didn't one of you other bad kids die instead?"

Special challenges such as these may require you as a parent to give more reassurance than normal to the surviving siblings. See "Helping the Surviving Siblings Grieve," later in this chapter, for details on how to give this kind of reassurance and support.

The types of sibling survivors

In her excellent book on sibling grief (see "Resources for Healing the Loss of a Sibling," later in this chapter), P. Gill White identifies the following seven types of sibling survivors based on research done on families with children grieving the loss of siblings:

1. **Haunted child:** This is the surviving sibling who lives in a family that doesn't talk about the death of his brother or sister. He has no real opportunity to grieve the loss as a child (a true disenfranchised griever), so the grief may resurface during some crisis, trauma, or other death he experiences as an adult.

2. **Overprotected child:** This is the surviving sibling whose parents become overprotective as a result of the death of his brother or sister in the hope that they never have to suffer such a terrible loss again. In so doing, the parents can interfere with the child's sense of self-reliance and independence.

3. **Lap child:** This is the child whose brother or sister suffers from a long illness before death and whose mother curtails the child's activities and keeps him close in order to make it easier to tend to the ill sibling. This kind of treatment sometimes fosters a sense of passiveness and helplessness in the surviving sibling.

4. **Replacement child:** This type of child may be the result of two different circumstances: He's born or adopted after the death of a brother or sister and then is treated as a replacement for the deceased sibling; or he tries to act like his deceased brother or sister and therefore become the deceased sibling's replacement in the family.

5. **Lonely child:** This surviving sibling either is neglected during the dying and grieving of a deceased sibling or is the last surviving child and therefore grows up as an only child.

6. **Later-born child:** This is a child who's born into the family sometime after the death of a brother or sister. He can feel a variety of emotions regarding the deceased sibling.

   • He may feel resentful of other surviving siblings who had an opportunity to know the deceased brother or sister.

   • He may see the deceased sibling he never knew as some type of guide or guardian angel.

   • He may resent the deceased sibling for dying and therefore making his parents sad.

7. **Scapegoat child:** This is the surviving sibling who bears the brunt of the parents' unhappiness and hostility brought on by guilt and regret after the death of his brother or sister.

As you may imagine, each type of child in this list has his own special burden to carry when attempting to grieve the death of a sibling. For many types, the actual grieving of the deceased sibling can't take place until he's on his own as an adult. In many cases, the experience of another profound loss in the surviving sibling's life triggers his grieving for the lost brother or sister.

Experiencing the death of a sibling as an adult

Losing your brother or sister as an adult is hard enough. The experience is made more difficult when the preponderance of other people's condolences and sympathy for the loss goes to the surviving parents, spouse, and children of the deceased, bypassing you and any other surviving siblings (see the sidebar "Adult sibling loss as the epitome of disenfranchised grief" for more on disenfranchised grief).

How much the loss of your deceased sibling affects you depends in large part upon how close you were to your brother or sister prior to his or her death. It also depends upon how close you were during your childhood and the amount and quality of experiences you shared.

Regardless of how intimate or distant your relations were as adults, the loss of a sibling is bound to bring up all sorts of memories of shared childhood experiences. The death may also stir up memories of conflicts and sibling rivalry, perhaps even particular incidents for which you feel particularly responsible and somewhat regretful.

If you harbor some childhood resentments against your deceased brother or sister, you may relive the conflicts and incidents that gave rise to these feelings, and your memories may rekindle anger against your deceased sibling.

It's very important that you deal with any guilt and anger that you feel toward your deceased brother or sister so that you can then get on with the work of healing from the loss of your sibling. Find appropriate ways to express your feelings both physically and creatively, as well as through ritual and memorial. As well, find ways to forgive yourself (in the case of guilt) and your deceased sibling (in the case of anger). Granting forgiveness clears the way for feeling the sorrow associated with loss and incorporating the loss into the rest of your life. See Chapter 2 for ideas on how to deal with guilt and blame. Check out Chapter 14 for suggestions on ways to express the feelings that arise when you lose a loved one and Chapter 15 for ways to memorialize your relationship.

Experiencing the death of a twin

Twins form a unique family unit: They're the two siblings in the immediate family who grow and develop together, keeping pace with one another as well as competing voraciously for parental attention and family resources.

Adult sibling loss as the epitome of disenfranchised grief

Ken Doka, a renowned grief researcher, coined the term *disenfranchised grief* in 1963 to describe the experience of surviving divorced spouses who, in grieving the loss of their former life partners, weren't treated as legitimate mourners because they were no longer married. Since then, grief professionals have widened the scope of this term to include a number of other types of mourners (such as grandparents, gay and lesbian life partners, and friends, the subject of Chapter 8). Recently, as grief research finally has started taking a long, hard look at sibling grief, disenfranchised grief has broadened to apply to surviving siblings, especially adult siblings.

As an example of how society devalues and fails to recognize the grief of adult siblings, T.J. Wray (author of *Surviving the Death of a Sibling;* see the section "Books," later in this chapter, for details), refers to the frequency of what she calls *dismissive condolences* that surviving adult siblings routinely receive after they tell friends and colleagues of the loss of their brothers or sisters. These trivializing condolences include such responses as "How awful — your parents must be heartbroken!" "Thank goodness it wasn't your wife (husband) or one of your children!" and "Well, you lived so far apart and saw each so infrequently, you must not have been that close."

Twins, especially identical twins, form a kind of symbiotic union that represents something larger than just two people who happen to be siblings of the same age. When one twin dies, the surviving twin doesn't simply lose a brother or sister but also a part of his or her very own identity.

As you may expect, some twins are so competitive with one another that, when one dies, the other actually may feel relieved on some level that he no longer has to strive so hard for his parents' attention. He may have initial feelings of being released from the struggle to be an individual in the eyes of family and friends.

However, the surviving twin's feelings of relief and release are usually short-lived and often are accompanied by huge regret over having to live without the one person who understood him as no one else could and the one who completed him in so many ways.

Consequently, it's completely understandable that a surviving twin, regardless of how young or old he is when he loses his other half, can have great difficulty grieving his loss. Healing this kind of sibling grief may take a great deal longer than healing nontwin sibling losses. In fact, I think the death of a twin is more akin to losing a spouse or life partner whom you considered to be your soul mate. This is a case where you may need to seek out professional help in getting through the loss (see Chapter 14 for suggestions on locating a professional grief counselor).

Helping the Surviving Siblings Grieve

There are two potential sources of help in grieving the loss of a sibling: the parents who lost a child in this death and the other surviving brothers and sisters who lost a sibling. If the death occurs when the surviving siblings are children, then they must look more to their parents than to each other for guidance and help in grieving the loss.

Leaning on parents

For the most part, parents can help a child grieve the loss of a sibling in the same way that they help the child grieve the loss of any other loved one (see Chapter 7 for specific suggestions). However, because some specific fears and doubts are attached to this type of loss, there are a couple of additional things you may need to do to support a child grieving a sibling's death:

- Explain to your child that in no way is he responsible for the death of his brother or sister. Children often feel that they caused the death either by wishing at some point that the sibling were gone or by doing something bad that somehow caused the death.

- Comfort your child both emotionally and physically, and assure him again and again of your love even in this terrible time of sorrow. Make sure that he doesn't get any hint that you would have wished him to die rather than his sibling.

- Reassure your child that his sibling's death doesn't mean that you'll die or that he's in danger of dying. Children often fear that the death of a sibling will be followed by the death of themselves or one or both of their parents.

Getting comfort from other siblings

If you experience the death of a sibling when you and any other surviving siblings are adults, then you're likely to look primarily to one another for help and guidance in your grieving. Surviving parents are often too frail and devastated by the loss of their adult child to be of much help.

Although they may be suffering a great deal of grief, surviving siblings are usually a good source of mutual comfort. They often understand the depth of the grief caused by this particular loss and relate to childhood memories involving the deceased sibling, all while still being able to communicate and share their feelings regarding the personal significance of the loss of their brother or sister.

Resources for Healing the Loss of a Sibling

Print and online resources to help you heal the loss of a sibling are readily available and of very good quality (although they aren't nearly as numerous as those for parents grieving the loss of children or resources that cover children's grief).

The print resources that I recommend include those targeted to adults surviving the loss of a sibling as well as those addressed to surviving siblings of any age. Some of the books offer very concise how-to guidance, whereas others contain moving and personal recollections of what it was like to mourn the loss of a brother or sister.

The online resources recommended here range from Web sites containing solid information on the idiosyncrasies of grieving a sibling as well as online communities where you can share your grief with others suffering the same type of loss. Of particular interest is an online support group for surviving twins who have lost twin brothers or sisters.

Books

For a while, sibling grief was a much overlooked area of grieving; however, in recent years, good solid books from grief professionals have started to appear in some number. Great books recounting the personal sagas of the death and mourning of siblings have been around for some time.

My recommended book list mostly includes books by professionals describing the phenomenon of sibling grief. (However, all the authors without exception have suffered the personal loss of a brother or sister as well.) The exception in the list is the very personal and moving *Letters to Sara: The Agony of Adult Sibling Loss* by Anne McCurry.

Here are my recommendations for some of the great books on healing the loss of a sibling:

✔ *Sibling Grief: Healing after the Death of a Sister or Brother* by P. Gill White (iUniverse): At the age of 15, P. Gill White lost her younger sister and later became the founder and director of the not-for-profit organization The Sibling Connection. This book contains valuable and insightful information about grieving the death of a sibling during childhood, adolescence, and adulthood. This slender volume also contains practical suggestions for healing loss through creativity, memorials, and dreams. The book concludes with ideas on how to use further reading about sibling loss to help heal the grief (what White calls *bibliotherapy*) followed by a book list that's worth the entire price of the book. The list is organized into age-appropriate categories, fiction and nonfiction, and memoirs.

✔ ***Surviving the Death of a Sibling: Living Through Grief When an Adult Brother or Sister Dies*** by T.J. Wray (Three Rivers Press): T.J. Wray suffered the loss of her only sibling, her adult brother, and eventually founded an online community for surviving adult siblings (see the next section for Web site details). Her book uses the structure of the Kübler-Ross Five Stages of Grief (see Chapter 11) and quotes from many case histories to illustrate the impact of losing an adult brother or sister. This book also explores the spiritual and religious ramifications of sibling loss and ends with practical suggestions of activities that you may undertake to mitigate the grief and aid the grieving process.

✔ ***Recovering from the Loss of a Sibling*** by Katherine Fair Donnelly (toExcel): In this book, Donnelly, a surviving sibling, compiled stories of other surviving siblings of all ages. These personal narratives are arranged thematically and cover such topics as denial, anger, coping with holidays and anniversaries, families that suffer multiple losses, and problems that grieving children typically encounter at school and grieving adults at work.

✔ ***Letters to Sara: The Agony of Adult Sibling Loss*** by Anne McCurry (Authorhouse): Anne McCurry lost her only big sister, Sara, after her long struggle with breast cancer. This book consists of a series of deeply personal letters written to Sara that chronicle Anne's tremendous grief over her death. This book is not only a great resource on sibling grieving but also a living example of how journaling all the feelings associated with the loss can help transform the grief.

✔ ***The Empty Room: Surviving the Loss of a Brother or Sister at Any Age*** by Elizabeth DeVita-Raeburn (Scribner): At age 14, the author lost her only sibling, her older brother Ted, after an eight-year illness. DeVita-Raeburn very skillfully weaves this personal story into the larger fabric of losing a brother or sister and its often devastating effects on the surviving siblings. Of particular interest are the author's coverage of sibling grief as disenfranchised grief, the importance of claiming and telling the story of your sibling's death, reconstituting yourself in light of the loss (a process that she calls *re-forming your identity*), and "carrying" your lost sibling forward into your present-day life.

Online resources

The online resources for help in healing the grief of losing a sibling include a great many sites where you can share your feelings and communicate with others suffering the same type of loss. In addition, you'll find sites that are full of good insights into the particular problems you may face.

My list of recommended online resources is as follows:

- **The Sibling Connection** at `www.counselingstlouis.net/index.html`: This Web site was founded by author P. Gill White (see the preceding section for my recommendation of her book, *Sibling Grief: Healing after the Death of a Sister or Brother*). This site is chockfull of good articles on sibling grieving, and it also contains a bulletin board where you can post your story about the death of your sibling and share your feelings.

- **Adult Sibling Grief** at `www.adultsiblinggrief.com`: This Web site was founded by author T.J. Wray, who appears on my book list as well (refer to the preceding section). This site contains a chat room and message board where you can post messages and share feelings with other surviving siblings either in a scheduled, moderated chat or a new chat that you start on your own. Click on Memorials and Tributes to view as well as post your story, poems, eulogies, and any other written tributes to and memorials for your deceased brother or sister.

- **TCF Sibling Resources** at `www.compassionatefriends.org/Siblings/Sibling_Entrance.html`: This resource page on The Compassionate Friends (TCF) Web site contains links to articles on the effects of losing a sibling as well as to a chat room and forum (only for registered members) where you can share your story and feelings. In addition, this page contains links to TCF sibling newsletters and an online pen-pal program where surviving siblings can e-mail one another.

- **Death of a Brother or Sister – Sibling Grief** at `www.griefworksbc.com/siblingdeath.asp`: This page contains general information on sibling loss that's aimed at teenagers along with links to recommended videos and books, articles on various types of grief, and a page of suggested activities that you can do to help heal the feelings of loss.

- **Sibling Survivors of Suicide** at `www.siblingsurvivors.com`: The site is dedicated to siblings who suffered the loss of a brother or sister due to suicide. It contains general information on sibling loss and links to sites supporting survivors of suicide. In addition, the Sibling Quilt link leads you to information on submitting a memorial quilt square that can be added to the Faces of Suicide Sibling Quilt.

- **Twinless Twins Support Group** at `www.twinlesstwins.org`: This site provides an online community for surviving members of fraternal and identical twins where they can share their feelings and stories about their twin loss. Members can share ideas in a forum as well as link to online information about twin loss for both surviving twins and their parents. You also can find information about regional meetings and national conferences where members of Twinless Twins Support Group International come to together to learn about being a surviving twin and to share their stories.

Chapter 6

The Loss of Children

*T*he loss of a child is possibly the most difficult loss to endure and surely among the most difficult to integrate into one's life. The death of a child is unlike any other loss because children are an enormous part of your legacy, and in their deaths, a large part of your own future dies. This makes the task of incorporating and integrating the loss of a child a lifelong endeavor, and it means that, for many parents, the grieving doesn't end even after they've learned to live with the loss.

This chapter looks at the loss of a child from many perspectives. It begins by examining the general nature of this singular type of loss in terms of the questioning, second-guessing, and guilt that often accompany it. The chapter then investigates the effects of losing a child under different circumstances (abortion, miscarriage, and so on) and at different ages (from infant to adult). It ends by examining the effects that losing a child can have on the family structure before covering a variety of resources you can turn to for more information and guidance in dealing with this particular kind of grieving.

The Cruelest Loss of All

In the natural order of things, children are expected to outlive their parents. When parents end up outliving their children, this natural order is turned topsy-turvy. Therefore, it's not surprising that parents who face this grim reality routinely question the justice of the cosmos as part of their grieving process. This kind of questioning is spurred on by the fact that children are synonymous with innocence; as such, there seems to be no way to defend their deaths as justified.

Parents suffering this type of loss often not only question the type of world order that can allow this kind of calamity to occur but also undergo a total crisis of faith that may result in a repudiation of both their religious traditions and communities. This crisis of faith is sometimes initiated through the use of pious clichés by well-meaning clergy, family members, and friends.

"God never gives you anything that you can't handle" or a variation thereof ranks as one of the more common and particularly cruel clichés. (See Chapter 20 for a bunch more of these beauties and the reasons they're so destructive.) This one's so cruel because there's no comfort in being strong *and* being without your child; worse yet, it gives the parents the impression that if they weren't so strong, then maybe God would have spared them this tragedy. And by this twisted logic, grieving parents can take away the worthless idea that they're somehow responsible for their child's death.

Any attribution, however subtle, that the parents are in some way responsible for their child's death is particularly perilous because, more often than not, the parents are already second-guessing the circumstances and feeling some sense of guilt over the death. This is true even if the parents are in no way responsible for the death and only did everything within their power to keep their child safe, secure, and healthy.

Guilt and the death of a child

When someone close to you dies, you're very likely to feel some sense of responsibility even if you clearly bear none. You can hear it in "If only I'd done this . . ." or "If only I hadn't done that . . ." thoughts or statements that you make. This tinge of guilt is so common, in fact, that it feels like a part of the usual grieving process, like the similarly logic-defying stage of denial (see Chapter 11). This being said, feeling guilty is all the more common with parents who've lost a child, especially a young child.

This guilt in the loss of a child probably stems in no small part from the understanding that parents' primary responsibilities are to nurture and protect their children from harm and the subsequent feeling on the parents' part that, when their child dies, they've failed in these duties. Another reason may be that, because the parents can find no ready-made cosmic justification for the untimely death of their innocent child, their minds naturally explore ways in which they may have contributed to the tragedy inadvertently.

Feelings of guilt and recrimination over the death that you hold onto can overshadow and eventually overpower the grieving process. If you find yourself caught up in "if only" statements, reliving the facts of the death in order to figure out what you could or should have done differently, and, worse yet, beating yourself up over what you did or didn't do, you need to deal with the guilt.

One of the most effective ways to deal with guilt (even though it may be misplaced) is through forgiveness. Chapter 10 has suggestions on ways to work on forgiving yourself, God, the universe, the doctor, the medical system, your clergyman, and whoever else needs pardoning in your particular situation.

Coming to terms with the loss in moral and philosophical terms

Whatever the reasons, a parent's need to justify the loss of a child and the unbearable grief is exceptionally strong. The need can manifest itself not only in undue guilt on the parent's part but also in fierce anger with the cosmic order that enabled this disaster to occur. Very often, anger takes the form of a quarrel with God (even if the parent wasn't overly religious or worried about the moral state of the universe prior to the child's death) in the form of some variation on the theme of "How could God allow this kind of thing to happen?" or "How could He have created a world in which innocent beings suffer and die before their time?"

Of course, these questions are just variants of the essential question "Why do bad things happen to good people?" that I discuss briefly in Chapter 1 (in the Western guise of the biblical book of Job and in the Eastern guise of the theory of karma). Because the untimely death of a young child who's clearly innocent represents the quintessential example of bad things happening to good people *and* because so many parents wrangle with this question as part of their grieving a child's death, I revisit this question in this section.

In his wonderful book, *When Bad Things Happen to Good People* (Anchor), Rabbi Harold Kushner takes up the question "Why do bad things happen to good people?" both in terms of the book of Job and in light of the suffering and death of his own son at age 13 due to illness. In his book, Kushner comes to the rather astonishing conclusion that God must *not* be all powerful. The rabbi refuses to believe in a God who is not all good, so in his estimation, God can't be both all powerful and all good and still allow the suffering of innocents.

I think that more important than the rabbi's rather unorthodox interpretation of the book of Job is his reminder that an answer to a question doesn't have to be a *reason*. Rather, it can be a *response*. Here's what I mean:

- There's clearly no answer to why a child should suffer and die in the sense of a reason because there's no moral justification for it.
- There is, however, a response to this unjustifiable heartbreak; the response is found in the path that the parents take in grieving the lost child in which they incorporate and integrate the loss into their lives.

Rabbi Kushner's extremely important point about the answer to the death of a loved one coming in the form of a response to the tragedy rather than as any kind of reason explaining or justifying it has some bearing on the theory of karma as well (the premise that what goes around comes around).

Exploring the Impact of Losing a Child

The loss of a child of any age is a parent's worst nightmare. No other profound loss seems quite as difficult to integrate into one's life because the loss of a child represents both a cosmic injustice and a forfeiture of a potential and anticipated future. When a child dies, the parents must mourn not only his passing but also the demise of all the hopes, dreams, and plans that they had for the child. In the event that the child is an only child, the parents also may mourn their legacy to a future generation.

This section looks at the impact of losing a child at various stages and ages, from conception all the way to adulthood. I start with the loss of a child before or at birth, including the grief caused by a lack of fertility and the ability to even conceive and have children. Then I profile the grief caused by the death of a child after birth — as an infant, toddler, young child, teenager, and finally as an adult.

Experiencing the loss of fertility

No one feels the loss of a potential and anticipated future more than a couple who desperately wants to have children but finds out that, for whatever reasons, they're infertile. Instead of mourning children that they've cared so much for, they mourn the children they will never meet and never have a chance to care for.

On the surface, the pain of the inability to have children may appear not as great as that caused by the loss of living children; however, by no means is that the case. After all, infertile couples have no body to bury, no memories (however many or few) to look back on and find comfort in, no support groups to shepherd them through the acute stages of the grief, and very few sympathetic folks who can or want to understand and console them.

The only thing that can mitigate this loss at all is translating this longing for children into some sort of other parenting experience, such as foster care, adoption, or even mentoring children in the community. The only problem with this compromise is that, although these solutions can fill the parenting needs for some couples, they can also be a reminder of what the couple can't have in their lives. As such, the alternate parenting experience can be a cause for renewed grief as well as for joy.

If you find yourself in this situation, grieve the loss of fertility as you would mourn the loss of any loved one before you undertake any alternate parenting experiences. With the right preparation, the alternate experience has a chance to become an integral part of your healing as well as a way of incorporating the loss into your life.

Experiencing the loss of a child through abortion

Abortion is one of the thorniest issues facing modern society. It raises deep philosophical and religious questions about both the sanctity and the autonomy of human life (that is, the fetus's right to come to term versus the woman's right to control her own body and determine her own future). It's also one of those hot-button issues about which people on both sides usually feel so strongly that they're much more apt to hurl slogans back and forth than engage in a meaningful debate and civil discussion.

Keep in mind that, for most women, deciding to abort is an agonizing and extremely difficult decision. Reasons for going through with the procedure run the gamut from the baby's high risk of serious birth defects and a critical threat to the woman's health during the pregnancy or at childbirth to facing severe economic and domestic adversities that make it nigh onto impossible to support and rear the child.

A woman who mourns the loss of her pregnancy as a result of an abortion is not in the same position as a woman who loses it on account of a miscarriage (which I discuss later in this chapter). Because the abortion procedure is the result of her own decision, the woman must often deal with her ambivalence about making that choice as well as her grief over the loss of the child. This grief is often complicated by any guilt she feels about terminating the pregnancy as well as any shame that she takes on as a result of disapproval expressed by her family or other members of her community.

Mizuko Jizo and the Mizuko ceremony

Jizo is a Bodhisattva (kind of like a saint) in Mahayana Buddhism who is known as the protector of all innocents and travelers in both the physical and spiritual realms. In particular, Mizuko Jizo (*Mizuko* literally means water-baby and is the name given to the fetus) is the guardian of stillborn, miscarried, and aborted fetuses and shepherds them in their journey through the spiritual realm. Modern Japanese have developed a Mizuko ceremony that enables families (particularly mothers) to participate in a rite that honors their unborn children or children who died at birth. This ceremony is conducted in a memorial garden and usually involves prayers and chants and placing a stone with a carved statue of Jizo as a grave marker

for the child. Families can return to the memorial garden to honor and remember their lost children by decorating the stone marker, bathing the Jizo statue, or burning incense and lighting candles before it.

In America, more and more Buddhist temples and Zen centers are setting up memorial gardens and conducting Mizuko ceremonies for grieving mothers and their families. Contact your nearest Buddhist temple or Zen center to find out if it has such a memorial garden and conducts this type of memorial service. Also, visit www.jizo.org for more information on Jizo Bodhisattva.

If you have an abortion for medical reasons and are part of a couple who otherwise would have had the child, you and your partner can support each other in your grieving. However, if you're on your own with limited or no support from the biological father or your family, you're left to grieve the loss alone. Experiencing grief alone is particularly difficult at any age, but if you're still a teenager or young adult (as many are who undergo this procedure), you may lack some of the emotional maturity necessary to deal with this burden. This is definitely the time to seek out the help of a professional grief counselor (see Chapter 14).

In grieving this type of loss, you have to confront any guilt you feel over your decision before you can begin grieving the loss of the prospective child. Separate your feelings about abortion from those of your religious tradition and society at large. Doing so may require the help of a professional counselor or therapist who's skilled in dealing with this type of trauma.

Experiencing the loss of a child through adoption

Women who decide against abortion (or have no access to the procedure) but who aren't in a situation in which to raise their babies are faced with the heartbreak of losing their children through adoption. As with a decision to terminate pregnancy, the decision to give up one's baby for adoption is never an easy one. And although this decision is almost always made in the hope of giving the child the best possible future, it's one that more often than not is fraught with second-guessing and self-doubt on the part of the mother.

Grieving the loss of a child that, though unplanned, you wanted but just couldn't keep can be a lifelong endeavor. The only memory that you may have of your baby is giving birth to him or her. Each anniversary of the baby's birth and each Mother's Day is an occasion to grieve the loss as well as an opportunity to wonder about what has become of your child and whether or not you made the correct decision.

Adding to this sense of sorrow and uncertainty, you may wrestle with the following issues:

- ✔ Whether you'll ever be reunited with your adopted child
- ✔ Whether, if you are reunited, the child will rebuff you for giving him up for adoption or will find it in his heart to understand the situation and forgive you

Keep in mind that many adopted children elect not to contact their birth parents, so many mothers never find out whether or not their children experienced the futures that they had hoped for when giving the children up for adoption. As a result, these mothers are plagued with a real sense of ambiguity regarding the wisdom of the original decision.

See Chapter 10 for suggestions on how to deal with guilt and forgiving yourself if you're having doubts about your adoption decision and if your feelings are hampering your ability to grieve the loss of the child.

Experiencing a prenatal or perinatal loss

Prenatal loss of a child occurs during pregnancy as a result of a *miscarriage* (a loss of a fetus before it has developed enough to live on its own). *Perinatal loss* of a child occurs during birth (in which the child is considered stillborn) or shortly thereafter (most often because the child is very premature or suffers from some birth defect).

Both types of child loss are extremely grueling for the prospective parents (especially for the mother, who carried the baby). After time spent preparing for the new baby and the anticipated joy of his or her birth, the parents are left only with heartbreak. They leave the hospital alone and often return to a home with a fully equipped nursery where they must bear their disappointment and grief.

Your grief is made more difficult in the case of miscarriage if you don't have a burial or funeral ceremony for the child. (Note that most funeral homes are prepared to conduct funerals and memorials for children who die under any circumstances.) You and your partner don't have that public acknowledgment of your loss or the comfort it brings to parents whose children died in childbirth or shortly thereafter and were then buried. Refer to the sidebar "Mizuko Jizo and the Mizuko ceremony" for information on a ritual for honoring and remembering children lost from a prenatal or perinatal loss.

If your pregnancy was public knowledge, you can expect people outside the immediate family to ask you about your baby after you experience a loss. Answer this simple but dreaded question with an equally simple answer that you had the baby and that she or he didn't survive. The problem is that this kind of innocent encounter brings up the pain of the loss and may cause the questioner to become embarrassed (when there's really no reason for it). As a result, you can find yourself in the position of trying to allay his discomfort, which is awkward and difficult given your own feelings.

Keep in mind that you're not responsible for another's feelings of awkwardness or discomfort around death and grief. If it feels appropriate, you can let the other person know that it's okay if he doesn't know how to express shock and sorrow over your loss.

Experiencing the death of an infant

Babies are the most innocent and pure beings one can conceive of. (Just thinking about a baby let alone being around one brings a smile to most people's faces.) Therefore, any *neonatal loss* (the death of a baby within the first month of his or her life) or loss of an infant is associated with a loss of innocence. (A child who is unable to walk and talk is considered an infant. The term literally means "incapable of speech.")

Perhaps the most common and most alarming type of infant death is SIDS (Sudden Infant Death Syndrome). SIDS is frightening not only because it occurs without warning in otherwise healthy babies but also because its causes are unexplained. Given the mysterious nature of SIDS, parents who experience this type of loss can be plagued with a lot of doubt that can easily turn into guilt and blame finding.

How deeply the loss wounds the parents and immediate family is often a function of the cause of the infant's death. When the death is clearly not in the hands of the parents, as in the case of an unpreventable disease or birth defect, it can be much less injurious than when the parents bear some or all responsibility, such as in the case of neglect or abuse of the baby. Of course, a gray area exists in cases where the death is due to a preventable accident and poor judgment or a total lack of it contributed to the baby's death.

If you, as the parent, feel guilt over the death of your infant (even if your guilt is completely unwarranted), it's likely that your feelings are amplified by the fact that a total innocent died with his whole life before him. Grieving the loss of an infant, then, is a lot like grieving infertility in that you mourn the loss of anticipated futures — both the baby's and your own as you would have experienced the joy of parenthood.

Because you're in high nurture mode when your baby is first born, it's natural that you view your infant's death as the result of your inability to properly care for your child. You must deal with such feelings as part of your grieving, especially if you have other children who need nurturing or if you're planning to have more children in the future.

Experiencing the death of a young child

By the time your child progresses from infancy into the toddler stage (between 1 and 3 years of age), he's well on the way to becoming an individual with his own personality expressed in language, movement, and beyond all else, disposition. From then on, you're confronted with spurts of growth and development.

The loss of a young child within the age range of toddler to preteen is compounded by your familiarity with the child's personality and nascent abilities. Unlike experiencing a neonatal or infant loss, in which parents lose the opportunity to really get to know their child, the parents of a young child who dies lose the opportunity to get to know how their child turns out.

Using an analogy to writing, losing an infant is like a promising story where just the beginning gets written and you're left to wonder what the tale would have been like. Losing a young child, on the other hand, is like a story where the first part is written but you're still left to wonder how the tale turns out.

Certainly, depending upon the circumstances of death, you may not only grieve the loss of your child but also question what you could have done differently to prevent the death. Keep in mind that feelings of guilt and second-guessing, while certainly understandable, aren't conducive to grieving the loss. Often you need to attend to these feelings before the real grieving can begin.

Because parents who lose a child have a definite image of the person they've lost, it's all the more important for them to memorialize the child. When creating this memorial, you can make it something physical, such as a special Christmas ornament, memory book, and the like (see Chapter 19 for ideas on memorials). You also may make this memorial something intangible, such as remembering the lost child at all family celebrations and gatherings and including him whenever you mention the order of all your children.

Experiencing the death of a teenager

As anyone knows who has a teenage child or even remembers what it was like to be one, teenagers are absolutely convinced that they're indestructible. Unfortunately, parents who have experienced the loss of a teenage child can attest that this belief couldn't be more false.

Regardless of how or why the death occurs, the loss of a teenager is devastating given that the child was in the prime of life and poised to become an independent adult. Going back to my analogy relating the death of a child to writing, it's as though the story comes to an abrupt end after the personality of the story's character was fully developed, the story's beginning was told, and the middle of the story was just about to commence.

Teen suicide is a special case. In most cases, suicide is not accidental and is considered preventable. It frequently comes as the conclusion of a long struggle with depression. Suicide may be completely unexpected, but it also may be preceded by unsuccessful attempts to take one's life.

Because society in general and many religions in particular look down on suicide, this type of death carries a stigma that other types of death do not. As a result, a family dealing with the death of a teenager by his own hand has to deal with a lot more than simple grief. Turn to Chapter 2 for more on suicide and its aftermath.

Experiencing the death of an adult child

No matter how old their children get, parents continue to see them as kids in great need of parental guidance. When an adult child dies, whatever the cause, the overwhelming feeling is that nature's order has been turned upside down; in other words, in a perfect world, children would always bury their parents and not vice versa.

The death of an adult child is often accompanied by a deep questioning of natural order and the innate justice of the universe (expressed in terms of God's plan in the case of religious people).

Because adult children often have families of their own, their deaths also may bring about a profound change in family dynamics. As a grandparent, you may be confronted suddenly with the challenge of helping your child's family cope with the loss financially as well as emotionally. In some cases, you even may be called upon to take your grandchildren in and raise them.

These kinds of challenges compound the wound that you feel over the unfairness of a world in which children don't always outlive their own parents. Many times, parents who lose adult children have to deal with their feelings about the inequity of the death as part of grieving their loss.

Adult children, especially when they've just started their careers or families, are lost right at the time when their lives have the most impact on their communities. This factor plays into the sense of tragedy and injustice that parents and other family members associate with the untimely death.

The Impact of a Child's Death on the Parents' Relationship

Regardless of the age of the child or the reason for his or her death, the loss of a child inevitably has a profound impact on the immediate family. The surviving children have to deal with the loss of a sibling as well as a change in the pecking order (see Chapter 5 for details). The parents have to deal not only with their grief over the profound loss but also with the challenges this loss presents to their marriage or partnership. They also may suffer a loss of identity as parents accompanied by upsurges of grief at what would otherwise have been milestones in the child's life (graduations, proms, and so on).

Even if the partnership didn't suffer from serious communication problems prior to the child's death, such problems can arise easily after the loss of a child. Many times, this is the first occasion for the parents to grieve the same profound loss. It even may be the first instance in which either of the parents has experienced any kind of profound loss and experienced this kind of intense grief.

The different manner in which you and your partner each express your grief sometimes leads to misunderstandings and, in some cases, even to a breakdown in communication. This communication breakdown is compounded when either of you becomes withdrawn from the other, which is common when trying to process this type of profound loss.

More often than not, the father tends to keep his emotions to himself, while the mother expresses her emotions more openly. Mom may come to the conclusion that Dad isn't grieving as much as she is. Things can go downhill quickly if Mom starts questioning whether Dad's lack of outward mourning means that he didn't really loved their child. Mom may then question whether or not Dad really loves *her*. Misunderstanding and lack of communication are ingredients in the perfect recipe for a marriage disaster.

As a parent under the strain of dealing with the loss of a child, you must be very careful not to alienate your partner as part of processing your own grief. Although grieving the loss of a child can bring couples closer together and strengthen their marriage, it also can open rifts that eventually threaten the very existence of the relationship. The intense emotions and deep hurt brought on by the loss can become destructive to the marriage when they're leveled at one of the partners.

If you're part of a couple grieving the loss of a child, be very aware of the danger of blaming your partner in any way as you question whether or how this loss could have been prevented. Given the intensity of emotions on both sides, you run a great risk of isolating yourself from your partner and eroding (and perhaps even permanently damaging) the trust you've cultivated in one another.

Because grieving a child as a couple is fraught with many twists and turns, consider seeking professional counseling to help you and your partner stay in communication with one another. If you decide to make use of a marriage counselor, try to find one with some experience counseling couples in crisis over the loss of a child. If you can't find such a marriage counselor, consider using the services of a bereavement counselor with experience in family counseling. Turn to Chapter 14 for more information on locating and making use of professional support and counseling.

Resources for Healing the Loss of a Child

Resources for guiding and supporting you through the loss of a child are numerous and include some very good books on the death of children as well as some very solid online resources. In addition to consulting the resources listed in this section, you may want to join a local grief support group that deals specifically with the loss of children or participate in one-on-one sessions with a grief counselor in your area. Chapter 14 contains general information on grief support groups and counseling along with suggestions on how best to go about locating these resources in the area where you live.

Books

Loss of a child is one subject in the bereavement arena on which there's no shortage of written materials. Books on the death of a child abound, with many dedicated to particular types of child loss, especially prenatal or perinatal losses. The following list represents just a portion of books available:

✔ *After the Death of a Child: Living with Loss through the Years* by Ann K. Finkbeiner (Johns Hopkins University Press): This book is written by a medical writer who experienced the loss of her 18-year-old son in a train wreck. The book examines the long-term effects of losing a child based on interviews conducted with 30 couples at least five years after the losses of their children.

✔ *The Death of a Child: Reflections for Grieving Parents* by Elaine E. Stillwell (ACTA Publications): This book is written by a diocese bereavement coordinator who lost two adult children in a car accident. It covers a wide range of topics related to the loss of a child, including anger with God, communication problems with a spouse, and coping with holidays and anniversaries.

✔ *Beyond Tears: Living after Losing a Child* by Ellen Mitchell, Carol Barkin, and others (St. Martin's Griffin): This book is written by nine mothers who have experienced the loss of an adult child. It speaks eloquently to their anger over the losses, problems that arose in their marriages, and ultimately how they coped with the losses.

✔ *Grieving the Child I Never Knew* by Kathe Wunnenberg (Zondervan): This book reflects the author's personal journey through grief over three miscarriages and the death of an infant son. Her insights into her grief are interwoven with scriptural passages and prayers, and the book provides journaling space for the reader to add his or her own comments and insights.

✔ *Gone but Not Lost: Grieving the Death of a Child* by David W. Wiersbe (Baker Books): This book gives simple, down-to-earth advice, coupled with relevant biblical scripture, on how to process the grief of child loss.

✔ *Jizo Bodhisattva: Guardian of Children, Travelers, and Other Voyagers* by Jan Chozen Bays (Shambhala Publications): In this book, Zen master Jan Chozen Bays introduces the reader to the practices and rituals associated with Jizo Bodhisattva in Zen Buddhism. These rituals include Japan's Mizuko (water baby) ceremony dedicated to the children who were never born as the result of abortion or miscarriage.

✔ *Facing the Ultimate Loss: Coping with the Death of a Child* by Robert J. Marx and Susan Wengerhoff Davidson (Champion Press): This book covers the range of emotions that comes from losing a child. It draws upon the authors' experiences as well as those of the parents they've counseled.

- ✔ *Help Your Marriage Survive the Death of a Child* by Paul C. Rosenblatt (Temple University Press): This book is based on in-depth interviews with 29 couples who chronicle the various marital challenges they faced after the death of a child.

Online resources

Online resources dedicated to grief support for the loss of a child are much more limited than print resources. The following Web sites are among the best in terms of this very special type of loss:

- ✔ **UNITE** at www.unitegriefsupport.org: This site is dedicated to helping parents cope with prenatal and perinatal loss. It offers information on grief support and a parent support forum in which grieving parents can share their experiences.

- ✔ **The Compassionate Friends** at www.compassionatefriends.org: This site offers a wide range of support services for bereaved parents, grandparents, and siblings. It includes information on grief resources, memorials, and a chat room where parents can share their stories and offer each other support.

- ✔ **Loss of a Child: Hope for Grieving Parents** at www.lossofachild.org: This Web site offers support for grieving parents and has links to other resources and books. This site also hosts a memorial wall where parents can remember their children and commemorate their losses as well as link to other memorial sites on the Web.

Chapter 7

Children and Grief

. . . .

In This Chapter

▶ Knowing how to explain and discuss death with a child

▶ Exploring children's emotional, physical, and behavioral reactions to death

▶ Helping your child grieve

▶ Knowing what to expect from grieving adolescents

▶ Checking out resources for guiding a child through grief

. . . .

*H*ow children understand the profound losses they suffer is closely related to their mental and emotional development, which is most often a direct function of their age. Generally speaking, the younger the child, the more concrete the thinking, so younger children have more trouble understanding the concept of death. Older children and adolescents, who conceptually comprehend death, often still have difficulties accepting its reality, especially when it happens to an immediate family member or a really close friend.

Occasionally compounding the problems that children naturally have with first understanding and then accepting the loss is the reluctance that many families have to include children in the formal mourning of loss. Children often are excluded from funerals as well as less formal mourning rites such as visiting grave sites because of the belief that doing so protects the children from undue and unnecessary pain.

This chapter examines the grief that children undergo when they suffer a profound loss. I divide this important topic into two parts: how children look at and understand profound loss in their lives, and how you can help them actually grieve these losses.

Helping Children Understand Death

Even adults who have a firm grasp on the notion of death and its permanence often have trouble accepting the reality of a profound loss when it first occurs. Just imagine how much more difficult it is for a child whose concept of death is every bit as vague as his understanding of forever.

A child's understanding of death is often a function of his age and how he experiences and comprehends time. Younger children live almost totally in the present, so they have no way to grasp a permanent, lasting change like death. They only see things in terms of what is or isn't directly in their environments, understanding that a loved one who has died is now no longer there for them to love.

As children grow older and have explored the concept of time in the future and past, they begin to grasp the irreversible nature of death. As a result, they have to come to terms with the idea that the losses they suffer are ones from which there is no reprieve and ones that they'll have to live with the rest of their lives. As you may expect, this more complete understanding of death brings a new level of grief with it: In addition to the anxiety that naturally arises from the absence of a loved one, the child also feels the stark pain that comes from the realization that this loss is one that will never change.

Children's different concepts of death

Adults tend to think of death as being quite a concrete phenomenon, but to young children, death is often one of the more abstract, challenging concepts they encounter. Part of the problem is that they're far too young to have a clear understanding of anything that's irreversible and lasts forever. Another part of the problem is the way that they see death portrayed in some of the cartoons and digital games — a character can be laid flatter than a pancake or blown to smithereens in one moment only to return to the screen right as rain in the next moment.

Table 7-1 gives you a general idea of the prevailing views and feelings that children in different age groups have concerning death. Note how the views move from the more concrete to the more abstract as the child gets older and he becomes aware of his own mortality and fear of his own death.

Table 7-1	Concepts of Death by Children of Various Ages
Age Range	*Prevalent Views and Feelings*
Infancy to toddler	No concept of death; reacts to the grief expressed by others in the immediate environment, especially parents
3 to 5 years old	Vague concept of death; denies death as a final process; often equates death with sleep from which one will awaken; believes in degrees of death (from kind of dead to really dead); may understand death as something that happens to other people
6 to 9 years old	Clearer concept of death; understands that he and people he loves can die; often sees death of a loved one as a punishment for his own behavior and not being good
10 to 12 years old	Sees death as final and inescapable; is curious about biological aspects of death; hides fear of death by joking about it; may feel some responsibility for death of a loved one
Teenage years	Vacillates between seeing death as final and feeling immortal; can become preoccupied with death; may engage in high-risk behavior to defy his own mortality

Explaining and discussing death with a child

If you can help it, don't wait to discuss death with your child until he experiences the profound loss of a family member or close friend. By explaining death to your child before a loss, you ensure better communication with him when a loss does occur. You also stand a much better chance of helping him through his grief.

When you set out to discuss death with your child, follow these guidelines:

- ✔ **Use the death of a family pet or even the passing of the seasons to illustrate the concept of death and as a natural segue into the discussion.**

- ✔ **Don't use euphemisms for death.** State clearly that so-and-so has *died* instead of "passed away," and never tell a child that the person is "lost to us" (unless you want your child to wait patiently for the person to be found or to actually set out looking for him).

- ✔ **Don't equate death with sleep (unless you want your child to expect the dead person to wake up one day and return).**

- ✔ **Discuss death openly with your child, answering whatever questions that he has honestly and with whatever amount of detailed information he wants that's appropriate to his level of understanding.**

- ✔ **Avoid using clichés.** The judgments behind clichés such as "God wanted him to be in heaven" and "It's always for the best" can distort the child's view of grieving as well as discourage him from discussing the subject with you. (See Chapter 20 for more on clichés and why they aren't helpful.)

Informing a child about a death

Parents often have questions about how and when to inform their children about the death of a loved one. They want to know whether there's a right time to tell children about a loss as well as how much detail about the event they should give.

By and large, professionals who deal with children and grief recommend the following guidelines regarding informing a child about the death of a loved one:

- ✔ **Inform the child of the death as soon as you possibly can.** You don't want to child to hear about the death from someone outside the family.

- ✔ **Explain what happened to the loved one as clearly, simply, and factually as you can.** Keep in mind that the language you use in describing the cause of death needs to be appropriate to the child's age and development.

- ✔ **When answering a child's questions regarding the cause of death and what happened to the body, ask the child what he really wants to know and give only the information necessary to answer that particular question.** Some kids want to know every detail whereas others only want and need certain information.

- ✔ **If you have spiritual beliefs regarding life after death, discuss them with your child, but be aware that if you make it sound like the death is God's doing, you run the risk of prejudicing the child against God.**

When discussing a death with a young child (especially one between the ages of 3 and 5), be prepared to answer the same questions over and over again (some kids are relentless in this regard). Also, be aware that this is the age of "magical thinking" when children often feel as though they caused the death simply because they thought it or wished it would happen. Therefore, they may feel a great deal of guilt over the death of a loved one (sometimes much more than adults) and may need plenty of reassurance that they were in no way responsible for the loss. (You may need to repeat this message over and over again and be relentless in this regard.)

Understanding How Children Grieve

The first fact about how children grieve that you need to understand is that children grieve the profound loss of a loved one just as much as (and sometimes more than) adults. However, because their verbal skills are usually less developed than adults', children tend to display the emotions surrounding their grief in more concrete ways.

This means that you can expect to see more-acute physical and behavioral changes in a grieving child than you would see in a grieving adult. A child's emotional response to the loss may manifest and play out in more physical than verbal ways.

The fact that children may not be all that verbal with their emotions doesn't mean that speaking with your child about his feelings about the loss does no good. Just keep in mind that talking about the loss may not be as beneficial for your child as it may be for you as an adult. Suggest and participate in other activities in which the child can express his feelings (check out the section "Helping Your Child Grieve," later in this chapter, for some specific suggestions).

Common emotional reactions to death

No matter how well you explain death and how openly you discuss it with your child, he'll exhibit his own response to a profound loss according to his age and related stage of development. Table 7-2 gives you a general rundown of the common reactions to death that you can expect from children in various age groups.

Table 7-2	Common Reactions to Death by Children of Various Ages
Age Range	**Responses**
Infancy to toddler	Cries easily and clings more to parents; experiences a regression of toilet habits; has more digestive and stomach upsets
3 to 5 years	Regresses to more-infantile behaviors; asks repeated questions about the person who died; becomes especially fearful of being separated from parents; shows no concern over the death
6 to 9 years	Demonstrates high anxiety surrounding death; becomes unwilling to talk about the death; experiences intermittent grieving

(continued)

Table 7-2 *(continued)*	
Age Range	**Responses**
10 to 12 years	Develops separation anxiety; loses manual dexterity; has difficulty concentrating (school grades may suffer); becomes emotionally distant
Teenage years	Assumes an adult role with younger siblings; angers quickly and shows aggression easily; becomes preoccupied with death; may become suicidal or attempt suicide as a gesture

As you can see in Table 7-2, anxiety is the common reaction to death in all age groups. Therefore, regardless of the child's age, as a parent or guardian, you need to be particularly available to the child during this stressful time. One of the most effective ways to do this is by frequently reassuring him both physically and verbally whenever you can. In other words, hold him more and let him know that you're there to listen to his feelings and even share your own.

In addition to heightened anxiety, children also feel all the other emotions that adults contend with during grieving. These may include any of the following feelings:

- ✔ **Sadness:** Children commonly feel sad over a death and may become melancholy and down in the dumps, if not weepy, at the drop of a hat. Teenagers can become despondent and even suicidal in some cases.

- ✔ **Loneliness:** Death often makes children feel abandoned and alone. They may alienate themselves from the rest of the family and even from their friends and schoolmates.

- ✔ **Apathy:** Children often become lethargic and feel emotionally flat after the loss of a loved one. They may lose interest in school as well as activities they enjoyed before the death. In some cases, a child may become clinically depressed and need professional and medical help (see Chapter 11 for more on death and depression).

- ✔ **Relief:** Older children may feel secretly relieved over the death and then feel very guilty about feeling that way. Feelings of relief may result from the end of a loved one's suffering as well as from no longer being subject to the loved one's strictures and influence (this is especially true when child abuse is involved).

- ✔ **Helplessness:** The general sense of powerlessness that children feel is often heightened by the loss of a loved one (especially a parent). As a result of this new level of vulnerability, they can become quite clingy and emotionally needy.

✔ **Impatience:** Children often become much more easily frustrated and less able to cope with changes and new challenges after a death. They may be easily aggravated by setbacks of any kind and easily stymied by problems they encounter.

✔ **Anger:** Anger is a recurrent emotion that both children and adults experience when grieving the loss of a loved one. In children, the anger often presents itself in the form of resentment, although it also can show up as a full-blown rage directed at the loved one for dying and leaving them alone.

Common physical reactions to death

Emotional responses to grief often have physical manifestations in children. When dealing with a child who's grieving a loss, you need to pay attention to any new physical problems that your child experiences so that you can determine whether or not these physical reactions are related to the child's grief and get him the appropriate help.

Some of the more frequent physical problems that grieving children experience can include:

✔ Headaches

✔ Stomachaches, nausea, and diarrhea

✔ Heart palpitations (often as a racing heart)

✔ Nightmares

✔ Shortness of breath and tightness in the throat

✔ Teeth grinding and tightness in the jaw

✔ Shortness of breath, dizziness, and feeling faint

✔ Tightness in the chest and muscle tension and pain (especially in the neck and shoulders)

✔ Fatigue and general weakness

In addition to the general ailments in this list, teenage girls who are grieving may experience irregularity in their menstrual cycles. The stress and anxiety from grief may cause a teenage girl to skip her period for several months in a row after the death.

Sometimes when a loved one dies from an illness, a child may become fearful that the physical problems he's experiencing as a result of the stress of the loss and grieving are actually symptoms of the same disease. He may even secretly question whether he'll also die from the same disease. This may be a situation where you want to be very clear about the cause of the loved one's death and give extra reassurance to the child that he's in no danger of dying from the same illness.

Common behavioral reactions to death

Behaviors rather than words are the hallmarks of childhood. Therefore, it's highly unusual for your child to go through grieving a loss without manifesting some behavioral changes. Naturally, some of the behaviors that children exhibit when under the stress of a loss and grief are more disconcerting and more dangerous than others.

Some of the more common behavioral changes you may notice in your child can include:

- ✔ **Accident-proneness:** Grieving children (especially adolescent boys) are much more prone to accidents in the first year after the death than nongrieving children. This increase in accidents may be related to an increase in absentmindedness as well as an inclination toward riskier behaviors.

- ✔ **Weepiness:** Some grieving children exhibit this behavior through sudden outbursts of crying, whereas others show it through a more general tearful state. Weepiness can indicate both that the child misses the loved one and that he feels anxiety over the changes that this loss has brought to his life.

- ✔ **Clinginess:** This behavior is common in the case of a child who loses one parent and then becomes exceedingly anxious over the possibility of losing the other one. As a result, he becomes overly protective of the surviving parent and often quite distressed at being separated from him or her.

- ✔ **Absentmindedness:** Concentration routinely suffers in grieving children (and adults) as a result of the shock of the loss and the energy required to deal with it. For many children, this behavior becomes most noticeable when they have trouble keeping up and completing schoolwork and their grades go down.

- ✔ **Listlessness:** Often referred to as depression, a child can exhibit this behavior through a general lack of energy and increased fatigue as well as a decided lack of interest in his normal activities.

- **Hyperactivity:** Older children and adolescents may feel the need to become superbusy after a death. This heightened level of activity is usually related to additional school and extracurricular activities. Often, the child's hyperactivity is a defense against having to feel the pain of the loss and suffer the grief, and it can become a problem if it blocks the grieving process.

- **Regressive behaviors:** Normally seen in younger children, these can include behaviors such as thumb sucking, taking a teddy bear to bed, and even bed-wetting that your child has long since given up but that he returns to in this time of great stress.

- **Risky behaviors:** Normally seen in teenagers (especially boys), these behaviors can include indulging in alcohol and drugs, undertaking activities that purposely place the adolescent's life at risk, such as death-defying stunts, reckless driving, and engaging in unsafe sexual activity, and making gestures of or actually attempting suicide.

Of all the risky behaviors in this list, the threat of a teen suicide after a death calls for the greatest concern. Suicide rates are already high enough among teenagers who haven't suffered such traumas; the extra strain of the loss and despair from the grief (not to mention any guilt surrounding the death) can be a deadly catalyst that turns a teen's idle talk into an actual attempt. If your teenage child talks about or threatens suicide, take it very seriously and don't hesitate to get the help you need (either from a suicide prevention organization or a professional grief counselor) to deal with this threat before an attempt actually happens.

Helping Your Child Grieve

Before you can help your child grieve a loss, you need to believe that he's entitled to it. Until very recently, many families routinely excluded children from all formal mourning (see the sidebar "Children and funerals: To go or not to go") and even some informal grieving for immediate family members on the false assumptions that

- Children don't need to grieve losses in the same way as adults.

- Children are protected when they aren't drawn into grieving the loss.

In response to this type of thinking, certain grief professionals and groups such as the American Academy of Bereavement have developed a so-called Bill of Rights for Grieving Children.

Children and funerals: To go or not to go

One of the big questions that parents frequently have after a death in the family is whether the children should be involved in formal mourning rites such as attending the funeral. Some parents feel very strongly that their child needs to attend the funeral in order to make the death real and to toughen him up and introduce him to the harsher realities of life. Others feel just as strongly that the funeral is no place for a child and that attending this sad event will only further traumatize him after the death.

Current thinking is that you include the child in the funeral only if he wants to attend. The thinking is that forcing a child to attend a funeral when he's really uncomfortable with the idea is the only way in which the event can be traumatic. Nowadays, many families include their children in all the mourning rites in the belief that doing so affords the children an opportunity to say goodbye as well as lets them know that death, although sad, isn't the frightening taboo that it may otherwise seem to be.

In short, this bill of rights says that a child not only has the right to grieve but also has the right to grieve in his or her own way. Also important among the principles in the Bill of Rights for Grieving Children are the tenets that the child has the right to question the cause of death and the right to memorialize the lost loved one. This right to remember the deceased includes being entitled to speak about the loved one as well as visit the grave site or cemetery on special anniversaries.

The family's influence on children's grieving

Immediate families exhibit different styles of behavior that make up their characters (and their quirks). For example, some families are open in terms of communicating feelings, and others are closed. Some families are emotionally warm and supporting of each other, whereas others are cooler and more distant.

How the parents in a family work as a team to adapt to change and deal with crises often determines how well the family functions in an emergency. The parents' ability or inability in this area has a great influence on how readily children accept the loss and how easily they deal with it.

Most families fall into one of the following categories, which are determined by how the family behaves in the face of a crisis, such as a death in the family:

- **Rigid:** In this inflexible family style, the family tries to resist a crisis most often by assigning blame. Fault finding and guilt remain the primary behaviors during the emergency.

  This family style makes children's grieving the most difficult because the blame game and guilt doom efforts to accept the loss and deal with the feelings that come from it.

- **Reserved:** In this stoic family style, the family tries to endure a crisis with a stiff upper lip. Denial and emotional detachment are the primary behaviors during the emergency.

  The second most difficult family style for children's grieving often makes it impossible for children to express their feelings of grief. The more reserved the family's response is to a death in the family, the more difficult grieving is for the children.

- **Chaotic:** In this disorganized family style, the family simply attempts to get through a crisis any way it can. Confusion and upheaval are the primary behaviors during the emergency.

  The family's emotional turmoil isn't conducive to helping calm the children's anxiety over the loss, but it doesn't have to be detrimental provided that the parents can remain emotionally open and accessible.

- **Open:** In this accessible family style, the family tries to remain open and caring during a crisis. Intimacy and communication remain the priorities during the emergency.

  Naturally, the more open and emotionally supportive that a family is to each other during a crisis caused by a death in the family, the easier it is for the children to get in touch with their feelings and grieve.

Together, the characteristics of rigid and reserved types of families form a lethal combination that can completely shut down the grieving process, forcing children to carry unresolved grief with them sometimes all the way into adulthood.

Guidelines for supporting grieving children

Anxiety is a principal emotion for children newly saddled with the grief from a profound loss. The first thing that parents can do to help their grieving children is to reassure them and do everything they can to reduce this anxiousness.

Here are a few hints on how you can help reduce the level of anxiety initially caused by a profound loss:

✔ Stay close to your child, reassuring him of your love and sharing activities with him. He'll benefit from your physical presence and lots of extra hugs and kisses.

✔ Speak with your child as openly as you can about what has happened, always keeping in mind his current stage of development (refer to the section "Understanding How Children Grieve," earlier in the chapter). Share your feelings when appropriate, and if you don't know something, be honest and tell him that.

✔ Maintain as much of the normal family routine as possible, including dinnertime, chores, homework, bedtimes, and the like.

✔ Be prepared to break with the normal family routine as soon as you see your child is having real trouble maintaining it. (For example, many times, a grieving child has difficulty concentrating on homework and sleeping through the night.)

✔ Spend extra time quiet time with your child at bedtime. This quiet time can include reading his favorite bedtime stories (you may even want to include some age-appropriate titles about death; see the section "Books for young children who are grieving," at the end of this chapter), playing his favorite games, or talking about the deceased.

✔ Safeguard your child's health by seeing to it that he continues to get the nutrition, exercise, and rest he needs. (This is often a tall order and a real challenge, especially during the acute phase of grieving.)

✔ Speak with your child's teachers and appropriate staff at his school about the loss, and enlist their help in reporting any changes in behavior that may be linked to the loss and indicate difficulties in dealing with it.

Whenever possible, postpone making big changes in your family's life for at least a year and a half or more after the death. For example, the hardest change for a grieving child is moving to a new residence, especially when this entails having to attend a new school and make new friends.

Activities to facilitate children's grieving

Because children are such concrete thinkers, having activities to do often helps them with the grieving process. All these activities should have one of two purposes: to encourage the child to express his feelings over the loss or to memorialize the lost loved one.

To help children express their anger and frustration over a death, many parents organize an area or a room in the house, basement, or garage where the children can vent their feelings. If you create such an area, stock it with items that make noise and enable the children to act out safely, including:

- Old pillows for them to punch
- Old telephone books, newspapers, and magazines for them to rip apart
- Foam bats for them to hit the floor and walls with
- Punching bags for them to hit and kick
- Puppets, dolls, or stuffed animals with which they can interact and express their feelings

To help younger children express their feelings about the loss and remember their loved ones, gather paints, rolls of paper, and other artistic materials so that they can paint or draw pictures to express their feelings. Supply older children and adolescents with journals in which they can record their feelings.

To help children of all ages, collect family photos that include the lost loved one and create albums together that you can look at later while sharing favorite stories and memories. Do the same with family videos, creating movies of family events and vacations that incorporate the loved one's favorite songs and music.

You can still memorialize your loved one even if you don't have photos for scrapbooks or videos for home movies. Simply arrange times when the family gathers and each family member shares a favorite memory or relates an important or amusing story that involves the deceased.

Holding memorial storytelling events is a crucial element in successfully surviving the holidays and anniversaries after a death. They allow you to honor and remember the absent loved one as well as make him present and part of the event. See Chapter 16 for more suggestions on getting through holidays and anniversaries after the loss of a loved one.

Getting children involved in new outside activities

Very often a death in the family leaves a child feeling particularly helpless. To help combat this feeling and boost his self-esteem, get him involved in some new activities outside the home. These activities can be physical or creative in nature depending upon his interests and natural inclinations.

Such outside activities can include:

✔ Art or drama classes

✔ Music lessons

✔ Team sports such as softball, soccer, and basketball

✔ Martial arts classes such as karate, judo, and tae kwon do

✔ Volunteer activities in the community such as visiting seniors or helping at an animal shelter

Volunteering in the community, although usually open only to older children and teenagers, can be a really marvelous way for grieving children to reconnect and heal their grief (it also works wonders for grieving adults). Check out Chapter 18 for more suggestions on ways to help out and integrate your grief all at the same time.

Creative projects for grieving children

The ability to express one's feelings through art is really not a function of a person's age or literacy. That being said, expressing one's feelings through art offers a particularly effective way for children to convey and reflect upon their grief.

Here are some artistic and creative projects that you may suggest to your child or even do with him:

✔ Draw a picture of the way he's feeling today.

✔ Draw a picture depicting a favorite activity he shared with the family member who died.

✔ Create a collage with photos and other objects that remind him of his favorite times with the family member who died.

✔ Plant a memorial garden with the family member's favorite flowers or in his favorite colors.

✔ Create a pendant or paint a stone that your child can carry around to remind him of the family member.

✔ Make a rock garden with stones representing each member of the family that depicts their relationships to one another and especially to the deceased.

Older children and adolescents can express their grief not only through art projects such as these but also through writing about their feelings and experiences. You can suggest any of the following writing activities to your child:

- A letter in which he expresses how much he misses the family member who died or says farewell to this person if he wasn't able to do so before death.

- A story in which he relates a favorite memory involving the family member who died.

- A daily journal in which the child communicates to the family member who died his changing feelings and thoughts.

Dealing with problems in children's grieving

A child's grieving process, while similar in nature to an adult's (and often modeled after the way the parents and other adults in the family grieve), doesn't always follow the same general pattern. For example, children (especially in the age range 6 to 9) have an amazing capacity for grieving intermittently. One moment they can be quite downcast from the grief and quite literally the next moment be running around and playing as though nothing in the world were wrong.

Your child's uncanny ability to suddenly turn off grief and act as though nothing has happened isn't a sign of a real problem in his or her grieving process. Nor is it a sign that the child's grieving is over. It's most likely just a self-protection device that enables the child to take a small vacation from the uncertainty and sadness so that it doesn't become too much to handle.

That's not to say that children don't have problems grieving. They do, especially in households where intense emotions aren't readily displayed and adults have trouble with their own grief from the same loss.

Here are some signs that your child's grieving process may be hitting some snags:

- He acts as though nothing out of the ordinary has happened (in other words, he shows no signs of grieving).

- He becomes easily and often panicked.

- His schoolwork takes a real nosedive, he starts cutting classes, or he even refuses to attend school.

- He has lots of trouble getting along with classmates and friends and even gets into fights.

- ✔ He uses inappropriate language, commits delinquent acts, or is cruel to animals.
- ✔ He talks about killing himself or threatens suicide.
- ✔ He becomes involved with alcohol or drugs.

If your child starts exhibiting one or more of these signs, you need to get outside help. Turn to a grief counselor, family counselor, or psychologist as long as the professional has some experience in grieving and is trained in dealing with children who have suffered trauma. You can find out more about finding grief counselors and support groups in Chapter 14.

Helping grieving children deal with dreams and nightmares

Children quite commonly have trouble sleeping through the night after a death occurs in the immediate family. They often no longer want to sleep alone or are unable to sleep without a night light on.

Moreover, many children have vivid dreams about the deceased and/or death. They may even have nightmares in which they, other surviving members of the family, or classmates and friends are harmed or are no longer secure.

In trying to help a child with problems sleeping, consider doing the following:

- ✔ Spend extra time putting your child to bed by reading his favorite non-scary stories.
- ✔ Turn on a night light and play soft, soothing music in his room at bedtime.
- ✔ Limit his viewing of scary movies and violent computer games during the day.
- ✔ Make sure that your child is as physically active as possible during the day.

When you're dealing with a child who's having dreams about the deceased, don't automatically assume that these are bad dreams or particularly frightening to the child. They may be attempts to stay in contact with the lost loved one (a very common occurrence among grieving people of all ages) that the child actually finds quite comforting.

Be certain to discuss these dreams with your child to determine how he feels about them. If the child is older, consider talking to him about what he thinks these dreams mean — such as whether they represent an attempt by the deceased to contact him or simply longing on the child's part to be in contact with the deceased (or both).

When you're dealing with a child who's having repeated nightmares, discuss the bad dreams with him. If he's reluctant to discuss the nightmares with you, seek out someone (perhaps a professional grief counselor) he feels comfortable talking to. Sometimes, simply talking about the dreams with someone the child trusts makes them less scary.

Some parents try to help their grieving children get over their bad dreams by putting up dream catchers, either above the child's bed or at the entrance to the child's room. If you do this, explain to the child that Native Americans believe that the net of the dream catcher captures all the bad dreams that might come to him, letting only the good dreams get through the spaces in the net.

Working through regrieving the loss

A child is a person in development. As children reach milestones on their way to adulthood — proms, graduations, weddings, the birth of the first child, and so on — they're often vividly reminded of the losses they experienced as youths, and they relive the grief they suffered.

Regrieving a childhood loss is quite common, especially during significant events at which the loved one's absence is particularly conspicuous (for example, a deceased father's absence at a daughter's wedding or a deceased mother's absence at the birth of a daughter's first child).

Normally, the regrieving that an adult experiences isn't nearly as intense and long-lived as it was in childhood. Nevertheless, the pain and sorrow are just as real, and many of the same emotions that the bereaved experienced as a child (anxiety, insecurity, and the like) can resurface.

Keep in mind that regrieving a loss represents just another step in terms of integrating the original loss into one's life. If at all possible, the bereaved should welcome this ensuing part of the grieving process that he began as a youth as yet another way to remember and honor his loved one.

One of the most important and poignant milestones for a person who lost a parent as a child is the birthday at which he reaches the same age that his mother or father was when she or he died. The bereaved may find it hard to believe that he's made it to the age of his deceased parent. He also may question whether he'll live beyond that age or, if he's the same gender as the parent, how he'll get by without any further model of motherhood or fatherhood to follow.

Adolescents and Grief

As you may recall, the teenage years are an awkward and turbulent time when you seem to be caught in a nether region somewhere between childhood and adulthood. No longer wanting to be seen as a kid, you're very seldom considered an adult capable of making rational decisions. As the parent of a grieving teenager, it's important that you keep these feelings in mind.

Adolescence is also the time when being liked by one's peers and being accepted by them is all important. Because the experience of a death and the grieving that comes with it makes a teen different from his peers, a support group with other teens who are also experiencing a profound loss may be most beneficial.

Grieving a profound loss as an adolescent, always tricky at best, can be particularly difficult when any of the following conditions apply:

- The teen feels as though he must be a role model for his younger siblings (the children in the home).

- The teen feels as though he needs to be stoic to protect the feelings of other family members. (This is especially true when the deceased is one of the parents and the teen feels as though he needs to shield the surviving parent.)

- The teen's intensely sad emotions brought on by the grief get mixed up and come out as anger and frustration (especially in emotionally cool households).

- The teen's relationship with the deceased was problematic and marred by intense conflict.

- The teen is preoccupied with his mortality or immortality and starts engaging in high-risk (perhaps death-defying) behaviors or even becomes suicidal after the death.

The best way to help a grieving teenager cope with his feelings is to be honest about your own feelings and provide as much honest information about the death and the current situation as you can. Also, try emphasizing the positive legacy of the lost loved one, and suggest creative ways in which the teen can memorialize and honor the loved one (see Chapter 19 for ideas).

Resources for Guiding a Child through Grief

Children's grieving is one area in which (thankfully) a great deal of research has been done and in which there's a great deal of interest. As a result, you can find a lot of solid support for helping yourself and your children grieve fully and successfully.

Books

The books on children's grieving are numerous, so you shouldn't have any trouble finding the right book for you and your child's situation. In this section of recommended books, I divide the print resources into three categories: books for younger children, books for adolescents, and books for parents and other caregivers who are dealing with grieving children.

Books for young children who are grieving

Many books are written for young children to help them understand death and grieving. Some of these books are perfect for reading to children who aren't yet reading on their own. Many are well illustrated and worth reading over and over again. My favorites include:

- ✔ *Water Bugs and Dragonflies: Explaining Death to Young Children* by Doris Stickney (Pilgrim Press): This small paperback uses a story about a water bug that turns into a dragonfly to help young readers understand death and life after death. (For ages 3 to 8.)

- ✔ *When Dinosaurs Die: A Guide to Understanding Death* by Laurie Krasny Brown (Little Brown & Co.): This book covers every aspect of death from old age to suicide, so I recommend that you read the book before you choose appropriate parts to read to your child. (For ages 4 to 8.)

- ✔ *Badger's Parting Gifts* by Susan Varley (HarperTrophy): This book covers the subject of remembering a lost loved one through the story of a badger whose friends recall a special memory of him after his death. (For ages 5 to 10.)

- ✔ *When Someone Very Special Dies: Children Can Learn to Cope with Grief* by Marge Heegaard (Woodland Press): This workbook lets children use artwork and journaling to express their grief. (For ages 6 to 12.)

- ✔ *Saying Goodbye* by Jim Boulden (Boulden Publishing): This workbook has activities and a coloring book that enables children to understand death and begin to deal with the feelings caused by grief. (For ages 5 to 10.)

✔ *Charlotte's Web* by E.B. White (HarperTrophy): This award-winning story of a little girl, her piglet, and a spider illustrates the poignancy of friendship and death. (For ages 7 to 10.)

Books for grieving adolescents

There are many good books on teenagers and grieving that you can turn to if you're a parent, friend, or caregiver of a grieving adolescent. Among my favorite titles are:

✔ *Fire in My Heart, Ice in My Veins: A Journal for Teenagers Experiencing a Loss* by Enid Samuel Traisman and Ben Seiff (Centering Corporation): This workbook for teens enables them to journal and write letters to their lost loved ones.

✔ *Straight Talk about Death for Teenagers: How to Cope with Losing Someone You Love* by Earl A. Grollman (Beacon Press): This book contains a wide array of advice for teens who have lost someone they love as well as answers to the questions they're most likely to have.

✔ *Facing Change: Falling Apart and Coming Together Again in the Teen Years* by Donna B. O'Toole (Compassion Books): This book covers typical losses that teens may face on their way to adulthood (death of a classmate, sibling, parent, or close friend). The book's full of suggestions of coping strategies that teens can develop to get them through the ensuing grief.

Books for adults with grieving children

The books in this section are written specifically for parents and caregivers of grieving children. These books can give you clear information on how to talk with children about death as well as guide and help them through their grieving.

Among the best books in this category are:

✔ *When Children Grieve: For Adults to Help Children Deal with Death, Divorce, Pet Loss, Moving, and Other Losses* by John W. James, Russell Friedman, and Leslie Landon Matthews (Harper Collins Publishers): This book can help you shepherd a grieving child through all sorts of losses in addition to the death of a family member or friend.

✔ *Talking About Death: A Dialogue between Parent and Child* by Earl A. Grollman (Beacon Press): This book is a classic not only for explaining death to children but also for understanding children's feelings during the grieving process. Rabbi Grollman also includes information on how children respond to particular kinds of deaths and a section on how to seek professional grief help.

✔ *Helping Teens Cope with Death* by Dougy Center for Grieving Children (Dougy Center): This practical guide to the kinds of responses that adolescents normally have to loss has plenty of advice on how to help them through their grieving.

✔ *The Grieving Child: A Parent's Guide* by Helen Fitzgerald (Fireside): This book provides easy-to-digest and useful information on how to explain death to a child and deal with his emotional responses.

✔ *Children and Grief: When a Parent Dies* by J. William Worden (The Guilford Press): This book is an excellent reference for supporting a child who's lost a parent. It also includes information on helping a child who's lost a sibling or suffered the loss of a parent through divorce.

Online resources

While not nearly as numerous as print resources, there are some very good online resources that caregivers supporting bereaved children as well as the grieving children themselves can turn to in their time of grief.

Among my favorite Web sites that provide information and resources for and about grieving children are:

✔ **The Dougy Center for Grieving Children and Families** at www.dougy. org: The center supports bereaved children and their family members, and this Web site provides targeted information on grieving for children, teens, and adults. (The center was founded in 1982 in tribute to Dougy Turno, a young man who died at age 13 from an inoperable brain tumor after writing to Dr. Kübler-Ross questioning people's inability to speak with him about his impending death.)

✔ **Children's Grief Education Association** at www.childgrief.org: This site contains pages specifically for grieving children and teens as well as a page for military families and one on suicide, both of which give 800 numbers for crisis hotlines that you can use in an emergency.

✔ **KIDSAID** at www.kidsaid.com: This Web site operated by GriefNet offers a safe place where grieving children can communicate with one another and share their stories and their feelings about the losses they've experienced.

✔ **Highmark Caring Place** at `www.highmarkcaringplace.com`: From the home page, you can link to information specifically for grieving children, grieving adults, and grieving families as well as information on the impact of death and grief.

✔ **Centering Corporation: Your Grief Resource Center** at `www.centering corp.com`: This online resource center contains category links for children and grief and teen grief, among others. The great thing about these links is that they take you to pages with listings of books specific to the type of grief. Click on a book title to get a synopsis and order it online.

Chapter 8

The Loss of Friends

In Chapter 5 on grieving the loss of brothers and sisters, I explain that grief professionals generally consider sibling loss to be a kind of disenfranchised grief, meaning that society often overlooks the grief of surviving siblings and therefore undervalues or trivializes their losses. Well, if that's the case, the loss of friends produces the kind of grief that, up to now, society has never even bothered to recognize.

The death of a friend, however, is a profound, grievable loss. In the modern world, nuclear families tend either to be spread hither and yon or fragmented and dysfunctional beyond repair; as a result, friends often act as your surrogate family. Friends may accept, support, and love you in ways that your blood relatives don't. I guess that this is to be expected: After all, your friends are the people who *you* choose rather than ones who fate chooses for you.

This chapter begins with a look at friends and all the various functions they fulfill in your life. It then examines the impact of losing a good friend, first as a young person and then as an adult. I cover the particular difficulties of grieving the loss of a friend before concluding with a few resources available to help you heal this type of loss.

The Importance of Friends

Friends run the gamut from casual acquaintances with whom you get together occasionally to lifelong buddies for whom you'd literally give anything you had. When you describe a particular friend to other people, you invariably add some sort of adjective that encapsulates the nature of the relationship, such as "my new friend," "childhood friend," "good friend," "best friend," or "close friend," to name the most obvious.

Your friends, at least the ones you consider to be close friends, actually may furnish you the greater part of the emotional support and love that you'd otherwise expect to get from either your family or your spouse. In an age when adult family members often live in different cities, states, or countries and when people often are between spouses or not in any kind of committed romantic relationships, you probably rely upon your close friends to fill many of the significant support roles in your life.

Close friends not only provide you with much needed companionship but also support and challenge you. These friends are the ones you can count on to tell you their woes as well as listen to yours. They're also the folks you can be honest with when you believe they need to rethink a position or revisit a particular viewpoint, and you expect them to do the same for you.

Good friends also may understand you better than your own family does because they're the ones with whom you share many interests and experiences. They're also the ones in whom you can confide all your triumphs and joys along with your worries and aggravations.

In many ways, friends are an extension of family, creating your family of preference rather than a family of legal and genetic ties. Friends are often your first line of support in life and are sometimes even more dependable than your very own kin. In short, the importance of friends, especially given the hurried pace and the complex nature of modern life, can't be understated.

Exploring the Impact of Losing Friends

If close friends are such a vital part of your life, it stands to reason that the loss of such friends can bring every bit as much grief as the loss of a family member. The loss of close friends is definitely a profound loss that needs to be grieved like any other, regardless of how indifferent society is about this kind of loss (it's that old issue of disenfranchised grief again).

Just as with the loss of siblings or any other family member, the impact of the death of a friend depends to some extent upon the age at which you suffer the loss. Young people who suffer the loss of a close friend may have less chance of grieving if the loss isn't publicly mourned through the school or a local church. Older people who suffer the loss of a good friend may have less of an opportunity to grieve that loss if they're not also associated with members of the deceased friend's immediate family or part of a close-knit group of friends for whom the loss is mutual.

Experiencing the death of a friend as a youth

Thankfully, most people seldom experience the death of the friends they make as children (that is, the friends they grow up with). This doesn't mean that young people don't suffer the loss of friends, though. Unfortunately, far too many teenagers and college-age young people lose friends to illness, accidents (teenagers and cars are often a deadly combination), drug use, or violence (including war).

If you experience such a tragic death, you may be aided by some sort of public mourning that's organized through your school or a local church. Because it may be your first experience with profound loss and the grief that accompanies it, public mourning provides you a way to memorialize your friend as well as to express your deep feelings over the loss.

If you're the parent or a friend of a young person who has lost a close friend, be sure to reassure that person that his grief is natural and something that honors both the lost friend and the friendship that they shared. If the friend died as the result of suicide, be sure to discuss any feelings of guilt related to not having been able to recognize the signs and prevent the death. Also, encourage the young person to find ways to express his grief for the lost friend, maybe through attending the funeral or visiting the grave site, and memorializing his friend, such as by writing about the nature of the friendship or by putting together a memory book for his friend's family.

Experiencing the death of a friend as an adult

Very few people make it through their adult years without experiencing the loss of at least one good friend, if not more. The deaths of friends may be the result of all the awful and tragic things that take young people (refer to the preceding section), although illness tends to figure in the mix a bit more prominently with age (too often in the form of a heart attack, stroke, or that old killer, cancer). The death of a friend of the same or similar age as you may be particularly difficult because it can bring up fears and issues that you have about your own mortality.

In some cases, you may find yourself actively supporting your friend during his illness. You may even go so far as to become a part-time caregiver in lieu of family members who live too far away to be able to provide day-to-day care. In such a case, you may suffer anticipatory grief (see Chapter 2) in addition to the grief that you suffer over the loss of your friend.

If you weren't part of your friend's support system during his final days, or if the death occurred suddenly and unexpectedly, you have to deal with a certain amount of shock over the loss. If it has been some time since you visited or talked with your friend and he was the picture of health and vitality at that time, the shock of the loss and your feelings of regret that you never had the chance to say goodbye are probably your paramount emotions (see Chapter 14 for hints on how to deal with these emotions).

If you're close to any of the surviving members of your friend's immediate family or are part of a group of mutual friends, contact them immediately and offer any support that you can. In offering support to the fellow mourners of your close friend, you'll undoubtedly receive a great deal of emotional support and validation for your grief. Reaching out to others affected by the loss is an excellent way to avoid feeling disenfranchised when it comes to grieving the loss of your friend.

Dealing with the Difficulties of Grieving a Friend

The difficulties normally associated with grieving the loss of a close friend stem directly from society's belief that only the members of the immediate family (including spouses) constitute the rightful mourners and are therefore deserving of the condolences and support (slim though they may be) that society normally affords to those it considers bereaved.

Sometimes you're left out

As I explain in Chapter 5 on the loss of siblings, not all immediate family members feel equally included in the circle of rightful mourners. Siblings of the deceased often feel undervalued as legitimate grievers and overlooked when it comes to the condolences that other family members (parents of the deceased, the spouse, and surviving children) receive. (They point to the general lack of sympathy cards for surviving siblings in the Hallmark card line as just one very obvious symptom of this disenfranchisement.)

Well, when compared to surviving friends (for whom no Hallmark sympathy cards now exist or are likely to in the near future), siblings have it really good. After all, no one would ever think of not informing brothers or sisters of the death of their sibling or not inviting them to the funeral. (An exception would be the direst of circumstances in which an insurmountable rift exists between the surviving sibling and the other family members.)

Contrast this to the predicament of close friends who may not be informed of the death at all. If you don't find out about your friend's death when it happens or shortly thereafter, you lose the opportunity to attend the funeral.

If you don't find out about the death of a dear friend in time to attend the public mourning services such as his wake or funeral, you'll have to find a way to privately mourn his passing. One good way to do this is by organizing your own memorial celebration to honor and remember the life of your deceased friend. This celebration can include as many of his other friends whom you know and as many members of his family who wish to participate. In planning this memorial celebration, you have a great opportunity to review your friendship and all that it means to you. In inviting and involving the other participants, you have a great opportunity to find out more information about your friend's passing and to discover ways you can help support the others grieving this loss.

Participating in the family's mourning

If you're in close contact with the family of your deceased friend, you're likely to be invited to participate in the mourning. For example, the family may give close male friends the opportunity to be pallbearers at the funeral if the deceased didn't have brothers or male cousins who can perform this task.

In addition, the family may give you the opportunity to speak about your friend and the relationship you shared either at the funeral or at some type of memorial service held afterward.

Finding appropriate ways to support the immediate family of a dear friend during and after his funeral can really help you in your own grieving as well as eliminate the feelings of being left out. When you contact the family to offer your condolences, be sure to ask how you can be of help. Before the funeral, check to see whether you can help with any of the many details related to the funeral service or any gathering planned afterward. After the funeral, look for practical ways to help the family get on with their day-to-day activities; for example, it may be helpful if you perform simple household errands that need doing and send over a favorite prepared meal.

When you have to mourn on your own

If the family or the circumstances under which the funeral is conducted don't permit you to eulogize as a close friend of the deceased, you need to find your own way of telling the stories and remembering your lost loved one. One way to do this is for you to gather with other friends to hold your own memorial service during which everyone has a chance to speak about the deceased and their relationships with him. This memorial service can be conducted both in a spirit of lightheartedness and seriousness and can do a lot to help legitimize your grief and bring the surviving friends together. Check out Chapter 14 for more on how to express your grief over the loss.

One of the trickier challenges associated with grieving a friend's death is finding ways to mourn the loss that don't interfere with grieving or further the pain of your friend's family. Following are two possible scenarios:

- ✔ In cases where the family is dealing with the loss as best as can be expected and the death has brought the family members closer together, they may find some solace in the expressions of grief by their loved one's close friends.

- ✔ In the case where the family is having great trouble dealing with the loss and the death has opened up old wounds and reactivated deep-rooted feuds, the family may not welcome such expressions of grief, misinterpreting them as outsiders' attempts to upstage their rightful grief.

On the whole, bereaved friends still remain the proverbial fifth wheel when it comes to grieving the loss of a close friend. The best advice I can give you is to remain sensitive to the situation both in terms of your own pain and need to grieve and in terms of the way in which you remain at the mercy of the immediate family's wishes when it comes to being included in public mourning.

Resources for Healing the Loss of Friends

Print resources that focus on healing the loss of friends are downright paltry, and online resources on the topic are completely nonexistent (how's that for disenfranchised grief!). In a field of limited options, here are my recommendations:

- ✔ *Grieving the Death of a Friend* by Harold Ivan Smith (Augsburg Fortress Publishers): This book acknowledges the death of a friend as a significant loss and attempts to help you with the grief. Smith examines this unique type of grief as a progression that begins with the building of the friendship and ends with remembering the friend and friendship and reconciling the loss in your life. The text is full of quotations — some from the Bible and many from other authors who have written about grief — that enhance the author's description of the feelings you endure as you deal with the passing, burying, and mourning of a good friend. Two sections of this book are particularly noteworthy:

- Cherishing the Memory: This section is chockfull of suggestions on how to honor and memorialize your deceased friend.

- The Naming of the Names: This section contains the text of a ritual for remembering any loved one whom you've lost. This ritual is perfect for memorializing your deceased friend in lieu of or in addition to a traditional funeral or memorial service.

✔ *Friendgrief: An Absence Called Presence (Death, Value, and Meaning)* by Harold Ivan Smith (Baywood Publishing Company): This is Harold Ivan Smith's most complete book to date about grieving the loss of a friend. In it, he covers all aspects of grieving the death of friends, including lots of good advice on how to be supportive after the death as well as how to honor the friendship as you grieve the loss.

✔ *When Your Friend Dies* by Harold Ivan Smith (Augsburg Fortress Publishers): This is Smith's shortest and most recent book to date about grieving the loss of a friend. In it, Smith introduces his concept of friendship and "friendgrief" as he outlines the basic ways you can honor your friendship by grieving the loss.

✔ *When A Friend Dies: A Book for Teens About Grieving and Healing* by Marilyn E. Gootman and Pamela Espeland (Free Spirit Publishing): This compact book addresses the subject of grieving the loss of a friend directly to adolescents. The authors aim to help teens validate their typical responses to this type of loss, including guilt, anger, confusion, fear, and numbness. This revised edition also addresses the subject of losing a friend through violence. Each chapter addresses a particular question and includes practical advice interspersed with quotes from other bereaved teenagers as well as from famous writers and philosophers.

✔ *Healing a Friend's Grieving Heart* by Alan D. Wolfelt (Companion): This little gem of a book contains 100 suggestions of things that you can do to help a friend who's grieving the loss of a loved one. At the end of each suggestion page is a Carpe Diem section that contains a related idea of something else you can do. Although this book isn't specifically targeted to people grieving the loss of friends, I think many of the author's suggestions are quite apropos if you read them as things you can do for yourself to help in grieving the loss of your friend.

In lieu of Web sites devoted to the loss of a friend, you have to make do with Web sites for bereavement in general. See Chapter 22 for my top ten general grieving Web sites. Also, you may want to check out Alan Wolfert's Web site for his Center for Loss and Life Transition, www.centerforloss.com. This site offers information on other titles in the 100 Ideas book series and Dr. Wolfelt's workshops on grief as well as information on how to contact him for one-time or short-term counseling.

Chapter 9

The Loss of Pets

For some people, it's a real shock to discover that the loss of a pet brings on a grief every bit as deep and challenging as what they experience after losing a close family member or a very dear "human" friend. In fact, sometimes the grieving is even greater in the case of pets. But if you stop to consider that most people consider their pets to be members of their families and very dear friends, this fact doesn't seem nearly so surprising.

Pet loss is the only profound loss that doesn't deal with grieving the loss of another human being. This chapter begins by examining some of the unique characteristics of the relationships people build with pets. Then I turn to the impact of losing a pet, first as a child and then as an adult.

The chapter also takes up the difficult topic of euthanizing pets (usually called putting a pet down) and how this decision can add regrets that make grieving your loss more painful and difficult. You discover the problems that can arise when you openly grieve a pet but the people around you have little understanding of pet grief and even less sympathy for it. The chapter concludes with a listing of both print and online resources to turn to for help dealing with the loss of your pet.

Always There for You

It's very telling that if you have a pet these days, you're much more likely to be described as the pet's "parent" or "guardian" than its "owner." So too, even though you technically own the pet (at least in the eyes of the law), you're said to have adopted the pet, just as you would adopt a human baby. I think that this change in language mirrors a change in the type of relationship people have with their pets. In the main, dogs and cats are companions looked at as treasured members of the family. Fewer and fewer animals function solely as nonhuman helpers that work as some sort of guardian and attendant.

Regardless of whether your pet works for you in some capacity or you feel as though you work for it, there's no denying the depth of the bond that grows between you and your pet. Many describe this relationship as unique because the pet — be it a dog, cat, bird, reptile, snake, or other animal — gives its love to its human unconditionally and completely (something you don't find too often in relationships with fellow humans).

The way I describe the relationship between pet and human is that it feels like your pet is always there for you, giving you total devotion. And while cynics may counter that pets have to behave in this manner in order to survive (how else are they going to get you to feed them and take care of them?), I know that the kind of loyalty and love I get from a pet is quite unlike the love I experience from any other source. In turn, the kind of love and caring that I have for my pets is very different than what I have for other people to whom I'm close; somehow the love feels purer and less complicated even if it's not necessarily any deeper.

Exploring the Impact of Losing a Pet

Dealing with the death of a pet is almost always difficult and challenging — even if the death is anticipated and the pet has lived a long and happy life. Others may not understand the intensity of your grief (especially if they aren't "pet people"). Nevertheless, your grief is a testament to the strength of the bond you created with your animal and the breadth of the experiences and love you shared.

Given the fact that the life spans of pets usually are much shorter than those of humans, when you adopt a pet, you also sign on to be there at its death and undergo whatever grieving the loss brings. In addition, in the event of a serious injury or illness, you may be called upon to make a decision regarding euthanizing your beloved pet — a difficult decision regardless of the circumstances that you never have to ponder when dealing with a human family member who's dying unless you're put in the very difficult position of having to decide whether or not to shut off life support in accordance with a loved one's wishes.

Just how difficult and challenging your grief is over the loss of a pet is a function of a couple of factors:

- ✔ Your age at the time you adopted the pet and at the time you lost the pet, as well as the challenges you faced during the time you shared together

- ✔ The circumstances surrounding the pet's death: Was the death anticipated or sudden? Did it occur after a short or long life? Did you have to decide whether or not to euthanize the pet?

I begin this section by looking at how age can influence the intensity of your grief over the loss of a pet before exploring the issue of how having to make a decision either to prolong or terminate the pet's suffering can make grieving the loss more difficult.

Experiencing the death of a pet as a child

As I point out in Chapter 7, how well children comprehend the death of anything or anyone is a function of their maturity, which most often is a direct function of their age.

It's like losing a friend or even a sibling

For most children, the death of a beloved pet is the first profound loss that they experience in life. Of course, if your child is too young to understand the concept of death, he may simply think that his beloved cat or dog has gone away for a very long time. If he's old enough to understand death conceptually, the loss of his pet will be accompanied by feelings of confusion, anger, and hurt — the same feelings that he'd manifest at the death of any other family member.

Because children aren't normally the primary caretakers of family pets (even when the pets are nominally considered theirs), they're likely to feel the loss of a pet as one would feel the loss of a best friend rather than a family member. In the case of an only child who loses a beloved pet, especially a dog with whom he shared a lot of experiences, the death can feel more like losing a sibling (see Chapter 5) than simply losing his very best, and perhaps only, friend.

Helping your child grieve

As when your child is grieving the loss of a human family member or close friend, it's very important that you find ways to enable the child's expression of grief over the loss of a pet. One of the best ways is to enlist your child's help in creating rituals that commemorate the pet and the child's relationship with it. Ideas for rituals include

✔ Having your child officiate at the pet's funeral in which both of you bury the pet's body (if it's a small animal) in the backyard or spread the ashes if the pet was cremated. If the pet's remains aren't available for this ceremony, you can help the child honor the passing by planting a tree or flower in the garden and/or placing stones decorated with messages and, perhaps, a picture of the pet alone or with the child.

✔ Helping your child create artwork that remembers the pet and depicts its unique place in the child's life

When helping a child grieve the loss of his pet, especially when that pet was the first one of any real importance in his life, you need to be very mindful *not* to rush the grieving process. Following are a few don'ts to steer clear of:

✔ **Don't try to mitigate the loss by prematurely suggesting that you get a replacement for the pet.** This well-meaning gesture can send the message that the pet isn't worthy of grieving.

✔ **Don't tell the child that he shouldn't feel so bad about the loss of the pet.** Instead, reassure the child that his sad feelings are a natural way to honor the love he has for the pet and that they'll diminish in time.

✔ **Don't try to hide your sad feelings over the loss of the pet in an attempt to spare the child.** Masking your own emotions can send the message that crying, pouting, and being confused about the death are not okay.

Experiencing the death of a pet as an adult

It may surprise you to find out that, for an adult, the death of a beloved pet can be not only bewildering but also downright devastating. In fact, sometimes adults take the death of a longtime pet companion a lot harder than their children or than they would take the loss of some of their human family members.

The reasons a pet's death can be so overwhelming for you are often unambiguous. They can, however, include any and all of the following:

✔ You regarded the pet as a surrogate child, and the pet was your one true loyal companion that you could look to for unconditional love.

✔ The pet represented the only constant during a time of particular stress and change in your life.

The break in your routine of caring for your pet day in and day out and constant reminders of the loss can all too easily lead to depression (see Chapter 11 for details on this stage and Chapter 12 for ideas on what to do about it). Keep in mind that the best way to deal with a period of depression is to use it as time to actively grieve the loss. You can do this not only by expressing your emotions — sadness, anger, and fear for the future (see Chapter 14) — but also by reminiscing about the pet and reviewing what it meant to you and what you shared together (see Chapter 19).

Pets as eternal children

At one time or another, friends and family accuse almost all people who are really into their pets of treating them like children (and in some cases, of treating their pets better than their human children). This idea may seem over the top, but pets really are like small human children in their inability to fend for themselves and their need for guidance due to an inability to understand the consequences of their actions.

Pets differ from human children significantly in that they don't grow out of this type of dependence as they mature, and they mature and grow old and die much faster than their human guardians. As a result, even if you don't actually see your cat or dog as any kind of substitute child, when you lose a pet of many years, you suffer a loss somewhat similar to that of a parent losing a small human child. In losing the animal, you lose the benefit of being surrounded by this purity and innocence.

The losses of a pet and a human child are very different, however, in that the pet has lived its life to its full potential (assuming that it's lived a fairly normal span of years) and the young child has not. When a young child dies, the parents lose all the dreams they had for the child and are left to grieve not only the child's companionship but the child's unrealized life. When a pet dies, the pet parents likewise are left to grieve the pet's companionship, but they can take comfort from knowing that the pet lived a full and rewarding life (for which they were responsible in no small part).

Pets as constant companions in an ever-changing life

As a pet parent, even if you clearly regard your pets as pets and not as any kind of furry or feathered children, grieving the loss of a pet can still be difficult because of the type of constancy it represents in your life.

Because a pet is such a constant companion, its absence is immediately apparent in your life and keenly felt every day after its passing (from the time you get up until the time you go to bed and especially when you come home from work). This loss also makes itself known in the rupture of your daily routine as you find yourself no longer having to do regular tasks such as feeding your pet or, in the case of a dog, taking it out for an evening walk.

The great thing about pets is that they're always happy to see you and always want to spend time with you (something that's not always the case with your family and friends). Moreover, they want to cheer you when you're down and still love you just the same even when you're on less than your best behavior.

This kind of loyalty and constant love, which is so important in everyday situations, can assume tremendous importance in your life when you're undergoing any type of life change, especially the really stressful ones like moving, ending a love relationship, or changing careers. Your pet can come to represent an emotional constant that's very difficult to be without.

After you come through a major life change with your faithful pet by your side, you naturally may identify the pet's steadfast and unswerving love as a key element in helping you making it through. You even may feel as though you couldn't have gotten through the change without the emotional support afforded by your pet. If this is your experience, after your pet dies, you're flooded not only with the regrets associated with being separated from this loving support but also with a nagging doubt about how you'll get through future changes — especially grieving your pet — without your pet to support you.

When you feel lost in the storm of such emotions, remember all the loyalty and love your pet afforded you and try to derive whatever sustenance you can from the strength of the unconditional love and support. You may realize how well placed your pet's confidence was in you and use this realization to find the strength to carry on to another day.

Dealing with Regrets over End-of-Life Decisions

No regret can make your grief over your pet's death more difficult than that associated with euthanasia. The decision to have a veterinarian terminate the suffering of a beloved pet is one of the most difficult that anyone can face; it's such an onerous decision that it commonly haunts both pet parents who have refused it and pet parents who have authorized it, all for the best reasons.

Fortunately, when all medical options for treating an injury or illness are exhausted, you have the option to terminate your pet's suffering through euthanasia. Unfortunately, it's not always clear when all the medical options are exhausted, and euthanasia is one of those actions that can't be undone.

When confronted with the decision of whether or not to euthanize your pet, it's important that you're able to see it as a way to end your pet's suffering rather than an act of giving up on your pet. If you're not able to see it as a gift of supreme love that you're able to give your suffering pet — regardless of how difficult and painful it is for you — then chances are good that you'll end up seriously second-guessing your decision if you move forward with euthanasia.

If you're ever faced with having to make this very difficult end-of-life decision, before giving your approval, be sure to ask your veterinarian all the questions you have about the chances of your pet's survival and the quality of its life if your pet does survive. Also seek out the opinion of a specialist or other veterinarian to corroborate your doctor's prognosis. That way, at least you'll know that you've based your final decision on the best information that was available to you.

Many pet parents are bedeviled by regrets and guilt after euthanizing their pets. You may find yourself asking the following questions:

- ✔ Were there other medical options I didn't explore before opting for euthanasia?

- ✔ Did I give the okay to euthanize too soon, not trusting in my pet's ability to recover and thus ending its life too soon?

- ✔ Did I wait too long before giving the okay to euthanize, thus making my pet suffer needlessly?

- ✔ Did I give the okay to euthanize because I just couldn't afford any more expensive treatments?

- ✔ Did I delay giving the okay to euthanize for purely selfish reasons or was there really a chance to save the pet?

Like all the coulda, woulda, and shoulda notions that you can come up with while grieving the loss of a loved one, the ones in this list are predicated on many factors that are well beyond your or anybody else's knowing. And more importantly, they all serve only to obscure the loving and caring that motivated whatever decision you ultimately made at whatever time you made it.

Keep your focus on the fact that your pet is no longer suffering and is at peace. That way, you don't get lost in regret and can prepare to start the hard work of grieving the loss.

For more information on pet euthanasia and the death of a senior dog, check out *Senior Dogs For Dummies* by Susan McCullough (Wiley).

Grieving a Pet Loss in an Unsympathetic World

The world is somewhat short on tolerance when it comes to human grieving, so tolerance is in even shorter supply for those grieving their pets (at least among those who don't have pets as well as those who don't see pets as family members).

Overlook those who can't understand

Realize that people who haven't experienced a close relationship with a pet just can't begin to fathom your grief. All too often, they see caring for animals simply as self-indulgent sentimentality on the part of the pet owner. In fact, some of these people ridicule the bond between humans and their pets, considering it to be beneath the dignity of a human.

Don't expect to turn to people who don't comprehend the bond between humans and their pets for any kind of understanding and sympathy for the grief you're suffering.

When you meet up with someone who has no patience for grieving the death of pets, you're best off not challenging his position or trying to change his opinion. Obviously, he's missed out on a lot of love and genuine feeling if he never experienced a bond like you had with your pet and therefore doesn't have any idea of how much it hurts to lose it. In such a situation, concentrate on taking care of yourself and safeguarding your feelings rather than wasting energy confronting him on this issue and trying to change his mind.

Tell the story of your relationship

Although it's important for all people to tell the story of the relationship and love that exists between them and the lost loved one as part of their grieving process, this exercise is doubly important for people grieving the loss of a beloved pet. (The importance of sharing may be related to the problems of grieving the loss of a pet in a particularly unsympathetic world.) Describing the relationship with your pet along with its meaning and depth can be as healing as outwardly expressing your sorrow over the loss.

If you don't have friends and family who can empathize and are willing to listen to your story, and if you find that journaling and scrapbooking (see Chapter 14) aren't enough, you definitely should seek out a pet grief support group in your area. For ideas on how to find and get in touch with a grief support group or counselor, refer to the next section.

Resources for Healing Pet Loss

As I indicate earlier in this chapter, although you may encounter some folks who just don't understand your grief over the lost of a beloved pet, you're apt to find a whole bunch more who do, especially if you use the resources that I list in this section. These resources include some very excellent and easy-to-read books and Web sites frequented by caring people.

Books

Although they tend to be fairly short, books on pet grieving are filled with great information that's very much to the point. By and large, these books rely upon the stories and anecdotes of pet parents to illustrate their points about pet grief and recommendations of how best to process it. The following are my favorite books on pet grieving:

- ✔ *Grieving the Death of a Pet* by Betty J. Carmack (Augsburg Books): Betty Carmack's gem on pet grieving loosely follows the famous verse from Ecclesiastes 3:1–8 ("To everything there is a season . . .") to present the process of grieving a pet in five parts stretching from a time to love to a time to heal. In between, she tackles the subjects of getting ready to say goodbye, actually letting go, and then grieving the loss.

- ✔ *Saying Good-Bye to the Pet You Love: A Complete Resource to Help You Heal* by Lorri A. Greene and Jacquelyn Landis (New Harbinger Publications): This book on grieving the loss of a pet is wonderful because of the range of its contents. It contains great information about the bond between humans and their animals and insights on the grieving process, but it also has exercises that prompt you to reflect upon and write your feelings (something that many people find very healing).

✔ ***Goodbye, Friend: Healing Wisdom for Anyone Who Has Ever Lost a Pet*** by Gary Kowalski (New World Library): The Reverend Gary Kowalski very sensitively explores and validates the bond between humans and their animals. In addition to good information on pet grieving, Kowalski includes some very touching poems. Kowalski also has written a book on the spirituality of animals entitled *The Souls of Animals*.

✔ ***When Only the Love Remains: The Pain of Pet Loss*** by Emily Margaret Stuparyk (Hushion House Publishing): This book consists of a collection of inspiring poems about the pain of pet loss and the strength of the human-animal connection. Stuparyk wrote the book after the death of her beloved rabbit, Poochie.

✔ ***How to ROAR: Pet Loss Grief Recovery*** by Robin Jean Brown (Lulu Press Inc.): Robin Brown's book on pet loss and grief recovery is unique not only in its insights into the pet grieving process but also because of its workbook approach that encourages journaling as a way to work through the heartache and grief associated with losing a beloved pet.

✔ ***Absent Friend: Coping with the Loss of a Treasured Pet*** by Laura Lee and Martyn Lee (Ringpress Books): Coauthor Laura Lee has many years of experience in bereavement counseling, and her husband and co-author Martyn Lee is a veterinary surgeon. Together they created a great source book on the trauma of losing a beloved pet and grieving the loss. This book has a great chapter on the subject of euthanasia as well as one on the subject of finding an appropriate resting place for your pet's remains. It also examines the issue of whether surviving pets grieve the loss of one another in a household.

Online resources

The online resources on pet grieving that I list in this section are among the very best grief support sites you'll find anywhere on the Web. The first two sites contain important listings of pet grief support groups and counselors arranged by state; use them to find understanding people with whom you can share your loss. The last two sites in this list offer more-direct support: the first in the form of pet memorials and the second in the form of a wonderful audio book to which you can listen again and again.

✔ **Pet Loss Support Page** at `www.pet-loss.net`: This Web site contains a state-by-state guide to pet grief support groups and counselors, a list of books on pet grief, information on grieving the loss of a pet, and links to various memorial Web sites.

- **Association for Pet Loss and Bereavement** at www.aplb.org: This site is run by a Brooklyn-based nonprofit dedicated to helping people cope with the loss of their pets. It contains a chat room as well as links to approved pet grief counselors in a number of states.

- **The Nikki Hospice Foundation for Pets** at www.pethospice.org: This site, run by the Nikki Hospice Foundation for Pets (NHFP), is unique in its hospice support for people whose pets are facing the end of their lives. NHFP can help you locate a veterinarian in your area who is willing to give end-of-life care to terminally ill pets in the home and, many times, euthanize them there, if and when that difficult decision is made. In addition, this Web site offers resources and support for pet parents who've lost their loved ones.

- **Rainbows Bridge** at www.rainbowsbridge.com: At this virtual pet memorial, you can commemorate your pet for an annual fee (a portion of which is donated to various animal shelters across the United States) as well as have your pet remembered at a weekly candle-lighting ceremony.

- **Journey Through Pet Loss audiobook** at www.petlossaudio.com: This site contains information about and excerpts from Deborah Antinori's audiobook, *Journey Through Pet Loss*. This series of audiotapes addresses all aspects of pet loss and grieving. The information is a blend of therapeutic help and the author's own experiences with pet loss, and the overall tone is quite sensitive and soothing.

Part II
Experiencing Grief

The 5th Wave   By Rich Tennant

"After Harry was gone I started decorating the house as a distraction. It was around the time I was wallpapering the driveway that I thought I should seek grief counseling."

In this part . . .

Grieving frequently phases in and out of the various identified stages as it follows its own unique course and timetable. In this part, you find out how to support yourself when you're in the throes of grief as well as how to provide that support for someone you care very much about. You also get an opportunity to look at the common stages of grieving as defined and developed by a variety of experts in grief counseling and support.

Chapter 10

Doing Your Own Grief Crisis Management

*T*he period following news of the death of a loved one often is a time not just of shock but of personal crisis, when you feel that life has thrown you into the deep end of the pool without any sort of life preserver. It's also a time when you can feel most alone — even if you're surrounded by loving and supporting friends and family.

The focus for this period in grieving is purely your survival. Initially, this means finding ways to take care of yourself physically and emotionally as the loss becomes real and unavoidable. Ultimately, your survival means finding ways to begin the grieving process and start the long road to integrating the loss into the rest of your life.

Think of this chapter as your immediate survival guide for enduring the shock you get when you first find out about the death of a loved one as well as for riding the roller coaster of emotions that follow this terrible news. The ideas and suggestions that you find in this chapter are geared to these aspects of the initial stage of grieving.

Handling the News

The most common reaction to the news of the death of a loved one (even if the death has been anticipated for some time and you actually witness it) is disbelief! The inability to believe that someone you care so much about and who plays such a vital part in your life is now lost to you forever is somehow just too much to take in and initially accept as true.

This initial numbness and inability to accept the loss slowly wear off as your head's no longer able to deny the truth that your heart knows. This period of initial loss acceptance varies widely according to the person and the type of loss he's suffered. Sometimes, sudden losses take more time for certain people to acknowledge than the anticipated ones. And for other people, anticipated losses can take just as much time to feel real as ones that folks never saw coming.

Initially disbelieving the loss

Although no one actually knows why disbelief is such a common initial reaction to the death of a loved one, experts in death and dying as well as psychologists who specialize in this area are pretty much in agreement that it's a normal reaction (and perhaps even some sort of survival mechanism). They also agree that disbelief in no way signifies any sort of leave-taking from reality that you need to be concerned about.

Not surprisingly, while your head may be denying the reality of the death, your heart may be suddenly and immediately overwhelmed with emotion, struck with the enormity of the loss and in fear that the news is true. As a result, although you can find yourself completely distraught and expressing the most intense emotion at hearing of the death or even witnessing it, you still may be in a state of mental uncertainty.

Slowly accepting the loss as real

Note that the initial disconnect between the head's incredulity and the heart's sorrow can sometimes survive the loved one's funeral, even if the interment of the body is part of the ceremony. However, the disconnect usually starts to lessen for most folks in a fairly short time period (within weeks after the death, in most cases).

Slowly but surely, the hope that the loved one will suddenly show up on your doorstep fades as the reality of the loss becomes more and more real. As the death becomes more real for you, it's not uncommon for you to feel as though you've been in contact with the deceased. (This feeling is particularly common for surviving spouses.) This contact may come in the form of an intensely real nighttime dream in which you feel as though you're gently caressed or touched, or it may be in the form of some sort of daydream-type vision. No matter how or when it comes, this event often signals an acceptance of the reality of the death and, along with it, the onset of grieving over the loss.

Surviving the Grip of New Grief

When you first start grieving a profound loss, about the only thing you can focus on is the loss itself, and about the only thing you can do about it is just try to hang on and survive. Seeing as you've just received a major blow to your soul, you really need to concentrate your energy on taking care of yourself both physically and emotionally. (This advice goes double when you're responsible for taking care of others such as children — always remember the instruction from airline flight attendants to put your oxygen mask on first before you assist others in putting on theirs.)

While attempting to take care of yourself in this survival mode, you may have to deal with periods of extreme emotional turmoil as well as bouts of emotional deadness and depression. You may have trouble sleeping and eating along with concentrating and remembering things. (At times, you may feel like you've taken on some sort of senility as part of your grieving process.) Above all, you may feel as though you're surely going crazy. That's one of the most common worries voiced by those suffering acute grief as well as one of the most unfounded.

 It's at times like this that you need to take each day one at a time and break it down into smaller parts that you feel capable of dealing with at the time. Moments may be as brief as the next minute or even the next few seconds — that's fine provided that you can find the strength to get through those moments.

Dealing with overwhelming emotions

From the moment you get the sad news, you begin to suffer the emotions that come from that loss. This is the time when you're especially vulnerable to being overwhelmed by your emotions. These emotions can be contradictory depending upon the stage of grief you happen to phase into (see Chapter 11 for more on typical phases of grief and the emotions that normally accompany them). Your emotions are, however, almost always intense and often too powerful to resist.

Don't fight them

You feel the most out of control when you're newly bereaved. You may feel as though once you start expressing an emotion, you'll never stop (especially if you express your sadness through crying or your frustration through anger). This impression that you're about to lose all control and may not be able to regain it may make you fear the emotions and try to resist expressing them.

Many times, this resistance is as futile as the folks on *Star Trek: The Next Generation* trying to resist their half-machine collective enemy, the Borg. You need to understand that this fear that once you start expressing an extreme emotion you'll never be able to stop is unfounded. It's probably just an indicator of how intense the emotions are and how much you need to express them.

Get to a safe place

To deal with emotional onslaughts, it's critical that you be in a safe place at the time they come over you. For example, if you're driving down the highway and you feel a crying jag suddenly coming on, you need to pull over as the waterworks start. Likewise, if you feel a rage boiling up inside you, try to maintain your cool until you get yourself into a space where you can fume and rant without alarming others around you. (Even better, find a place where you can even tear up a few things or punch a few pillows without any possibility of injury either to yourself or anybody else.)

As for the concern that you'll never be able to stop crying, screaming, or giving flight to whatever emotions you need to get out, you needn't have any worries on this score. At some point in the emotional purge, probably right after exhaustion sets in, you'll run out of tears, cries, screams, wails, cusswords, and whatever else, and then just as suddenly as the onslaught began, it will end.

Get some rest

After an emotional onslaught ends, you'll probably be as limp as a washrag and feel pretty drained. This is a perfect time to take a break from grieving and set about restoring yourself both physically and emotionally. If you can manage it, take a short nap. At a very minimum, give yourself at least a few minutes (or better yet, 15 minutes) of quiet time before trying to undertake anything.

Depression and its relation to grieving

Depression is a term that has both a clinical and nonclinical usage in everyday language. Clinically, depression describes a psychological condition marked by a group of symptoms that include diminished motivation, interest, and energy levels, and dejected moods, all of which disrupt a person's ability to function normally. Nonclinically, depression generally refers to the emotional state in which you feel sad or low and often suffer a loss of motivation and physical energy.

As far as depression and grief go, most death professionals agree that the majority of bereaved people suffer symptoms of clinical and nonclinical depression without being officially depressed in the sense of requiring medical help (either in the form of psychological counseling or antidepressant medication). Fortunately, most bereaved people manifest the symptoms of depression only while they're actively grieving their losses, and their symptoms go away naturally afterward.

Dealing with your initial numbness

Not all newly bereaved people experience onslaughts of intense emotion that they just have to let out. And even those who do may find that there are times when they not only don't feel any strong emotions but also don't seem to feel anything. Emotional numbness can be the result of physical and mental exhaustion from the events surrounding the death and funeral just as well as the result of depression over the recent loss.

Regardless of their origin, periods of emotional numbness aren't a sign that you're going crazy. The only time you should be the least bit concerned about this lack of feeling is if it's the only state that ever manifests itself after your loss.

If you find yourself pretty much emotionally numb all the time and unable to feel *anything* for some time after your loss, don't ignore this condition indefinitely. It could be a sign that you're having real trouble grieving the loss and are in danger of shutting down the entire process. I urge you to seek out a grief counselor (see Chapter 14) to discuss your numbness in light of your loss and get ideas of what you can do to safeguard yourself while at the same time start grieving the loss.

Taking Good Care of Yourself

It almost goes without saying that the first thing you need to do at the outset of grieving the loss of a loved one is take care of yourself physically and emotionally. Although this advice may sound ridiculously self-evident, it's the one thing that a newly bereaved person can easily forget to do.

Forgetting to care for yourself is quite understandable given the stress caused by your loss (even if you anticipated it) and the fact that immediately afterward your attention is normally anywhere except on your needs. Add to this the fact that newly bereaved people frequently lose their appetite for food and have trouble sleeping soundly and through the night, and you have a perfect recipe for making yourself ill and making your grieving even harder than it has to be.

Eating right

To avoid getting ill while you're grieving and to maintain the strength you need to get through its ups and downs, you may need to consciously adopt an attitude that makes eating regularly a priority. You have to resist the urge to ignore food even if you don't have much of an appetite, aren't able to eat much at any sitting, and don't much enjoy the taste of the food.

Consciously watch the type of food you eat. You may find yourself reaching for comfort food with loads of sugar and carbohydrates. Sugar is just about the last thing you need during this time because it can depress your mood as well as interrupt your sleep. Regulate your sugar intake carefully, and make it a point to eat healthier.

Because you may lack the motivation to cook and prepare healthy meals during your grieving process, create a list of various delis and other restaurants that can supply you with food to go (assuming that you won't be in the mood to go out to eat very often). That way you can rely upon these resources for good and healthy takeout food during this time and thus avoid frequent stops at all those fast-food chains in your area.

Getting the sleep you need

Eating regular and healthy meals while you're actively grieving a loss is only one part of the battle for taking good care of your physical needs. In addition, you need to make sure that you get enough sleep, which is often more difficult than it sounds.

Nights are particularly hard for many newly bereaved people to get through. You may have a really tough time falling asleep because your mind's racing and you can't stop thinking about the loss you've just suffered and replaying different what-if scenarios by which it could have been avoided. And even if you do get to sleep without too much fuss, you may have trouble sleeping soundly through the night.

Short of seeing your physician and getting a prescription for sleeping pills or other types of sedatives, the most effective way to combat sleep disruptions is to engage in physical activity during the day so that your body is physically tired at night. Then, to stop your mind from racing and to resolve other problems you have falling asleep, try some meditation techniques that involve concentrating on your breathing (see the next section for more on mental alertness and focus).

To help you get the rest you need at night, it's often a very good idea to make sure that you get regular physical exercise during the day — and even increase your levels, if you're a regular exercise enthusiast. You'd be surprised at how much the need for physical rest can help calm the troubled mind even when dealing with such intense emotions. In Chapter 15, you can find information about using physical exercise to help you get through the grieving process.

Especially at the onset of the loss and during the first few weeks following, you may find that a prescription sleep aid or sedative is your only option for dealing with your stress-related sleep problems. When this is the case, be very careful not to abuse these pharmaceuticals; many of them are habit forming, and you may find yourself particularly vulnerable to dependence during this time of great emotional upheaval and sorrow (check out the section "Avoiding the tendency to drown your sorrows," later in this chapter).

Staying mentally alert and present

As if suffering loss of appetite and trouble sleeping weren't enough, many newly bereaved people also find that they have trouble concentrating and staying focused on whatever's before them. This is the case even when the folks had no such problems concentrating on things prior to the loss and were generally considered sharp as tacks.

Some of this lack of mental acuity may be related to your improper nutrition and sleep deprivation, but you may experience difficulty concentrating even if you're eating right and sleeping well. In fact, the problems with concentration that commonly strike newly bereaved people more likely relate to the person's overriding need to process the loss and make some kind of sense of it than to any other factor.

The good news is that this kind of difficulty concentrating and staying focused on a topic or task is a temporary condition for almost everyone. Usually, your ability to concentrate returns some time after you begin actively doing the grieving work.

Obviously, this reassurance is of little comfort when you have tasks you have to get done — related to your job or the estate of the deceased, for example — and you just can't focus. About the only thing you can do in this kind of situation is cut yourself some slack.

✔ Admit to yourself that, for right now, you're just not as sharp as usual.

✔ Let others know about your current (temporary) situation, and get them to help you complete the job at hand.

In the long run, the key to regaining your powers of concentration is to pay proper attention to the enormous distraction that's responsible for throwing them off so badly — namely, your grief over the recent loss of your loved one. You can facilitate this process by giving grieving your full attention whenever you can *after* you've taken proper care of your physical needs and fulfilled the unavoidable demands of your daily life. See the section "Giving Yourself Permission to Grieve," later in this chapter, for more on this subject.

Avoiding the tendency to drown your sorrows

The pain caused by the loss of a loved one can never be underestimated. As I mention earlier in this chapter, when first confronted by a profound loss, you basically go into shock, and as a result, you walk through your everyday activities in a kind of zombie mode.

During this period, you may find yourself trying to drown your sorrows (which are now extensive) with whatever "mother's little helpers" you normally turn to in order to take the edge off your anxiety. These helpers can be anything from junk food to shopping, although more times than not, they're alcohol and prescription drugs (often in the form of sleep aids and sedatives).

Be aware that acute grief makes you particularly susceptible to developing dependencies on all anxiety-reducing and pain-relieving substances and activities. This situation is somewhat analogous to the danger of dependency when you take strong pain relievers after a major operation or physical injury. However, you may be even more susceptible when grieving because this condition often brings up overpoweringly painful emotions that are harder to deal with and block than physical pain.

The bottom line is that, as part of taking good care of yourself during this time of acute anxiety, you have to balance your need for lessening the pain against your personal vulnerability to dependence on whatever actually lessens the pain. Some people have more-addictive personalities than others (and you probably already know your strengths and limitations in this arena), and these people have to be extracautious about using outside means to de-stress and lessen the pain. Because grieving is such a stressful process, it's also the time to err on the conservative side when it comes to masking or dulling the sorrow you're undergoing.

Don't mistakenly believe that you're going to find some great release from the pain of grieving through the use of drugs or alcohol. Instead, more often than not, these substances end up intensifying your sorrow instead of lessening it in any way. And even when you take these kinds of substances to excess and are able to block out all memory of the grief for a bit, the hurt only comes back worse afterward. This can easily lead to a cycle of addiction in which you have to keep medicating yourself more and more in a losing battle to block out the pain.

Taking on only one thing at a time

Strangely enough, the outset of grieving is a time when people are likely to take on too much despite the fact that it's also a time that they have the most trouble concentrating. This situation normally results from the demands placed on you to make funeral arrangements and deal with matters related to the death and estate (in which case, you want to delegate as much responsibility to trusted family and friends as you possibly can). But it also can result from the desire to stay busy so that you don't have to think about your present loss and suffer the pain it causes.

The problem with taking on too many things to avoid the pain (see Chapter 12 for more on this) is that it exacerbates your weakened condition. You're probably already at risk for getting sick from the general stress and fatigue brought on by loss. You're also too scattered to be at top efficiency in accomplishing the things on your to-do list.

Therefore, taking on just one task at a time is probably all you can manage safely. You may even find that it takes you longer and requires more energy than usual to accomplish just one task. This is perfectly natural considering the circumstances, and this is the time to be gentle with yourself and give yourself as much space as you need to deal with all the aspects of grief you're experiencing.

Giving Yourself Permission to Grieve

I believe that one of the most important things you can do for yourself at the outset of a profound loss is to give yourself permission to grieve the loss you've just suffered. At first, this whole idea may sound really strange. However, the reasoning here is twofold:

✔ You can't rely upon anyone else to give you all the time and space you need to grieve the loss and integrate it into your life.

✔ You're very well served by making an internal agreement with yourself by which you unequivocally acknowledge your need to honor your relationship with your loved one by grieving its loss fully and completely.

 Needless to say, you almost never have any clear idea of how much time and space you're going to need to grieve a particular loss. What you can count on, however, is that no matter how much time you eventually take, it will be more time than your friends and co-workers and even some of your family members think you should have spent and, frequently, more time than they can comfortably afford you.

In giving yourself permission to grieve your loss, you also

✔ Honor the relationship you had with your loved one

✔ Acknowledge that your feelings of sorrow over the loss are valid

✔ Recognize that the grieving of this loss is now of paramount importance in your life

 No matter how difficult and painful the process, by giving yourself permission to grieve, you actually begin the work of grieving, evaluating the importance of the person lost and the nature of the relationship you shared. In so doing, you also begin the process of finding out how the best qualities of both (the deceased and your relationship) can continue to live in you and influence the rest of your life.

I'm not suggesting that giving yourself the necessary latitude to grieve is always easy. You may come upon times when the sorrow is almost too much to bear and all you want to do is shut down all your feelings, but you also may feel quite a bit of pressure from the outside world to shut the grieving process down prematurely.

Staying in touch with your feelings for the duration

Staying in touch with your feelings all the while you grieve can prove more difficult than you expect. Because so many of the emotions associated with your loss are negative and overwhelming, you may find yourself doing everything in your power to shut them out. To protect yourself and facilitate this survival mechanism, you even may end up shutting down all your feelings, thereby running the risk of putting the kibosh on the entire grieving process.

Keep in mind that when you shut down emotionally and hold back the grieving process, you feel more wretched than if you were readily and openly expressing all your emotions. Feeling dead inside really isn't that much better than feeling all your sadness and anger.

In fact, because sadness and anger (and all the other emotions that may come up) are testaments to the bond you shared with your loved one, one could easily argue that the grief you suffer outwardly is not in vain: Even though you may consider the emotions negative, they serve the very positive purpose of helping you remember the loved one and value the relationship you had with each other. Remembering and valuing ultimately enables you to incorporate the best qualities into your life from both the person and your connection with him.

It's not possible to grieve a loss without feeling the grief that comes from it. And although grief work is by no means wholly emotional, a good share of it is, and if you shut down your feelings, you can't know when the bulk of the work is done and you've reached some sort of peace with the loss. Also, don't forget that you don't have to grieve 24/7 to get the job done. You will often need respite from the grief, whether you get it by taking a walk in the park, listening to some soothing music, or renting a dumb movie.

Taking time to grieve

In Chapter 1, I relate how modern society seems to be in such a rush to get everything over and done with that it has limited tolerance for grieving. Many people (and you may be one of them, especially if this is the first major loss you've suffered) think that grieving is (or should be) a very short and sweet process.

When your grieving doesn't prove so short-lived, you may end up feeling pressured by people around you to get the sorrow over with and move on well before you're ready. Even if this pressure isn't evident, you'll probably find that taking care of your economic needs and maintaining your other regular duties don't leave you all that much time and energy to devote to grieving.

The truth is that many people receive minimal leave from work after a death in the family and often find themselves busier than ever after the event (especially with estate-related matters with which they're usually totally unfamiliar). Although in an ideal world you would get all the time you need to work through your loss, the fact is that you'll probably have to strike a balance between the following:

✔ The time you must devote to all the practical obligations in your life

✔ The time you need to devote to grieving your loss (usually uninterrupted time when you can be completely alone)

Note that some folks benefit by getting back into the routine of work as soon as possible and others do not. If you're in the latter category and don't have any more bereavement leave, consider taking some extra days off before returning to work (assuming, of course, that you have some vacation or other leave that you can use or can afford the days off without pay).

If you're finding it difficult to get the time you need to grieve, you may have to set aside a particular hour in your daily schedule when you can count on uninterrupted time all to yourself. Although the idea of doing your grieving at a particular time of the day may strike you as really odd at first, you may find that this system not only allows you adequate time to express your emotions and concentrate solely on your loss but also enables you to function better in the world and perform the duties you can't escape.

Whatever you have to do to arrange your life so that you have ample time to grieve your loss, in the long run you'll probably find that this is time well spent. By taking time to grieve your loss when it's new, you may even speed up the process of integrating the loss into your life and thereby actually reduce the amount of anguish you have to endure.

Forgiving Yourself and Everyone Else

Seeing that a great many losses are accompanied by feelings of regret and sometimes downright guilt, forgiveness can play a big part in grieving. Forgiveness either jump-starts the grieving process when you're having trouble getting in touch with your sorrow or gets the process back on track if you've shut down your feelings (refer to the earlier section "Staying in touch with your feelings for the duration").

You may feel guilty about any number of things related to the loss of your loved one. Most often, guilt centers on things you either did to or didn't do for your loved one before he died as well as things that your loved one did to you or didn't do for you prior to his death. In short, the guilt stems from the things that you may consider to be weaknesses in the relationship, either on your part or the part of your loved one.

Forgiving yourself

Forgiveness when grieving can be tricky because often it involves forgiving yourself for not doing the things you imagine could have, would have, and should have prevented the loss of the loved one in the first place. It can even include having to forgive yourself for blaming your loved one for dying and leaving you with all this grief to deal with.

Because many people have more trouble forgiving themselves than they do other people, giving up all the regrets that you envision would have changed fate can be particularly hard to do. For some, giving up on ruminating over the things they feel responsible for and believe they could have changed is tantamount to making the loss real in their lives, something they're not yet prepared to do.

Forgiving others

Needless to say, some situations require forgiveness not for yourself but for others whom you hold responsible in the loss. The other may not be another person but rather God, the cosmos, or whatever you feel is ultimately responsible for the way things turned out.

This particular kind of forgiveness is tricky because it requires you to modify not just your relationship to another person but your entire relationship with the cosmos and your understanding of its justice, something that's hard enough to accomplish under ordinary circumstances and nearly impossible under the weight of a profound personal loss.

Trying to forgive God for a world in which you have to endure the pain of losing a loved one — especially under particularly traumatic circumstances — is often work best left until near the end of your grieving process. Waiting gives you a chance to really accept the loss as well as affords you the opportunity to express and work through the major part of your disappointment in the workings of the world and its creator. Moreover, as you come to the end of the grieving process, you usually feel a renewed connection to the lost loved one, which may mitigate your need to forgive the Almighty.

Seeing forgiveness as a release, not a pardon

When most people think of forgiveness, they naturally think of it in the sense of pardoning a guilty party for his offenses, as when you forgive a person who wrongs you. Such forgiveness is great when you can manage it because it can enable you to repair the friendship or relationship and move on.

When forgiveness is related to the death of a loved one, however, I think it makes more sense to think of it in the sense of a *release* than of a pardon. By releasing the regrets you have in relation to the loss, you free yourself up to grieve the loss without the burden of whether or not you're also ready to pardon the responsible parties.

At whatever point you're able to free yourself from the regrets surrounding the loss, you immediately assume a new phase in grieving that loss. As your concentration moves away from culpability for the loss, it moves toward appreciation of the person you've lost and the relationship you shared. And it's here that you do the work of incorporating the loss into your life.

Knowing When You Need to Share and When You Need to Be Alone

Although grieving is obviously something that you can only do for yourself, you don't have to go through the process all alone. In fact, you shouldn't even attempt to do so. It's quite common for newly bereaved people to vacillate between wanting to be left alone in their grief and wanting someone there with whom they can share their sorrow.

Although only you can be the judge of when you really need time to yourself and when you need to share your feelings with someone, be aware that opening up to others can be one of the most beneficial and therapeutic ways of working through your grief (see Chapter 14 for more on how this can work).

Companionship versus solitude: Either is okay

Some folks in the first stages of grieving really need constant companionship and actually are hesitant to be alone in their grief. (This is often the case with people who've just lost a life partner.)

Others shun interaction with others and crave time and space all to themselves in order to sort things out. (This is often the case with parents who've just lost children.)

It really doesn't matter where you fall along this spectrum. The important thing is that you recognize when you can benefit from sharing with others and when you can't. And when you feel like you need to share, it's also important that you have access to people who can support you in your grief and don't mind listening to your feelings.

Reach out when you're ready

Right after experiencing a profound loss, it's quite natural to feel more alone than ever before (see Chapter 14). These feelings of being isolated and alone can add to the burden of trying to handle the overwhelming emotions that come with the loss. During this grieving period, you need to find the courage to reach out to people who can support you, sometimes by listening to you or just by being there with you.

If you don't have friends and family members who can be there for you when you need to share feelings, consider turning to grief support counselors in your area. Although you may find the prospect of reaching out to total strangers intimidating at first, it's well worth the risk. Keep in mind that these people not only are trained to support those in acute grief but also really want to help the bereaved in any way they can. Turn to Chapter 14 for hints on locating and contacting grief counselors in your local area.

If you're the kind of person who doesn't readily share your feelings with others, you may find yourself naturally holding back from reaching out to others during your initial stages of grieving. The danger here is that you run the risk of making your grieving process a great deal more complex and difficult than it has to be. If you're having trouble getting beyond your feelings of anger and regret regarding the loss or expressing your feelings of appreciation for the one you've lost and the relationship you shared, it may be a sign that you're in trouble and that the tactic of keeping your feelings to yourself is not working for you. In such a case, you need to push yourself to seek out others who can support you and listen to your feelings.

Chapter 11

Working through the Process of Grief

Sometimes people liken grief to a physical injury that must heal, which means that the process of grieving compares to the healing process that takes place over time as an injury mends. Some people, however, aren't particularly satisfied with that analogy and believe that it demeans grief. Moreover, they don't feel that the grieving process can be equated with healing because a grieving person isn't unwell; rather, he's sad, and therefore his grief isn't in need of any type of a cure.

To help their patients understand and work through their grief, many noted grief professionals have developed useful models with milestones or tasks that they feel are normally part of this "healing" process. In this chapter, I present three of these grief models in most basic outline form. I present their information with an eye toward ways you may use their particular stages, tasks, and phases as a kind of map to help you navigate your way through your own personal grieving process. Then I use their particular steps as stepping-off points to give you my own suggestions on ways that they may guide you more effectively.

Just don't forget that the models I discuss in this chapter, with their various stages of loss and tasks and phases of grieving, do *not* describe sequential steps in a series that you will or must follow to get through grieving. They're merely signposts of phases that you may or may not encounter in your personal grieving process (or may even encounter more than once). Moreover, although I present these stages and tasks consecutively, you may not encounter or have to face them in the same order. There's absolutely nothing wrong with you or your grieving if you don't do them in the prescribed order or don't do each one.

The Five Stages of Loss

Dr. Elisabeth Kübler-Ross was a true pioneer in the field of death and dying. In her seminal work, *On Death and Dying* (Scribner), published in 1969, Dr. Kübler-Ross outlined what she typically witnessed in her clinical practice as the five stages of dying. In her final work, *On Grief and Grieving* (Scribner), published after her death in 2004, Dr. Kübler-Ross and her coauthor, David Kessler, adapted these five, now classic, stages of dying to grieving.

The classic Five Stages of Dying and Loss as outlined by Dr. Kübler-Ross are:

1. **Denial:** In dying, denial refers to a basic inability to deal with the reality of the impending death. In grieving, denial refers to an inability to believe that the death of a loved one has really happened.

2. **Anger:** In dying, this anger is all about the impending death. In grieving, this anger refers exclusively to loss of a love one. In both cases, this anger can be directed either inwardly at oneself or outwardly toward others.

3. **Bargaining:** In dying, bargaining refers to making deals (usually with God or the universe) that will spare a loved one his impending demise. In grieving, bargaining refers instead to feelings of regret expressed by "what if" and "if only" scenarios in which the death of a loved one could have been prevented.

4. **Depression:** In dying and grieving, depression refers to being overwhelmed by the reality of the situation as well as the resulting withdrawal and shutting down (this can be on both a physical and psychological level).

5. **Acceptance:** In dying, acceptance refers to acknowledging the reality of the impending death. In grieving, acceptance refers to acknowledging the loss and its repercussions in one's life. Note that in neither situation does acceptance necessarily mean that one is okay with this reality.

Given the widespread familiarity that health professionals and laymen alike have with these five stages as they concern the process of dying, I think it's useful to compare Kübler-Ross's Five Stages of Dying to her Five Stages of Loss. Therefore, the following five sections describe the meaning of each of these stages, first as it traditionally applies to a person who's facing death and then as it applies to a person who's grieving the loss of a loved one.

Dr. Elisabeth Kübler-Ross

Elisabeth Kübler-Ross (1926–2004) was a world-renowned medical doctor and psychiatrist who revolutionized modern thinking about death and dying. While in practice in New York and Denver, she was shocked by the way dying patients were shunned by medical professionals, especially doctors. In response, she began a series of lectures to medical staff in which she talked openly about dying.

In 1969, she published her first book, *On Death and Dying,* which was a bestseller and seminal work that remains required reading in most medical and psychology curriculums. Her legacy includes working directly with terminally ill children, AIDS patients, and the elderly, as well as helping to bring the hospice movement (which originated in England) into the mainstream in the United States. She and her work have also educated countless health professionals on the vital importance of dealing with the dying honestly and compassionately.

For more on Dr. Kübler-Ross, her work with end-of-life issues, and her classic stages of dying and grieving, visit her official Web site at www.elisabethkublerross.com.

Standing deep in denial

The first of the Five Stages of Dying and Loss is denial. A person in denial doesn't accept the reality of something unpleasant. That something unpleasant (the 2-ton elephant in the room, so to speak) is none other than death.

More specifically, in the case of the Five Stages of Dying, denial is an inability to admit that you're dying or that someone you really love is dying. In the case of the Five Stages of Loss, denial is an inability to admit that a person you love who has died is really gone.

Denial of death by the terminally ill

For someone who's been given a fatal medical diagnosis and whose death is therefore imminent (as opposed to the rest of us who naively think that we'll be here forever), denial refers to the state of utter disbelief with which the patient receives this type of diagnosis.

The rationalizations that can accompany this type of denial can run the gamut from "It's gotta be a mistake — you're looking at somebody else's X-ray" to "There's got to be a cure, a new drug, or operation that can beat this thing." So strong is a person's core belief in immortality (to say nothing of the human fear of death) that it's a rare individual who can stoically take the news that his life *really* is about to end. For most, the idea that they're going to die is simultaneously theoretically assented to and fundamentally denied.

I suspect that it's precisely this kind of denial that's responsible for so many terminal patients seeking out new experimental therapies and undergoing extra rounds of radiation and chemotherapy when they may benefit more from purely *palliative care* (care that has to do with pain management and comfort rather than with curing) and the support of hospice. However, folks who are placed on hospice care don't always deal with the stage of denial any better. I can't tell you how many people I've visited as a hospice patient-care volunteer (none of whom suffered from dementia) who continued to ask me visit after visit, "Why am I on hospice?" Ultimately, it's just not that easy for anyone to accept that his time is finally at an end.

The stage of denial isn't limited to the patient who's actively dying; sometimes the patient's family is in much more denial about the impending death than the patient is. The family's denial can become a huge problem when it means that the patient doesn't fully come to terms with his own death. To accommodate his family's state of denial, the patient may not speak with his family members about issues of real concern related to his dying in order to protect their feelings by keeping up the façade that everything will be okay.

Denial that a deceased loved one is really gone

For grieving people, denial refers to the air of unreality that accompanies the knowledge that someone they love has died.

This kind of disbelief is almost never an actual denial that your loved one is really deceased but rather an inability to take in the full reality of his death. Rather than being some sort of delusion on your part, this type of denial is more like a defense mechanism that protects your psyche from the full trauma of the death.

The inability to fully grasp the idea that your loved one is truly gone appears even when the death is fully anticipated, as it is in the case of a death from a long-standing serious illness or from old age. Denial is also equally prevalent whether you actually observe the person's death or you only hear the sad news from a trusted medical professional or family member.

Most often, a grieving person's denial of a loved one's death takes the form of intermittent forgetfulness that the person is deceased, thus allowing you to slip up and anticipate again being in his presence. This is most likely to happen to you when you first wake in the morning and return home from a day at work only to find your expectation dashed. As time goes on, however, this little charade becomes more and more difficult to keep up as it becomes more and more disappointing and hurtful. Slowly but surely, the sad and bitter truth that your loved one will never return comes home to roost, and this denial stage of loss loses its energy and finally plays itself out.

This type of denial is unrelenting in cases where a loved one goes missing and there's no independent confirmation of his death. The hope springs eternal that a loved one who's missing in action, has run away, or has been abducted is still alive somewhere and will return some day. For many caught in this terrible situation, accepting an unconfirmed death of a loved one is tantamount to dishonoring that person by giving up hope. The people left behind can't allow themselves to move out of this stage and complete their grieving; they need professional help to develop ways to deal with the conflict between the need to continue to honor the missing loved one and yet grieve the loss.

Cooling the secondary stage of anger

Anger is a fairly multifaceted emotion. When you characterize someone as being angry, you may mean that he's simply annoyed and frustrated with the situation, or you may mean that he's completely riled up and therefore furious over it. The emotional intensity of anger runs the gamut from a mild irritation to a full-blown rage.

Anger in the sense of annoyance is connected with frustration. Anger in the sense of rage is almost always connected to fear. People can become easily angered in both senses of the word anytime they fear that they're no longer in control of their own futures. The timing and even the circumstances under which you die are so seldom in your control that some degree of anger over your own death or the death of a loved one seems almost inevitable.

Although anger is the second of Kübler-Ross's Five Stages of Dying and Loss, this doesn't mean that people always enter this stage after the initial stage of denial. In fact, it's quite possible for dying and grieving people to skip the denial stuff entirely and go directly to rage. (This is especially true when the circumstances of the death are deemed to be particularly unfair.)

Anger at dying

Because dying normally brings up feelings of both frustration and fear, one can reasonably expect people facing imminent death to feel angry about the situation at one time or another.

- ✔ Anger at dying may stem from exasperation with the patent unfairness of the situation, such as when the death is very untimely (as in the case of a dying mother with young children) or completely unwarranted (as in the case of a young man dying from a misdiagnosed illness).

- ✔ Anger at dying may stem simply from the fear that one feels at the prospect of soon losing all control over one's future and then having to face the unknown of death.

When dealing with a dying loved one who's particularly angry at the situa-tion, you need to be very patient and allow him to vent as much as possible in the hope that he can get beyond the anger before he dies. Be very careful *not* to engage in any arguments regarding the validity of his anger. The point here isn't whether the anger is justified but that your loved one gets out all these feelings before he dies.

Anger over the loss of a loved one

Often people who've just lost a loved one have to deal with their anger over the death as their initial task in grieving the loss. They may direct their anger at themselves or at others.

When your anger is directed at yourself, it's usually the result of some sort of guilt or regret that you have regarding the loss. The guilt may stem from something you did or didn't do that, in your mind, would have or might have prevented the loss from happening. (It's what I call the "coulda, shoulda, woulda" syndrome.)

No matter how strongly you feel that you may have been able to prevent the loss, you did the best you could at the time. Further, you need to appreciate these feelings as part and parcel of the entire remorse and sadness you have over the loss. Further, you need to understand that, guilt or no guilt, your remorse and sadness are necessary parts of grieving a loved one.

When your anger's focused on someone or some force outside yourself, it usually lands in one of two places:

✔ The social, medical, or even cosmic powers you hold responsible either for doing something that caused the death or for not doing something that could have prevented it

✔ The deceased loved one

When your anger's focused on other authorities whom you hold responsible for the death, you have to be particularly careful not to get caught up in an almost endless game of justification. In this game, all your energy goes toward recounting and elaborating on the injustice of the death, leaving you little or no energy for any other grieving work. To stop this process of recrim-ination and jump-start the rest of the grieving process, you may have to for-give the parties you hold responsible so that you can move on into other phases of grief (see Chapter 10 for more on practicing forgiveness).

It may surprise you to know that many bereaved people direct their anger at the loved ones they lost rather than at themselves or any other powers. The irrationality of such anger, to say the least, doesn't prevent the bereaved from feeling it. For example, when you consider the death to have been pre-ventable (as in the case of an accident caused by the deceased's own reck-lessness, suicide, or an avoidable illness or physical condition), you become angry because your loved one didn't exercise more caution, reach out and get the necessary help, or take better care of himself.

You can become angry at a loved one for leaving you even if you consider the death to have been completely unpreventable. Particularly if you lose your loved one as a result of an accident or illness before his time (as opposed to an accident or illness in old age), the anger you feel toward him simply may be misdirected. Instead of focusing your anger on outside authorities such as the doctors or God, you focus your anger on the loved one who has left you bereft.

Dealing with the stage of bargaining

Bargaining is the third stage in the Five Stages of Dying and Loss outlined by Kübler-Ross. Bargaining has a couple of interpretations, the most common of which is to haggle with someone to get them to meet your price (as in getting a bargain by bringing the price down). The second common meaning for bar-gaining is to get someone to agree to your terms for a purchase or contract (as in striking a bargain by coming to terms).

People who are actively dying engage in both types of bargaining: striking the best possible terms for dying as well as trying to strike a bargain that enables them to avoid death entirely. The bargaining, however, that bereaved people do is almost entirely of the latter type; they strike a bargain under which they're able to come to terms with the loss.

My anger over the loss of a loved one

In April 1998, I lost my life partner of 16 years from complications from hepatitis C contracted as a result of a blood transfusion given in an emergency surgery some 20 years before. At the time of his death, my partner was ninth on a waiting list for a liver transplant that could have saved his life.

In grieving this loss, I initially felt anger at the medical system for its inability to provide a liver replacement as well as at myself for not being more effective in navigating and working the system and getting my partner the necessary replacement. Near the end of my grieving process, however, I got angry at my partner simply for leaving me and putting me through so much grief and sadness. Oddly enough, in my case, this misplaced and totally irrational anger marked the final phases of my grieving this loss.

Bargaining the terms of one's death

By and large, dying folks who enter the stage of bargaining are those with fatal illnesses for which medicine can provide no cures. They believe in God or, at the very minimum, have some sort of belief in a higher power with whom they can strike deals.

People with curable illnesses normally spend their remaining time trying to obtain the cures and therefore don't enter the bargaining stage. And those who don't have a strong a sense of a higher power with whom they can negotiate have no need to enter the bargaining stage either.

The actual terms of the bargains that a dying person wants to make with a divine power depend on his particular condition. He may want to strike a deal under which he will mend his previous ways (in regard to either his health or morals) if only God (or the higher power) spares his life by curing him. In essence, he's asking for a pardon from the divine for behaviors that he believes have resulted in his illness.

In contrast, a dying person may bargain with God for less than a full reprieve, asking only that he be allowed the additional time needed to accomplish something that he feels he must do before he dies (such as see his children graduate or marry or visit his birthplace one last time). Many times, the only thing the dying person has to offer God in return is a promise that, if he gets the time he needs, he'll ask for nothing further. Of course, assuming he does get extra time, he probably can't resist asking the divine for just a little more.

The deals that people strike in the bargaining stage often have a similar structure and content to the regrets that their loved ones express in grieving their losses (see the next section). When you're dying, the bargaining is a way for you to express the misgivings you have about the quality of the life you've lived and the unknown nature of death; it's also a way to feel like you're avoiding your fate. When you're grieving, the regrets you mull over are very often a way for you to come to terms with the impact of the loss and a precursor to integrating it into your life.

Bargaining as part of coming to terms with the loss

For the person grieving the loss of a loved one, the idea of bargaining with a higher power for a different outcome doesn't apply. Seeing that the loss is already a fact (and assuming that the person's not in the stage of denying it), the bargaining that a grieving person does is quite different from that of a dying person.

Bargaining in this case refers to all the "what if" and "if only" type of regrets that so often plague your grieving. They represent all the "coulda, woulda, shoulda" doubts that so easily can overwhelm you and over which you probably agonize; they're the doubts about what you or anyone else could or should have done that would have prevented the death of your loved one and, more to the point, *spared* you all this grief.

I'm convinced that this type of bargaining can be very useful in grieving, if only as part of the process of really coming to terms with the loss. By evaluating (and yes, even agonizing over) all the conditions that you think may have resulted in a different, much-desired outcome, you eventually may come to realize that none of this very painful and distressing bargaining work changes the reality of your loss. You then can move on from "what if?" to "what now?"

In this way, the bargaining stage can be a very important part of your grieving work. Being able to come to terms with the loss is an important step (and a necessary precursor, for some) in really accepting the reality of the loss. And by accepting the loss, you give yourself the opportunity to move on to the final work of reconciling yourself to this acknowledged reality.

Coping with the stage of depression

Depression is the fourth stage in the Kübler-Ross Five Stages of Dying and Loss. In the context of these stages, depression refers to the symptoms commonly seen as part of clinical depression — diminished motivation, interest, and energy along with dejected moods — that result directly from facing death or dealing with a loss of a loved one.

Both of the stages of depression in Kübler-Ross's processes of dying and grieving are differentiated from clinical depression (as a psychological ailment) in that they're considered to be natural within the dying or grieving processes. Depression related to death and grief normally dissipates on its own without requiring the intervention of professional psychological counseling or antidepressant drugs.

Depression during the dying process

In the case of a person who's dying from a fatal disease and suffering depression, the symptoms of depression often are intertwined with the general physical discomfort and disability of the illness. In such a case, the depression symptoms also may be directly related to the medications that he's taking to fight the disease or to alleviate the resulting pain.

Bouts of depression are to be expected in any person facing death. After all, he's dealing with the idea of losing all control over his future and having to say goodbye to all he loves.

Interestingly enough, in many people facing death, depression seems to come and go in real bouts (like anger) instead of forming the general emotional background against which the death plays out.

Depression during the grieving process

Depression is a very common stage of grief. For some bereaved people, periods of depression marked by a general flatness of emotion and lack of motivation tend to follow periods of extreme sadness and emotional outbursts.

For others, depression is the general emotional background against which all the other stages and manifestations of grieving take place. For these folks, coming out of this general depression is often the harbinger of the end of active grieving and the onset of the stage of acceptance (which I discuss in the next section).

One of the suggestions that Dr. Kübler-Ross makes for bereaved people suffering depression in her book *On Grief and Grieving* is to welcome rather than fight the depression. How do you do that? By allowing the sadness and emptiness of the depression to cleanse you and by exploring your loss in its entirety. You shouldn't be overly concerned with the nature of your depression — whether it comes and goes in bouts or seems to form your general emotional background. Instead, keep in mind that this depression is not only a necessary part of grieving but also will most likely leave of its own accord after it has done its job.

Reaching the stage of acceptance

Kübler-Ross names acceptance as the final stage of her Five Stages of Dying and Loss. The only problem with calling this final stage "acceptance" is that the word sometimes gives the faulty impression that in order to reach this stage, you need to be 100 percent okay either with your imminent death or with the profound loss you've suffered. That simply isn't the case: You can tolerate your impending death or the loss you've suffered without ever feeling completely all right with it.

Indeed, reaching the final stage of acceptance simply signifies that you've learned to live with the new reality that life has forced on you, and you're ready to move on in light of the change. Therefore, the real power of this stage lies in the way it can enable you to acknowledge your fate while no longer being limited and entirely defined by it.

Accepting your own death

Accepting your own impending death is one of the most difficult things to do. In fact, it's so difficult that many people never make it to this state of acceptance until just before they die.

One way to look at acceptance is as a kind of state of grace in which the person facing death is released from the turmoil of anger and denial as well as the weightier emotions that accompany depression. For many people, the acceptance of death is as fleeting as the anger and sadness they feel from time to time about the situation. A special few, however, reach the stage of acceptance and never leave it; these fortunate people are able to tolerate their deaths and, in so doing, transcend them.

How long the stage of acceptance lasts depends a great deal on a person's character *and* the circumstances under which he's dying. It's an old adage among death professionals that "a person dies the way he lives." Someone who lived his life fairly conservatively, not welcoming many changes, is apt to find death very hard to welcome. In contrast, someone who continually took risks and always seemed to relish a new challenge is more likely to accept the reality of death. As for the circumstances of death, an elderly man who has lived a relatively full life and is leaving behind scores of children and grandchildren will probably find death much easier to welcome than a relatively young man who's just getting started in life and is leaving behind very young children.

Accepting the death of a loved one

Whereas reaching the stage where you accept your own death is not at all necessary in the dying process (you can die quite successfully protesting and even denying the whole thing up to your very last breath), this isn't the case when it comes to grieving.

In order to complete the grieving process, you must accept the death of your loved one. If you can't accept the death — at least in the sense of learning to live with it — you can't begin to integrate the death into your life and move on (creating what many grief counselors call a *new normal*).

As far as I'm concerned, the Kübler-Ross stage of acceptance is the most essential stage in the grieving process. If you remain unable to accept the loss, by definition, you remain unable to grieve the loss. Another way of looking at this is to consider the first four of the Five Stages of Loss as the normal phases that you pass through for the sole purpose of reaching the stage of accepting the loss of a loved one. In this way, denial, anger, bargaining, and depression are simply means to the end of attaining this acceptance.

Most people can't get to this place where they can abide the loss of a loved one until after they've experienced all the denial, anger, bargaining, and depression that the grief brings. The other four stages are the tools needed in order to learn how to tolerate and find yourself a place in the alien world into which the loss has thrust you.

The Four Tasks of Mourning

The Five Stages of Grieving that Dr. Kübler-Ross derives from her Five Stages of Dying is the standard way to evaluate the grieving process and one's progress with it. However, it isn't the only system available for this purpose. In place of stages of grieving, Dr. J. William Worden, a clinical psychologist with a specialty in terminal illness and bereavement, developed the Four Tasks of Mourning as a way to describe the grieving process and assess one's place in it.

The Four Tasks of Mourning as Dr. Worden currently outlines them are:

1. **Accept the reality of the loss.**
2. **Work through the pain of grief.**
3. **Adjust to a changed environment.**
4. **Emotionally relocate the deceased and move on with life.**

As you can see from this list, the Four Tasks of Mourning are much more proactive than Kübler-Ross's Five Stages of Grieving. In very general ways, the tasks outline the steps that, according to Dr. Worden, most bereaved people must undertake in order to deal effectively with the profound loss of a loved one. Again, remember that you may not accomplish these tasks in the order in which they are presented here — grieving just isn't that linear of a process for most folks.

Accepting the reality of the loss

In Worden's Four Tasks of Mourning, the first task that a bereaved person must take on is accepting the reality of the loss. This first task seems to be the equivalent of Dr. Kübler-Ross's fifth and final grieving stage (acceptance). So, at first glance, it would appear as though Worden begins right where Kübler-Ross leaves off.

Dr. J. William Worden

Dr. J. William Worden's research and clinical work over 30 years has centered on issues of life-threatening illness and life-threatening behavior. He has lectured and written on topics related to terminal illness, cancer care, and bereavement. His book *Grief Counseling & Grief Therapy: A Handbook for the Mental Health Practitioner* has been translated into seven languages and is used around the world as the standard reference on the subject.

For more on J. William Worden, his clinical work with end-of-life issues, and his publications, visit www.rosemead.edu/faculty_research/faculty_profiles.cfm and click the link Worden, William J. to open the page with his profile information.

Actually, the work that you do in accepting the loss in Worden's account of the grieving process is much more comparable to the work that you must do in Kübler-Ross's initial stage of denial.

According to Worden, all profound losses are surrounded by a certain atmosphere of unreality, a sense that the loved one isn't really gone. As a result, the initial task of grieving is to accept the death on both an intellectual and emotional level so that you fully acknowledge that your loved one is never coming back to you.

All the traditional mourning rituals, including such things as the public wake, funeral, and any type of memorial ceremonies, help you begin the process of accepting your loved one's death as real. Also, taking every opportunity to tell your story over and over again can help in this task, and there are no forums better suited for doing this than grief counseling and grief support groups (see Chapter 14 for more).

Working through the pain of the loss

Worden's second task of mourning is to work through the pain of the loss, which he specifically characterizes as the "pain of separation." By and large, this task requires you to feel all the emotions attached to the pain of your grief as well as find adequate and appropriate ways to express them.

It's one thing to feel tremendously angry at the death of a loved one but quite another to find the right time and place in which to vent your rage and frustration. For example, it's quite appropriate and beneficial to express your fury by beating a pillow in your bedroom or to go a few rounds with a punching bag in the basement, but it's quite inappropriate and counterproductive to express this anger by screaming at your children for playing boisterously in the house or to smash a favorite heirloom vase into smithereens in front of your family members.

Finding the right place and time to express your emotions is a really difficult part of working through the pain of grief. At the outset of grieving, waves of intense feelings, especially sadness, often come over you without warning. These waves of emotions are so strong that they threaten to overwhelm you.

If you're not with people with whom you're comfortable sharing these intense emotions, the best thing you can do when you're about to be overwhelmed by your emotions is excuse yourself and then literally head for cover (your own bedroom if you're home or the restroom if you're at work or in some other public place) where you can let the feelings out. (I promise you the emotions won't wash you away, no matter how fierce they feel.)

When it comes to finding appropriate ways to express the feelings that come from the pain of your grief, you're often guided by the kind of emotion you're feeling.

- ✔ **Anger** usually requires a physical outlet such as yelling, shouting, and even physical activity such as punching, flailing, and running.

- ✔ **Sadness** usually requires a physical outlet such as crying, moaning, screaming, and even wailing.

- ✔ **Guilt** can require the same types of physical outlets as anger and sadness. It also may require you to be with someone with whom you can freely express your feelings.

- ✔ **Anxiety** can require you to get to a place where you feel safe. It also may require you to be with someone you trust who can comfort you and with whom you can freely express your feelings.

Beyond these obvious physical outlets for your anger and sadness, you may find a number of less apparent activities that allow you to get your emotions out. For example, you may be able to work off some of your anger by doing manual labor. The energy of your anger also may motivate you to undertake a task such as cleaning out the garage or organizing your CD collection.

Give a voice to some of the sadness you're feeling through creative projects such as putting together memory albums with old photos or multimedia projects that incorporate digital photos, music, and video reflecting your relationship with your loved one and telling the story of his life. In this vein, you may also want to consider keeping a handwritten or online journal in which you can vent your feelings as well as reflect on your loved one. Some people also use journaling as a way to communicate with a lost loved one; flip to Chapter 14 for more on various types of memorials you can create that may help you express your feelings about the deceased.

Adjusting to the changed environment

The third of the Four Tasks of Mourning is to adjust to a changed environment both in terms of relating to the outside world as well as in terms of your own internal feelings and beliefs. When you lose someone you love, especially a member of the family with whom you lived day in and day out, adapting to the absence of the person is, to say the least, a major, long-term undertaking.

Coping with the absence of your loved one

If the person you lost is someone with whom you shared a lot of your time (such as your child, life partner, close sibling, or very dear friend), you're left with a whole bunch of empty time on your hands. And you have to find a way to fill this time with more than just your grief over the absence of your loved one if you're ever going to be able to adjust to living without him.

Some people attempt to fill the time that otherwise would have been spent with these loved ones by becoming closer to and spending more time with surviving family members and friends. Others occupy their time by taking up new hobbies, engaging in physical activities, and learning new skills.

Taking on new roles

If you're grieving the loss of a spouse, the adjustments that you must make aren't limited simply to filling the time you would have otherwise spent with your significant other. Often a spouse is a best friend, confidant, and someone with whom you're physically intimate as well as someone who provides economic and decision-making support.

In attempting to adjust to the world without your spouse, you have to come to grips with your entirely new role and responsibilities when it comes to making major decisions on your own and providing economic stability both for yourself and your family. Moreover, you're forced to fulfill this new and often very challenging role while struggling to reconcile yourself to being deprived of all the emotional and physical intimacy your spouse provided. (Refer to Chapter 4 for a more detailed discussion of the particular challenges involved with adjusting to the loss of a spouse or life partner.)

For most bereaved people, successful adjustment requires a significant change in attitude about the relationship with the deceased. You not only have to get used to being without the companionship of your loved one, but you also have to accept the fact that your relationship with that person is for-ever frozen in time. You also may have to ask for help from other people in your life whom you trust.

Even if you're left with many precious and worthwhile memories of the rela-tionship with your loved one, you still have to resign yourself to the fact that, from this time forward, you have to grow and develop independent of that person. The best you can do in this circumstance is see to it that you incor-porate the finest qualities from your relationship into all the new relation-ships you build.

Emotionally relocating the deceased and moving on

The last of Worden's Four Tasks of Mourning is to emotionally relocate the deceased in order to move on with your life. This last task is the most com-plex as well as the one that's the most difficult for most bereaved folks to accomplish. To be able to accomplish this task, you have to be ready to make the following two adjustments:

- ✔ Invest yourself emotionally in something or someone new.
- ✔ Shift your feelings for your lost loved one in such a way that allows you to move on with your life.

The phrase "move on" doesn't always sit well with people suffering profound grief. The problem stems from the supposition that moving on with your life means necessarily forgetting the loved one you've lost. This certainly is nei-ther the reality of incorporating loss nor Dr. Worden's intended meaning for the fourth task.

When you reach the point at the end of your grieving when you can move on in your life, most likely you've already incorporated the deceased person into your life in such a way that there's no possibility of forgetting him. As I explain throughout this book, one of the most effective ways to honor loved ones you've lost and to keep their memories alive within you is to incorpo-rate their best qualities and the finest aspects of the relationships you had with them into all the relationships you maintain and build.

Although moving on generally signals the end of acute or active grieving for most bereaved people, keep in mind that reaching this stage doesn't guaran-tee that you'll never again suffer grief over this loss. The original feelings of grief can well up suddenly long after you think that the grieving process is over and you're finally okay. They can even happen on occasion throughout one's life.

Sometimes these upsurges are triggered by particular events such as the dawning of another anniversary day or revisiting a location with special meaning in your relationship with the deceased. Other times, you don't realize any obvious triggers and don't understand why you're once again mourning the person.

The most important thing to remember about such an upsurge of grief is that it's a very temporary phenomenon. Unlike the emotional turmoil associated with grieving the person's loss, the sad feelings connected with it are very short-lived. And as time goes on, fewer and fewer events trigger upsurges until, for most folks, they eventually completely fade away.

The Six "R" Processes of Mourning

As if the Kübler-Ross Five Stages of Grieving and the Worden Four Tasks of Mourning weren't sufficient, Dr. Therese Rando developed yet another grief model system charting the phases that people normally experience in grieving a profound loss. Her model identifies six individual processes (which are a cross between a Kübler-Ross stage and a Worden task) that she calls the Six Processes of Mourning.

Rando's Six "R" Processes of Mourning are routinely called the Six R's because the first word in each process begins with the letter *r:* recognize, react, recollect, relinquish, readjust, and reinvest. (Come to think of it, this abbreviation is much more logical than education's more common three R's [reading, writing, and arithmetic] because only one of those even begins with the letter r!)

The Six R's as outlined by Dr. Rando's model of grieving are:

1. **Recognize the loss.** This involves acknowledging the reality of the death as well as comprehending what caused it.

2. **React to the separation.** This involves identifying and expressing all the feelings and psychological reactions associated with the loss.

3. **Recollect and re-experience the deceased and the relationship.** This involves reviewing and remembering the relationship as well as experiencing once again the feelings associated with it.

4. **Relinquish old attachments to the deceased and the old assumptive world.** This involves surrendering your old connections with your lost loved one and the world you shared before the death.

Dr. Therese Rando

Clinical psychologist Dr. Therese Rando is the clinical director of The Institute for the Study and Treatment of Loss, which provides mental health services through psychotherapy, training, supervision, and consultation. The institute specializes in loss and grief; traumatic stress; and the psychosocial care of persons with chronic, life-threatening, or terminal illness, and the care of their loved ones.

As a former consultant to the U.S. Department of Health and Human Services' Hospice Education Program for Nurses, Dr. Rando developed its

program for training hospice nurses to cope with loss, grief, and terminal illness. Her research focuses on the operations and courses of anticipatory and postdeath mourning, loss of a child, intervention with the traumatically bereaved, psychosocial stress in parents of infants in the NICU (neonatal intensive care unit), and outreach to mourners disenfranchised from treatment.

For more on Dr. Rando's clinical work, research, and publications on loss and grief, visit her official Web site at www.thereserando.com.

5. **Readjust to move adaptively into a new world without forgetting the old.** This involves developing a new relationship with your lost loved one along with adopting a new identity that includes new ways of being in the world.

6. **Reinvest in life.** This involves taking the emotional energy that you once put into the relationship with your loved one and putting it into new relationships that can bring you some type of gratification.

As you can see in this list, the work called for in some of these processes is very similar to that in the Five Stages of Loss and the Four Tasks of Mourning covered earlier in this chapter. What's different and of particular interest here is how specific the Six R's are and how their specificity can help you understand where you are emotionally and what work you still need to do.

Recognizing the loss

The first process in Rando's Six R's is to recognize the loss. This process is very similar to accepting the reality of the loss, which is the first of the Worden's Four Tasks of Mourning. However, Rando focuses on understanding what caused the death as well as acknowledging its reality in Worden's sense of accepting it as real.

I would like to suggest that this recognition can include more than simply understanding that death is real and the factors that caused it: It can also include an initial and rudimentary understanding of the death's lasting impact on your life. As part of the process of recognizing the loss, you may begin to appreciate its deeper significance in terms of the long-term changes it will affect in you and the consequences it will have on your life.

And I think that when you're capable of this broader type of recognition, you're in a very good position to be able to deal with some of the other Six R processes, especially relinquishing old attachments and readjusting to your new world.

Reacting to the separation

The second of the Six R's is to react to the separation from your loved one. This is the process that includes all the pain and sorrow of your grief along with your physical and psychological reactions to the loss. As part of this process, you need to identify your feelings as well as find ways to express them (see Chapter 14 for some ideas).

Going through this process of reacting to the separation from your loved one also includes identifying and dealing with all the secondary losses that result from his death. These secondary losses can be anything from a loss of emotional and financial security to such things as a loss of well-being and lack of continued faith in the overall goodness of the world.

Recollecting and re-experiencing the deceased

The third of Dr. Rando's Six R's is to recollect and re-experience the deceased. The recollecting part of this process necessarily includes remembering your lost loved one and appreciating the relationship you shared. This type of relationship review also includes reliving the feelings associated with these memories.

Personally, I see the re-experiencing process as also requiring something more because re-experiencing your lost loved one isn't always a simple matter of just recalling experiences frozen in time.

To fully re-experience a loved one after death, you also need to find ways in which to see that person in a new light as well as to stay in contact with him so that he's fully part of the new world that you face after your grieving is done. Here are a few suggestions for doing just that:

✔ Share the story of your relationship with anyone who will listen, noting how its details change over time and depending upon the person to whom you're telling it.

✔ Speak directly to your lost loved one in prayers, journal entries, or letters that you address to him.

✔ Do meditations on specific qualities that your loved one manifested (see Chapter 23 for specific meditation ideas).

For many bereaved people, re-experiencing the deceased is the greatest challenge in the entire process of grieving a loved one. It's just a lot easier to freeze your loved one in time (which too often can lead to ultimately forgetting him altogether). You may find it too arduous a task to probe and dissect your relationship with the loved one to determine the qualities that you want to continue functioning in your life.

Canonizing the deceased loved one by conveniently forgetting all about his failings and foibles and placing a halo on his head is too common when families remember their lost ones. It's as dangerous a practice as demonizing the deceased because the almost insurmountable gulf it creates between you and your loved one isn't conducive to recollecting or re-experiencing him. Remembering only the best things about your lost loved one is so easy to do in large part thanks to society's emphasis on always eulogizing the deceased and its general disparagement of speaking ill of the dead.

Relinquishing attachments to the deceased

The fourth process of the Six R's is to relinquish your old attachments to the deceased along with the old assumptive world. This process is really unique to Dr. Rando's grief model.

I assume that the idea of giving up your old attachments to your loved one in the first part of the statement is quite clear (although you may still question its value). I'll bet, however, that you're wondering what in the blazes it means to give up the old assumptive world.

Actually, this is just psychology talk for the basic idea that in order for you to move forward, at some point in your grieving process you have to let go of the things that linked you with your loved one.

Letting go doesn't mean that you forget your loved one or all the things that you shared together (indeed, doing so would violate the third of the Six R's discussed in the previous section). Rather, it means that you must eventually accept the following realities about the loss:

✔ The separation between you and your loved one is final.

✔ You can only remain in an emotional holding pattern for so long before you have to let go of the loss for the sake of your own health and well-being.

✔ Trying to resist your changed world by holding onto the past you shared with your lost loved one is not only an impossible feat but a self-defeating one as well.

As soon as you're able to surrender your old emotional attachments to your loved one (and this does take some time, so don't push yourself if you're not ready) and appreciate (or re-experience) your loved one anew, you've accomplished the major work of grieving the loss. At this juncture, you know that you'll be okay in your new world, and you can be grateful for the love and what you were able to share with your lost loved one.

Readjusting to move into a new world

The fifth of the Six R's is one of the more long-winded ones in Dr. Rando's grief model: Readjust to move adaptively into a new world without forgetting the old. As inelegant as this fifth process may sound, it's really quite a natural follow-up to the fourth process of relinquishing your old attachments to the deceased and the world you shared together.

In letting go of your old attachments and assumptions of how the world should be, you move almost by definition into a new world and in so doing, establish a new identity. However, once you make it to this new world, you still have to establish yourself there. In order to do so, you must remain open to change and once again be willing to invest yourself in it (the sixth and final R process).

It's worth noting that some grief counselors characterize the new world that you move into as your *new normal.* The basic idea is that the loss and grief that accompany it are so disruptive that almost nothing in the mourning period resembles the normal world you knew before. It also means that you can't go back to the ways things were before the death. Therefore, as your grieving comes to an end, you naturally establish another routine that forms the basis of your new normal.

The idea that you'll ever be able to consider anything as "normal" in a world devoid of your loved one may initially strike you as highly improbable. You may feel as though you've been so changed by the loss and all the pain you're enduring as part of your grief that you'll never see anything as normal again.

However, as you learn how to live in this new world and develop new relationships within it, you will also undoubtedly reconnect to routines that are filled to the brim with all that good, old-fashioned normality you missed so much during this dark time of grieving.

Reinvesting in your life

The final process in Dr. Rando's Six R's is simply to reinvest in life. This last process is my favorite, and it's a fitting way to conclude an explanation of the phases of grieving.

The word "reinvest" simply means to invest again. "Invest," however, has two basic meanings: The first, more common meaning is to endow in the sense of putting resources such as money, time, or emotion into some venture, and the second, less frequently used meaning is to empower in the sense of making someone powerful or giving one authority over something.

The idea of reinvesting in your life as the final process of grieving covers both of these meanings: You finally feel connected again with all the aspects of your everyday life and fully empowered to make the most of them.

During the grieving process, it's quite common for you to feel dissociated from the routines of your everyday life. As you try to carry on in strict survival mode, you may feel as though you're sleepwalking through all your daily tasks and social encounters. It may be only for the briefest moments that you're able to put aside your deep sorrow and overriding grief to truly engage in what's going on around you.

When it dawns on you, this final process of reinvesting in life may feel like waking up from a long sleep. You find yourself able to go off autopilot more and more as your interest in your new life (that new normal) grows.

Entering into this phase doesn't mean that you've forgotten your loss or that you'll forever be free of its grief. It simply means that dealing with this loss and feeling its grief are no longer in the forefront of your life, demanding most of your physical and emotional energy.

To me, this work is the most rewarding part of grieving (the payoff, so to speak, if something as painful and difficult as grieving can be said to have any such a thing). You go beyond the mere acceptance of the loss and moving on from it to using the loss to shape the course and direction of the rest of your life. As a result, your life after bereavement is a place not only where you recollect your lost loved one but also in which he can continue to have influence and provide guidance. (You can find more ideas on how to integrate a profound loss into your life in Chapter 18.)

Chapter 12

Troubled Grieving

● ●

In This Chapter

▶ Examining the relationship between trauma and grief

▶ Understanding and recognizing traumatic losses

▶ Getting to the roots of complicated grieving

▶ Identifying attempts to dodge the grieving process

▶ Exploring techniques for getting in touch with your grief

● ●

*H*eaven knows that, even under the best of circumstances, grieving a profound loss is very difficult. Despite this fact, most people are able to grieve the loss of a loved one successfully, by which I mean they're able to complete the process of grieving in due course. And it's understood as well that each person determines the exact course that this grieving takes as well as the timetable on which he completes the work.

Unfortunately, not everybody is capable of grieving each of the profound losses he experiences with the same aplomb. In some cases, the grieving is forestalled or becomes stalled shortly after the loss occurs. In such a situation, the grieving process becomes troubled in ways not usually associated with this always challenging work.

This chapter explores the subject of grieving processes that either have trouble getting started or get stuck at certain places by looking at how and why some profound losses are more complex and difficult to grieve than others. It also looks at some of the techniques you may employ to jump-start grieving a loss that you're having trouble grieving.

I begin this chapter with a brief introduction to trauma and its relationship to grief. Then I help you recognize when a loss is traumatic rather than simply complicated. I share some of the ways that people avoid starting the grieving process before looking at some of the techniques that you may employ to break through this kind of resistance.

Clinical trauma as a physical response

Trauma is a physical response to a situation that your brain considers seriously threatening to your well-being. The feelings of anxiety and stress come from the impulse to flee the threatening situation (that old "fight or flight" response) only to find that you have no way to escape. This anxiety plus the lack of a way out combine to make trauma so powerful both physically and emotionally. It's powerful enough, in fact, for the same feelings of anxiety and physical helplessness to manifest whenever your brain even faintly perceives a situation that may threaten your well-being in a similar way.

Relating Trauma and Grief

The word "trauma" has both layman's and clinical definitions. Most people think of trauma as either a physical or psychological injury or wound that one receives often as a result of a sudden or violent action. To a psychologist, trauma is more technical; it refers to an emotional or psychological shock or stress that results in disordered feelings or behavior or feelings of extreme anxiety.

The death of a loved one is surely traumatic in terms of the layman's definition of the word. However, the death isn't automatically traumatic in the clinical sense used by mental health professionals.

For the loss to be traumatic in the clinical sense of the word, your loved one's death itself must be either traumatic (as in the case of a particularly violent death, for example) or linked to some other traumatic events in your life. The traumatic events tied to the death may be indicative of a troubled or at least ambivalent relationship that you maintained with your loved one before his death.

Quite often clinical trauma is associated with the specific psychological condition known as *post-traumatic stress disorder* (PTSD). This condition typically is characterized by a number of symptoms that can include depression, anxiety, nightmares, and flashbacks as well as avoidance of all reminders of the event.

In terms of these PTSD symptoms, it's worth noting that flashbacks aren't like vivid memories but rather are more like actually reliving the original traumatic events. Along the same lines, avoiding all reminders of the event isn't the same as being somewhat uneasy with the subject but rather more like being completely unable to bring the subject to consciousness in any way.

Recognizing Traumatic Losses

More often than not, traumatic losses result from either of the following:

- ✔ Traumas experienced in the course of a very troubled relationship with the loved one
- ✔ Traumatic circumstances surrounding the death

Quite often in the case of a traumatic loss, grieving the death isn't possible because it means having to relive the trauma associated with the loss. Moreover, many people who suffer a traumatic loss avoid reminders of the death by continuing to deny its reality.

As I point out in Chapter 11 on the stages of grief, it's quite common for you initially to have trouble accepting the reality of the death (it just doesn't seem real at first). However, when the death isn't particularly traumatic (or complicated in some other way), you're likely to move beyond this initial stage of denial in due time. This isn't the case, however, if you suffer a traumatic loss and have a great need to avoid all reminders of the death.

Under these circumstances, you continue to deny the reality of the death, most often by attempting to freeze your life at a time before the loss. For example, you may never change a thing in your loved one's room or discard any of his belongings. You also may continue to pattern your life strictly according to the ways that your loved one would have preferred.

In addition, when you speak of your lost loved one, you're likely to canonize him or at least put him on a pedestal by speaking of him only in the highest terms and by always praising his outstanding qualities. Even if he was rather notorious for some less-than-perfect behavior, you speak nothing but acclaim.

Denying anything but stellar qualities in a lost loved one often is a defense against feeling anything having to do with the loss. In overlooking all negative qualities, you hope to maintain a block on all feelings of anxiety that naturally arise whenever you focus on the resentments you still carry.

Grieving traumatic relationships

When mental health professionals speak about trauma, they sometimes differentiate between the following:

✔ Impersonal trauma that ensues from events such as automobile accidents, fires, natural disasters, and the like that can result in a traumatic death that you must grieve (discussed in the section immediately following)

✔ Intensely personal trauma caused by the physical or emotional abuse at the hands of a loved one that can result in a traumatic relationship that you must grieve

Whereas both types of experiences can produce similar shock and stress, trauma related to abuse carries an added element: It sets up a traumatic relationship whose toxicity is bound to outlive the death of the abuser.

It should come as absolutely no surprise to find out that people traumatized by abuse from loved ones generally have great difficulty grieving the deaths of their abusers. What may surprise you is that these people often suffer greatly in their inability to grieve; they're unable to find solace in the fact that their abusers are now dead and gone with no way to ever harm them again.

If you're a survivor of a traumatic relationship, you may feel like you can't afford to express your true feelings regarding your abuser. To do so would put you at risk of being doubted by others as well as re-experiencing the trauma of the abuse you endured. You may not be able to express any emotions over the abuser's death, or you may only speak well of the dead, not daring to touch any of the rage and hurt you feel.

As the survivor of a traumatic relationship, you first need to grieve the loss of trust and safety that resulted from the abuse before you can seriously consider dealing with the death of your abuser in any way. With the help of psychological and professional grief counseling, you can develop the skills needed to cope with any recurring trauma and grieve the loss of your innocence. Only then can you take up the complicated task of grieving a loved one who failed so utterly in his obligation to protect and nurture you.

Grieving traumatic deaths

A traumatic death is quite simply any death of a loved one that produces trauma-like symptoms in survivors. Most violent deaths, especially those witnessed by a loved one as well as those involving intense media scrutiny and prolonged legal proceedings, fall into this category. Some deaths that place the bereaved under particularly unusual circumstances, including many suicides (see Chapter 2), also fall into this category.

A death doesn't have to be violent or particularly unusual to be traumatic to a loved one. In many cases, a traumatic death may simply be a death that the loved one considers either too upsetting to recall or too vivid to forget.

In trying to deal with a traumatic death of a loved one, you may find it too distressing to recollect anything about the death and speak about it in any way (an extreme form of denial). Or you may have the most difficulty keeping the death out of your thoughts. The death in all its horrible detail (real or imagined) keeps invading your thoughts, making you feel as though you're reliving the death. You end up in great distress and are unable to actually start coping with the loss of the loved one.

For all intents and purposes, both of the following responses to a traumatic death effectively grind the grieving process to a halt:

- ✓ **Blocking out all recall of the loved one's death:** Prevents you from doing any healing through expressing the pain of your grief as well as through telling the stories of your relationship with the deceased

- ✓ **Being completely overwhelmed by the horrible details of the loved one's death:** Prevents you from feeling the pain of the loss of the relationship as opposed to feeling the intense pain inherent in reliving the manner of death

You may get stuck continually reliving the traumatic death of a loved one because you feel some level of responsibility for the death. Often, these feelings of regret and guilt are undeserved. They say much more about your feelings of inadequacy in regards to caring for the loved one, especially if he assumed the role of a primary caregiver, than they say about your culpability in the death.

Identifying Complicated Grieving

Complicated grieving is the technical name that grief professionals give to a grieving process that gets stuck at some point, making it impossible for the bereaved to successfully start or conclude the grieving process. Complicated grieving is often a sign of unresolved problems in the relationship between the bereaved and the deceased that make it more difficult than usual for the bereft person to grieve.

Whereas a traumatic loss almost always makes for complicated grieving, you need to keep in mind that not all complicated grieving involves traumatic losses. Human relationships are sufficiently varied and complex to create all sort of snags (some traumatic and some not) that can interrupt the grieving process.

If you find that you're unable to start grieving the loss of a loved one or you aren't getting through the grieving process, I recommend that you stop and take stock of the relationship you had with your lost loved one. Depending upon the intricacy of the relationship and its particular problems, you may not be able to really assess it without the help of a mental health professional. However, by working through the issues that stand in your way of grieving a loved one, you not only ultimately free yourself from the grief but also create a new appreciation for yourself as you honestly face all the aspects (good and bad) of your erstwhile relationship.

Complicated grieving in one-sided relationships

Almost all the relationships you build with your loved ones are complex and multifaceted. Sometimes, however, these relationships aren't as balanced as you may like them to be. Unbalanced relationships — especially those in which one person doesn't have anywhere near as much influence or power as the other — can often result in some level of complicated grieving when the person wielding the greater influence dies.

Unfortunately, after the death, it's far too late to rectify the balance of power, and you're left to deal with whatever damage this imbalance caused. Bereft of a particularly powerful person in your life (whether a parent or a spouse), you may experience an overwhelming sense of abandonment and emotions that vacillate between great anger and acute apprehension.

Both the anger and the fear come from the same place of uncertainty — not knowing whether or not you have what it takes to survive on your own. Instead of focusing on grieving the loss, you can only focus on the predicament that your new status confers on you. Before you can feel the grief, you must first deal with your lack of confidence and all the emotions that your insecurity engenders. Many times, this requires the help of a mental health professional other than a grief counselor who can help you work on these aspects not entirely related to the pain of your loss.

Complicated grief in excessively dependent relationships

Relationships in which the two people are exceedingly dependent upon one another for emotional support (sometimes referred to as a *codependent relationship*) can also result in complicated grief when either person dies. This kind of dependent relationship may exist between a child and parent, but it more commonly occurs between spouses and life partners.

Queen Victoria and her perpetual mourning of Prince Albert

Queen Victoria of England (1819–1901) has the distinction of having the longest reign of any British monarch to date (64 years). She also holds the distinction of going into a kind of perpetual mourning for the loss of her husband of 21 years, Prince Albert. Upon Albert's death in 1861, Queen Victoria was so devastated that she went into mourning for him for the remainder of her life (some 40 years). She continued to wear black and remained in semiseclusion (after being in total seclusion for three years) until her death. Moreover, she kept her court in mourning, forbidding them to wear bright colors, and she kept Albert's room exactly as it was at the time of his death — clothes, furniture, and all.

Typically, the two companions are so close that one or both feel as though they couldn't live without the other. Then, when one of the two dies and this misgiving is finally tested, the survivor finds himself hard-pressed to grieve the loss.

Losing the person who defines you in so many ways is sometimes too much too handle. As a reaction, you refuse to acknowledge the loss in an effort to ward off grieving. More importantly, denial keeps you from having to admit that the loss is real and that you have to change a great deal in order to thrive rather than survive (see Chapter 11 for more on working through this stage of the grieving process).

Instead of continually denying the loss, some survivors of codependent relationships refuse to stop mourning the loss of their loved ones. In essence, they create a perpetual mourning in which they safely reside. This too is a defense against real grieving (a process that has a definite end, even when there's no set timetable for reaching it). Perpetual mourning represents an effort to keep the dependent relationship alive in some form and to insulate the survivor and keep him from having to adjust to the new reality. The only way for such a person to break through this kind of stalemate is for him to realize that the end of the grieving is not synonymous with the end of the relationship (see Chapters 18 and 19).

Typical Ways of Avoiding Grieving

There are probably as many ways to dodge grieving the loss of a loved one as there are ways to grieve the loss. The old adage "You can bring a horse to water but you can't make him drink" applies especially here: Life can bring you to the juncture of grief by taking a loved one from you, but it can't force you to grieve the loss.

This section looks at a few of the more common ways that bereft people avoid grieving: refusing to grieve, getting busy, and dulling the pain with drugs and alcohol. Keep in mind that these three reactions, while all too common, are only a sampling of the many methods that people come up with to avoid facing the very hard work of grieving a loss.

Claiming to be "just fine"

The first and most obvious way of avoiding grief is refusing to grieve. (This is technically known as *absent grieving*.) You can bet that a person's doing some mighty fine absent grieving when he tells you that he's really fine and everything's okay the moment you offer your condolences shortly after the death.

Many times, people who refuse to grieve have the naive notion that they can just leapfrog over the nasty business of mourning. If this is you, you may almost will yourself not to feel anything. You may not even show emotion at the funeral or memorial for your loved one. You may get busy right after the death and stay busy in order to avoid your grief (see the next section for more on burying yourself in projects).

As an absent mourner, you're extremely uncomfortable discussing the death of your loved one and usually refuse to discuss and acknowledge any feelings related to the loss. You meet any expression of sympathy and condolence with a quick change of the subject to something more positive. You no longer speak of your loved one (as though he never existed) and therefore never tell stories about the relationship you shared.

In extreme circumstances, you immediately clean out your loved one's closets and give all his stuff away. You also may turn right away to substitutes for the lost loved one, such as a new love in the case of partner loss or a new puppy or kitten in the case of pet loss.

If you're trying to help a loved one through his grief, don't mistake the absence of obvious emotion as an automatic sign of absent grieving. Some folks grieve mightily without ever breaking down in public and letting their feelings show. To count as a case of absent grieving, you have to witness more symptoms than just a lack of public emotion. The best indicator of absent grieving remains the tremendous discomfort and reluctance in discussing anything having to do with the death, the lost loved one, or anything about the relationship with the deceased.

People who refuse to grieve do everything they can to put the death behind them without doing any of the hard work of grieving. Essentially, you're in search of a nonexistent quick fix for your pain. The big problem is that even if you manage to successfully bypass grieving this loss, in due time you'll experience another profound loss, and then you'll have to pay the piper, so to speak, as the grief from this ungrieved loss arises with that of the new loss. Instead of grieving a single profound loss (which is hard enough), you have to contend with the almost overwhelming challenge of grieving multiple losses at the same time because it's very normal for a current loss to trigger other earlier losses, especially when those losses have not been successfully grieved.

Making sure you're just too busy to grieve

Another common technique for avoiding the pain involved with grieving the loss of a loved one is to become too busy to have any time or energy left for feeling the grief. You have to deal with a lot of financial and legal details following the death of a loved one. Therefore, it's very natural to become temporarily quite busy dealing with the estate and related affairs soon after the passing. But what I'm talking about here isn't just attending to the business that naturally arises from settling the estate; rather, the problem is avoiding grieving by throwing yourself into big projects that keep you super occupied shortly after the death (it's what I call the Winchester syndrome; see the sidebar "Mrs. Winchester and her ongoing construction project").

Projects that keep you from grieving can be anything from getting the family business or home ready to sell to overseeing extensive home or business improvements. Often, these projects were planned before the death, so you're left to undertake them alone, sometimes in honor of the lost loved one or as part of the legacy of your relationship.

Becoming too busy to grieve by immersing yourself into one or more of the projects isn't especially dangerous as long as you take the time to grieve when the project winds down. Most often, a person avoiding grieving in this manner secretly hopes to keep the pain at bay long enough for it to fade completely. When the pain doesn't go away, he's forced to finally confront the grief or come up with a new strategy of avoidance (which means that this can become a vicious cycle).

Anesthetizing the pain

Perhaps the most common way to avoid the pain of grieving is to turn to alcohol or the use of other drugs to dull the pain. This tendency isn't surprising given that the temptation to drown your sorrows exists even when you're not suffering a loss anywhere as serious as the death of a loved one.

Mrs. Winchester and her ongoing construction project

After the death of her husband, gun magnate William Winchester (of the rifle fame), and her daughter, Annie, Sarah Winchester (1839–1922) supposedly consulted with a medium who told her that her family was haunted by the spirits of those killed by the Winchester rifle and that Sarah was to move to the West and build a house for herself and the spirits. Further, the medium told Sarah that she would die if construction ever ended on the house.

Accordingly, in 1884, Sarah Winchester purchased an eight-room farmhouse in what's now San Jose, California. From that point until her death 38 years later, Winchester's house in San Jose was under constant construction and renovation. (Work went on 24 hours a day, seven days a week, year-round.) At the time of Winchester's death, the house had more than seven stories and 160 rooms with many oddities, including doors that open to walls, staircases that go nowhere, and windows that overlook other walls. Today, the Winchester Mystery House is a museum that's open to the public. Now that's what I call keeping yourself too busy to grieve!

When you're suffering something as devastating as a death, the lure of taking something to dull the pain can be very seductive. Many times, newly bereaved people aren't even aware that they're gravitating toward substances that anesthetize their constant anguish. All they're aware of is that they're in a pain unlike anything they've experienced before and they need relief.

Keep in mind that you may abuse prescribed medications in the same ways as alcohol and illicit drugs. You may have a great deal of trouble sleeping and therefore naturally seek out medications from your doctor to help you get the rest you need. Many prescription sleep medications quickly become habit-forming if you start relying on them not only to get to sleep but also to help you get through the pain of your grief.

If you have a newly bereaved friend or family member who you know already had a predilection for alcohol or any other mind-numbing drug before the loss, you definitely need to monitor his substance use, especially immediately after the death. The temptation to drown his sorrows will be strong, and one weak moment may lead to a downward spiral, especially if his coping skills aren't in top form.

This strategy for avoiding grieving may be the most common, but it's also the least effective. Many times, instead of dulling the pain, substance use actually aggravates the pain. This is particularly true in the case of alcohol, which as a depressant tends to make many people more emotional, not less so.

Therefore, the relief that you get from substance use is extremely fleeting at best. At worst, this technique actually may make your grief worse as well as make the grieving process more frightening and daunting than it ever could have been.

Strategies for Jump-starting Your Grieving

The fact that grieving isn't a linear process that proceeds evenly from start to finish almost goes without saying. Rather, grieving is a process that goes in fits and starts and one that more often than not goes every which way but forward. The suggestions in this section are for people who are having trouble getting on with their grieving or have gotten stuck somewhere in the process.

Note that stalling at some point in this process isn't tantamount to developing an aversion to grieving. It's also no indication that the process won't get going again at some point soon. However, there are some things that you can do to help jump-start the grieving process and get it back on track.

 If you've suffered a traumatic loss (see the section "Recognizing Traumatic Losses," earlier in this chapter), then you most likely need to seek out professional help to learn new ways to cope with the trauma that you've experienced and lessen its debilitating effects before you can start dealing with the grief process. Trauma is a condition that's too serious to ignore, and it's not one that you can cure yourself. After you've gotten help to deal with the trauma, you can work on grieving the loss.

Retelling the story of your relationship

Your grieving process may get stuck at a point where your feelings about your lost loved one or the relationship that you shared with him are completely ambivalent. Or your process may stall out because you can't find a way to get beyond a particular regret, guilt, or even anger that you feel.

When this happens, one way to get beyond these feelings and get the process back on track is to retell your story. (You can do this in a journal, in a support group, or even with a friend who's willing to lend an empathetic ear — see Chapter 14 for more ideas.)

In telling the story of your relationship many times to many different people, there's a good chance that you'll uncover some new, previously forgotten details. Especially if you tell your story in a group setting or to another friend or family member, their questions and comments can trigger you to remember things.

Moreover, other people's observations can help you gain a much needed new perspective on the relationship or an aspect of it. Sometimes this is all you need in order to gain a new and deeper appreciation of the person and the relationship you lost. This deeper awareness, in turn, gets the old grief machine working once again, and you're able to replace your feelings of regret, guilt, or anger with feelings of deep longing for your loved one and deep sorrow for the loss you've endured.

Working with the pain creatively

Try getting your grieving process unstuck by getting in touch with your creative side (and yes, you have one even if you haven't used it in a long time). By expressing yourself creatively, you can tap into feelings that you didn't even know you had, which can be a real boon when it comes to jump-starting your grieving process.

Expressing yourself creatively doesn't necessarily mean that you have to "do an art," although pursuing an artistic discipline can be a very effective way to get in touch with feelings. You can be creative in any activity that you undertake — from the most mundane task to the most artsy-fartsy discipline.

Here are some suggestions of creative activities that you can do, or learn to do, to help you get back in touch with your feelings:

- ✔ Write down your feelings about anything and everything in a daily journal.

- ✔ Write a poem about anything that comes to mind (and it doesn't even have to rhyme).

- ✔ Paint pictures in oil, watercolor, or acrylic.

- ✔ Draw pictures with pencil, charcoal, pastels, colored pens, or even crayons!

- ✔ Sculpt in clay, metal, or wood.

- ✔ Do calligraphy, decoupage, or collage.

- ✔ Make jewelry or pottery.

- Do woodworking or beading.
- Cook dishes in your favorite cuisine or learn to cook dishes in an entirely new cuisine.
- Sew, crochet, knit, or quilt.
- Make music with an instrument or anything you have that makes noise, sing in a choir, or just listen to your or your loved one's favorite tunes.
- Take photographs of anything you like or arrange existing photos into albums.
- Pursue a meditative body movement such as yoga or Taiji (t'ai chi) or a martial art such karate or tae kwon do (see Chapter 15).
- Create a grief altar, an altar to your patron saint, your ancestors, or whomever or whatever you hold sacred.
- Design and plant a garden of flowers or plants (use a container or terrarium if you don't have a yard).

When pursuing any creative activities, remember that you don't have to use the activities to overtly express your feelings about your loss. Trust that your feelings will surface effortlessly in whatever creative activity you undertake. The idea here isn't to push yourself back into feeling grief but rather to open a channel through which grief can naturally flow.

Also, it's no crime if these creative activities simply give you some much needed and deserved respite from all the stress and sorrow you've had to deal with. Getting a chance to recharge your batteries after the shock of the death also helps you get back on track with grieving.

Check out Chapter 14 for information on how to use creative activities such as the ones suggested here to directly express your feelings about your loss and help you work through your sorrow.

Chapter 13

When Someone You Care About Is Suffering Acute Grief

*M*ost people find themselves somewhat tongued-tied with feelings of helplessness when they're facing a person who's suffering acute grief. That's what makes finding constructive ways to support someone who's actively grieving a profound loss so important.

Feelings of helplessness stem from a number of fears, including:

✔ The fear that you'll say something wrong, embarrass yourself, and end up offending the person you're trying to support

✔ The fear that the strength of the emotions engendered by the person's loss may "get out of control"

✔ The fear that the bereaved's deep emotions will stir something up in you and you may lose control of your own emotions

✔ The fear that in trying to support this person's grief, your own fears and deep discomfort with death will surface

As I discuss in this chapter, strategies do exist for dealing with any and all these fears. But in order for these strategies to work, you have to be highly motivated to help the person who's grieving. With each of these fears, the focus is on you instead of on the person who's actually suffering. So obviously the first step in helping a bereaved friend or family member is turning the focus away from you and back onto the person you want to support in this crucial time of need.

What to Say to Someone in Acute Grief

The first rule to remember about saying the right thing to someone who's in intense grief is that there is *no* "right" thing to say. That being said, there are a number of rather insensitive platitudes, such as "I know how you're feeling" and "It's all for the best" (see Chapter 20 for a more complete list and discussion of their effects), that I urge you to avoid. They aren't supportive to the person in distress, and they tend to stifle the conversation by putting the person off, which is the last thing you want to do for someone you intend to help.

Instead, simply tell the person how sorry you are for his loss. Or, if you're not comfortable with that and don't have any words, simply be honest and tell him that you don't know what to say in the face of his sorrow. In most cases, the bereaved will find such honesty completely refreshing. This is especially true if he's been inundated with platitudes or, even worse (far worse), he's finding that people have suddenly started going out of their way to avoid saying anything to him at all.

Don't give in to the temptation to avoid saying anything to a bereaved person, mistakenly thinking that it's better to say nothing at all rather than risk saying something awkward or inappropriate. No matter how trite and superficial, any platitude you deliver sincerely is much less hurtful than no words of support at all. Even in acute grief, people can feel the sincerity in a comment; from silence, they can only deduce that you don't care enough for them to confront your own feelings of discomfort.

If you've never suffered a profound loss, you may underestimate how important the words, cards, and casseroles of sympathy and support are. Even though they can't begin to mitigate the situation, they're clear signals that the people suffering the grief aren't alone. And, believe me, the message that you're not alone is an incredibly important one to receive when you're faced with a profound loss because alone is often exactly how you feel.

How to Listen to Someone Who's Grieving

No matter how much you want to take away someone's pain from grieving a profound loss, you need to realize that you can't. Don't spend any time trying. Instead of fretting about a bereaved person's level of discomfort, concentrate on listening to the bereaved person as he expresses his feelings about the loss.

Unfortunately, listening isn't always as easy as it sounds. Most people have trouble really listening to other people even when they're expressing essentially positive feelings. When confronted with listening to what you normally consider negative feelings (sorrow, guilt, anger, and all the rest), it's easy to find that you're in over your head!

Cultivating active listening

One of the basic training techniques designed to help hospice volunteers really listen to the concerns and feelings of the people they visit and attend to is called *active listening*. Despite its name, active listening doesn't refer to listening in which you take charge of the conversation. It's quite the opposite: Active listening is a technique whereby you do everything possible to help the other person fully express his or her feelings without regard to your own feelings.

The key element to active listening is the suspension of judgments, at least as far as your verbal responses go. Instead of responding to the bereaved person by telling him what you think about the feelings he's expressing (which may be pretty intense and very dark), you simply ask him what he thinks about the feelings he's having. And even when you feel moved to counter a particular viewpoint or idea, you first acknowledge the person's feelings.

For example, suppose your recently bereaved friend tells you that, now that his wife is dead, he has no reason to go on and wishes only that he were dead as well. Instead of rushing to buck him up with reasons for going on living, first acknowledge his feelings and their validity — "Yes, I can really understand how losing her makes you feel right now as though you don't want to go on." After you grant the validity of his feelings, you give him your gentle advice — "But, you need to keep in mind that even feelings as deep as these are subject to change, and you may not feel so forlorn in time."

Keep in mind that your responses have to be genuine. Participating in active listening doesn't mean that you have to give up your honest feelings about an issue. It does mean, however, that you remain aware that the whole point of the conversation is to enable the other person to express his honest feelings about the grief — not express how you feel about his loss!

Coulda, shoulda, woulda and active listening

"Could have," "should have," and "would have" are highfalutin tenses frequently used to express wished-for states that didn't come true. In the world of active listening, they have no place, so you can just eliminate them from your vocabulary. Unfortunately, the bereaved person you're conversing with may have a great need to express his feelings in any or all of these tenses. A person's feelings of guilt over a death are especially strong in the acute stage of grieving. So you may hear a lot of feelings expressed as "He never should have done such and such . . ." or "If only he would have listened to me, he could have . . ." and the like. And, as you now know, the best thing you can do is to just keep the space open for him to express these kinds of feelings.

If you feel it's appropriate in the course of the conversation, you certainly can tell the other person how a similar experience you had affected you and how you learned from it, but be careful not to use this as an opportunity to shift the focus onto yourself and your story. I don't ever recommend responding with a hypothetical feeling. In other words, I might tell a bereaved family member how I dealt with similar feelings I experienced when my mother died, but I would never tell him how I think I would have felt in I were in his situation. If I've never experienced anything close to what the person is describing, I don't have any experiential wisdom to share and therefore have no business interjecting my two cents; I should just keep my mouth shut and listen (something that people who know me well know is not all that easy for me to do!).

At first, you may find active listening quite challenging, especially if you're someone with strong opinions who's quite used to sharing them freely. With time and some practice, however, you may find it as liberating as I do. Perhaps this is because I know going into the conversation that my only requirement is to listen from the heart. I don't have to have anything in particular to say; I don't have to have anything in particular to contribute. All I have to do is hold the space open for the other person so that he can openly express his feelings.

Empathizing instead of sympathizing

Listening without judgment is surely one of the most effective ways to hold the space open for a person to freely express his grief. Another effective method is to convey empathy rather than sympathy in your responses. What's the difference, you ask?

- ✔ When you empathize with someone, you identify with that person.
- ✔ When you sympathize with someone, you feel sorry for the person, and in turn, you feel for his predicament.

The difference really isn't in the feelings, their depth, or their sincerity because in both cases, you may commiserate genuinely with the other person and his situation. However, in the case of empathy, you're on the same level (as you have to be in order to identify with someone else's situation). In the case of sympathy (or pity), you can be safely on a different level, and without noticing, the focus can turn to the fact that it's the other person — and certainly not you — who's in the extremely unfortunate situation of grieving the death of a loved one.

In order to have empathy for another person's grief, you don't have to have experienced the same or a similar type of loss. You simply have to acknowledge fully that grief is the great human common denominator and that, although today it may be the other person who's lost a loved one, tomorrow it may well be you. Seen from this perspective, when you take the time to support a friend in his grieving by listening to him with your heart, you're really doing some of your own grief work.

What to do if your own grief surfaces

Sometimes just hearing someone else talk about his grief (much less express it emotionally and physically by crying) can trigger your own feelings of sadness over losses you've experienced. And it can happen even when you've long since finished actively grieving a loss. So what do you do if your own feelings of grief surface when listening to someone else express his grief?

When this happens to me, I simply regard it as a part of human empathy that enables me to connect deeply and communicate with another person about such issues. You, on the other hand, may have a very different take on it: Having your own feelings of grief suddenly triggered may make you feel very vulnerable and more than a little out of control.

The best thing to do in such a situation is to honestly acknowledge that it's happening. For example, you might say something like "Your story is affecting me so deeply that it's put me in touch with my own feelings of grief over losing . . . ." Of course, if you're welling up or actually starting to weep, you may not be able to get any words out. In such a case, it will be plenty evident that your friend's words have touched you deeply, although he won't know the reason for your tears.

If you find yourself totally overcome with emotion, just excuse yourself and go off and deal with your own grief (it's analogous to the airline instruction to put on your own oxygen mask before attempting to help anyone else put on theirs). You can always explain the reason for your abrupt departure at a later time when you're more in control. No one in the world will be more understanding than your friend who's undoubtedly often overcome in a similar way by his own grief.

Patience as the key

Keep in mind that many times a bereaved person needs to tell his story of loss again and again. If you're just a friend trying to support another friend, you may find it a bit tedious to hear the same story (or parts of it) over and over again. You also may jump to the conclusion that repeated storytelling means that your friend is stuck and in need of help in getting on with his life.

Although it appears from the outside as though the bereaved person is stuck and getting nowhere in telling the same story again and again, most often that isn't the case. Chances are good that he's working his way through the meaning of the loss or a certain stage of it (see Chapter 11 for details) as he goes over and over a particular incident or string of incidents involving the lost loved one.

In fact, if you have enough patience to sit with your friend through the telling and retelling of the same story, you may be surprised (pleasantly, of course) to find that, suddenly, one day your friend is done with the story and has absolutely no need to revisit it with you again. He's worked out whatever he needed to work out in the retelling (and, perhaps, rehearing) of the story, and he's ready to move on.

The challenge for you, the listener, is to manifest sufficient patience. Sometimes it's all too tempting to want to move things along after you've heard what sounds like exactly the same story over and over again. You may think that, now that you've heard your friend relate the same thing for the umpteenth time, it's high time to ditch active listening in favor of a more focused agenda that will move him along in his grieving. Again, I urge you to avoid the temptation to do anything more than support a bereaved friend through active listening. If you find that your patience has run out, it's clearly time to gently move your friend toward professional help.

The challenge of working with the dying and bereaved

Like many who work in hospice and end-of-life care, I'm regularly asked how I can do the kind of work that I do. It's tantamount to asking how I can handle working with the dying and grieving without being weighed down by it. The simple answer is that once I mastered active listening (and it took some time and loads of practice), carrying on conversations with people who were dying or grieving deaths became a whole lot easier and much less draining. In fact, I often find these heart-to-heart conversations uplifting and much less taxing than normal, seemingly more superficial conversations because they're so honest and because the spotlight's not on me and I'm not required to fix anything (which is not always the case in my regular day-to-day affairs).

Also, through my experience with people in acute grief (myself and others I've supported), I've come to realize that every person is quite capable of seeing his or her way through the pain of grief. Often, all they need is a way to tell their stories, express their grief, and be heard.

A professional grief counselor should be able to ascertain quickly where your friend is in his grief process. She'll also be able to determine whether your friend is stuck in a certain grieving stage or simply taking his own sweet time working through a particular part of the process.

If listening is not your forte

Not everybody is capable of listening (actively or not) to another person express his innermost thoughts and feelings about grief. If you're one of these people, don't feel at all bad about it. You probably know that you aren't capable of this kind of listening because you'd rather have a root canal than sit for an hour supporting a grieving friend. If, however, you don't recognize this inability before you attempt to listen, you'll discover your mistake quickly enough; in the course of the conversation, you'll find yourself very tense and emotionally shut down, having trouble hearing what your friend is saying, or you'll become impatient and maybe just a tad irritated at being subjected to these strong emotions.

If comforting a friend in acute grief isn't your strong suit, accept that and make every attempt to get the bereaved friend connected to someone who can provide comfort and attention (such as a professional grief counselor or support group as described in Chapter 14).

This pithy advice is all well and good provided that a dear friend isn't in acute crisis over his grief and you're seemingly the only one around who he can reach. In that situation, you have no choice but to tough it out and listen as best you can, however difficult you may find it. (Try looking at the situation from your friend's perspective: He didn't ask for this loss and probably feels totally unprepared to deal with the grief that comes from it.)

The best way to make it through a difficult support situation is to keep reminding yourself that you're not responsible in any way for making the situation better or for taking away your friend's pain. Your only job is to enable your friend to express his feelings and tell his story. Perhaps most important of all, keep in mind that listening to and even empathizing with another's pain doesn't entail taking that pain onto yourself. You're not there to shoulder a friend's pain but to help him shoulder it himself (and just being willing to listen is often a very effective way to do this).

Other Ways to Support a Bereaved Friend

Although I spend a great deal of space in this chapter discussing ways to effectively listen to a bereaved friend, I don't want you to take away the mistaken impression that talking is necessarily the best way to support your friend through acute grief. Regardless of the benefit, some people aren't able to discuss their feelings or aren't comfortable doing so. Moreover, in the first stage of grief, they may be in too much shock or denial over the death to be in touch with their feelings, let alone ready to share them.

If you're helping a friend through his grief, keep in mind these general guidelines:

- **Talk when it's time to talk.** Always follow the bereaved person's lead. If he wants to talk, talk. If he's reticent to talk, be quiet. Just realize that your presence and willingness to be with him in his pain is often the best support that you can give him.

- **Help out when talk isn't required.** If you aren't particularly comfortable with silence (not all of us are Zen trained), you may want to ascertain what, if any, chores you can perform to help out. This may be something as simple as helping organize your friend's mail, cooking him a few meals, or chauffeuring him around.

- **Be available.** Supporting your friend may entail doing nothing other than being prepared to be there or to talk should the need arise. In that case, check in, preferably by telephone, on a regular basis to see how your friend is and to ascertain whether there's anything you can do to help.

Like people who are actively dying, people who are in acute grief never know where they'll be emotionally at any given moment, much less from one day to the next. When you call to check in, be aware that you could catch your friend at almost any point on the emotional spectrum. Therefore, don't expect that, just because your friend sounded genuinely okay when you talked on Monday, he'll be in that state on Tuesday or vice versa. Try your darnedest not to anticipate — simply ask where he is at the time you actually make contact.

Often, at the time of the funeral and shortly thereafter, the bereaved almost has too many people checking in on him to find out how they can help. This support soon disappears, though, and the bereaved is left all alone to fend for himself. This is the time when *you* really need to remember to pick up the phone and check in and let your friend know that you're there for him and that he's certainly not alone.

Being Sensitive to the Factors That Affect Grieving

In trying to support anyone who's grieving, keep in mind the obvious fact that everybody grieves in their own ways. And there are a bunch of factors that can affect the way a person grieves. Among the most important are

- ✔ Type and nature of the relationship to the lost loved one
- ✔ Manner of the loss (for example, sudden versus expected or preventable versus inevitable)
- ✔ Accumulation of losses and experience with profound grief
- ✔ Personality of the bereaved person
- ✔ Culture of the bereaved person

This section looks at each of these factors with an eye toward how they work together to affect how someone grieves and how you can support a friend in his time of need.

The type and nature of the relationship

In Chapter 1, I suggest that the depth of the grief one undergoes is a direct function of the nature of the loss suffered. By this I don't mean that it's simply a question of the type of loss one endures — loss of a parent, child, sibling, friend, or pet; rather, the depth of grief also is related to the particular relationship that the person built up with his loved one.

For example, the death of a parent with whom your friend was close throughout every stage of his life can be expected to affect him far more deeply than the loss of an estranged parent whom he really never knew and who was unfortunately seldom or never an active part of his life. So too, the death of someone's best friend from childhood can be expected to affect a person far more deeply than the loss of a friend at work with whom he was just starting to become close.

When supporting someone in his grief, it's not enough to simply know who he's lost. You also have to know the nature of the person's relationship with that loved one. In the case of a close friend whom you're trying to support, you may already know quite a bit about the nature of this relationship.

No matter how much you think you may know about the nature of a friend's relationship with the lost loved one, you owe it to everyone concerned to check out your assumptions. Often, information about the relationship comes out as a natural part of the storytelling that your friend engages in as part of his grief process. Sometimes, however, you may find that your friend's story is oddly devoid of this type of concrete information and you have no choice but to question him about it.

The manner of the loss

The manner of the loss can influence the depth of your friend's grief (see Chapter 2). Expect your experience supporting your friend through his acute stages of grief to differ greatly according to whether the loss was sudden or anticipated:

- ✔ In the case of a sudden loss, your friend will be experiencing a great deal of shock and numbness. And you may hear more anger, recrimination, and perhaps even guilt expressed before this initial shock wears off and you start hearing stories about the relationship with the loved one, its depth, and how this loss is affecting him.

- ✔ In the case of an anticipated loss, your friend may have had to experience the decline and loss of his loved one's abilities. And you may hear many stories describing the extent and depth of his relationship with the loved one, with very little mulling over the manner of death after expressing the pain associated with having to witness this decline.

The effect of accumulated losses and grief experience

The older you get, the more losses and battle scars you naturally accumulate (hey, that gray hair has to stand for something). The first time you go through the grieving process, you aren't at all sure that the pain will ever end or that, if it does end, you'll make it through in one piece. The next time you experience profound grief, you still may not be sure how intense it will be or long it will last, but you're a little more certain that it will eventually end and you'll survive it.

Although grieving doesn't necessarily get any easier with experience, the process does become more predictable. And out of this familiarity can come some self-knowledge about how best to go about handling the process and even working through it more effectively.

Supporting someone grieving a first big loss

When trying to support a friend who has little or no previous experience with the grieving process and how to handle it, one of his overriding concerns is likely to be his ability to withstand the terrible pain and survive the process. Other important worries that you may hear about may include whether he's going crazy and whether the pain will ever go away and the grieving come to end (as in "Will I feel this bad all the rest of my life?" and "Will this pain ever end?").

When discussing such fears with your friend — in active listening mode, of course (refer to the earlier section "How to Listen to Someone Who's Grieving") — don't rush to reassure him that he's unquestionably strong enough to withstand the pain of this grief, that he's definitely not going crazy, and that yes, all this pain will ultimately end. Instead, consider using these steps:

1. **Let him know that you hear all his fears by actually mirroring each one of them back to him.**

   For example, say, "I hear that you're afraid that you're not going to be strong enough to get through the pain you're suffering now, that you're feeling like you're going crazy, and that you're very concerned that this grief might never end."

2. **Tell your grieving friend that you understand how he could have these feelings given the loss he's just suffered (provided you honestly feel this way).**

3. **Consider telling him that you read in a book on grieving (decide for yourself whether telling him that it was a *For Dummies* book will help or hurt your cause!) that it's not unusual for people dealing with the profound loss of a loved one at first to feel so overwhelmed by the depth of their feelings and sadness that they naturally doubt their ability to withstand the pain. They also often worry that they're going crazy and are deeply concerned about whether or not the grieving process will ever come to an end so they can feel connected to life once again.**

Supporting someone who's grieved multiple losses

You may get the impression that supporting a friend who has had multiple experiences with grief is bound to be easier than supporting someone who's grieving his first profound loss. Actually, one isn't necessarily easier than the other — it really depends upon how well your friend has handled each grieving experience.

If your friend has had the time and the courage to grieve each loss, then you may expect him to understand how he deals with the grieving process and have fewer qualms about surviving it. However, this doesn't mean that past grieving experiences are always good indicators of how one will deal with the next loss.

Even if your friend deems the present loss he's grieving to be somewhat minor when compared to some of those he has experienced in the past, the present loss may stir up extremely deep sorrow. The present loss becomes a vivid reminder of all the profound losses he's had, and he ends up grieving not only this loss but also those of the past.

Of course, your friend may be a person who hasn't dealt completely with all his past losses for a number of reasons. He may not have given himself sufficient time to grieve all his past losses. He may even have experienced multiple simultaneous losses or losses compacted within a very short time frame, so he simply didn't have the time to grieve each loss as thoroughly as he otherwise would have done.

Whatever the reasons, your friend's present loss may trigger unresolved grief from past losses that gets mixed in with the grief for the current one. You may even find that he starts talking about and expressing sorrow for past losses before he's able to deal with the sorrow caused by the present one.

When supporting someone who has dealt with accumulated losses, understand that you may end up listening to more than just his stories about the loved one he's just lost. Indeed, at least for a while, you may hear more about other loved ones long gone and emotions that their passing stirs up than you hear about the person recently deceased.

Provided that you're supporting your friend with active listening (and therefore without any agenda), his mixing of losses and grief should present no particular problem. Just keep in mind that his expressions of sorrow and feelings for past losses are all necessary in order for him to get to and properly process the present loss. In fact, not having someone like you who was willing to listen to his stories about past losses may be part of the reason that he still needs to tell them.

Personality and grieving

Think about the personalities of your friends: Some are probably naturally more outgoing and open with their emotions than others who are naturally more reserved and tend to keep tighter control over their emotions. A tendency toward a more or less extroverted show of emotions often is an indicator of how openly a friend will express his sorrow to you during grieving. However, it's no indicator of how deep his grief is over the loss or how long the acute phase of grieving will go on.

Helping extroverted people

When dealing with a friend who's naturally more expressive with his emotions, you may find that he has a relatively easy time opening up to you and expressing his feelings about his grief. Note that this may not be the case if your friend becomes concerned that, once he starts outwardly expressing grief (especially by crying), he won't be able to stop.

The fear of not being able to ever stop crying is quite a big concern for some people, especially when they first start grieving. Dealing with this fear can run the gamut from blocking the show of all emotions to just having a much harder time opening up. If a friend expresses this concern to you, you can safely reassure him that, although he feels sad enough to cry forever, his body will naturally stop when it runs out of tears. Also let him know that he's safe to let it all out with you (provided that's the way you really feel).

Helping introverted people

When dealing with a friend who naturally tends to keep a tighter rein on his emotions, you may find that he has a relatively difficult time opening up to you and expressing his feelings of grief. Of course, that's fine, and you should tell him so. In fact, he may find that your acceptance of his reluctance to share and show emotion eventually makes him feel comfortable enough to open up and unburden himself.

A person's openness or lack of it in expressing sorrow over a loss is no indicator of how deeply he's grieving. It only shows how comfortable he is publicly expressing his grief, and this comfort level is often just a function of the person's gender (on the whole, men have a harder time sharing feelings than women), socialization (some families and cultures are more stoic than others), and personality (extroverts are more open than introverts).

Culture and grieving

It's not only your personality but also the culture in which you're brought up that influences how easily and openly you express your grief. Some cultures naturally encourage public mourning and grieving for the dead (especially at the time of the funeral), whereas other cultures tend to frown upon public displays of grief and encourage people to mourn the dead in much more private and discreet manners. (For some specific examples of cultural influences on grieving, turn to Chapter 17.)

When trying to support a grieving friend who's been brought up in a culture different from your own, you may have some trouble understanding his responses to his grief. Ask him directly about the mourning practices of his native culture and/or family. If he's open and willing to discuss this subject, the information can go a long way toward helping you understand his response to the loss. It also may be the case that, by discussing his culture's or family's expectations and norms surrounding death, dying, and grieving, your friend gains valuable insight into his responses to grief.

Part III
Healing Grief

The 5th Wave   By Rich Tennant

"I usually mix my meditations. Today
I'm doing healing, insight, and bad hair
day meditations."

In this part . . .

Healing the grief you suffer from the profound loss of a loved one is often a long and challenging task. In this part, you find out how to support the process of healing through appropriate ways of expressing your grief. You also get a chance to investigate the physical aspects of grief and how you can use physical activities as tools to help you in healing. Finally, you're given some tips for developing strategies to help you through the pain and heartache that inevitably accompany the holidays and anniversaries after the loss of a loved one.

Chapter 14

Expressing Your Grief

· ·

In This Chapter

▶ Knowing that your grief isn't atypical

▶ Exploring ways to express your grief

▶ Releasing your grief so that you can move past it

▶ Turning to others for grief support

· ·

*E*xpressing your grief is really at the heart of the grieving process. By finding ways to express your grief, you're able to release the intense pain over time. And from there, you can begin to move from acknowledging the loss and all that it means to you to incorporating it into the rest of your life.

The chapter begins by examining some of the more typical ways you may experience the pain of grieving, especially at its outset soon after the death. I share typical strategies that you may want to use to help you communicate and get your feelings out; they include finding your own way to express your grief, grieving with others who are mourning the same loss, and expressing your grief through creative or artistic activities.

The chapter concludes with a look at various ways that you can get help in dealing with the pain of the grief and getting yourself through it, including relying upon the sympathetic ear of someone who's not mourning the same loss and can listen to you and seeking out professional help from a grief counselor or grief support group. This discussion covers how to locate grief counseling resources in your local area and how to choose between one-on-one counseling and a support group. Regarding grief support groups, I tell you how to choose the right support group for you and what to expect and what not to expect from the group experience.

Typical Grief Experiences

It may strike you as a bit odd to have a discussion about typical grief experiences. After all, isn't the entire grieving experience such a personal affair that the likelihood of typical experiences is pretty slim?

Strangely enough, although the grieving process is one of the most intensely personal experiences you can go through, there are some very general grief experiences that are common to most people's grieving. In this section, I review three of the more pervasive grief experiences, namely:

- ✔ Grief seems like an interminable experience that you fear will never end.
- ✔ Grief isolates you and makes you feel more alone than ever before in your life.
- ✔ You're plagued by remorse over not having had the chance to express all your feelings to your loved one before he died, adding to your grief and making it much worse.

Will this pain never end?

Grieving is really scary business for most people. And one of the most frightful things about grief is that it seems quite simply that the pain and misery will never end.

I think this fear may account in part for why so many bereaved people are reluctant to get in touch with and show their sorrow: They fear that once they start getting in touch with this profound pain, the feelings of sorrow will pull them under and they'll never again be able to resurface.

Yes, the pain will end

I know that it feels like the pain of your grief will never end and the grieving will go on forever. I'm here to reassure you that it will end: Grieving is a natural human process and not some crime that carries a mandatory life sentence.

Go directly through the pain and don't try to put it off or avoid it. By feeling the pain as deeply as you need to, you hasten the day when you'll be released from your grief. Trying to hold back the emotions or ignore the pain altogether only slows down the grieving process and makes it last even longer.

But sometimes the grief comes back

Just as it's imperative that you understand that one day you'll wake up and the intense pain of the grief will be gone, it's also very important to understand that this doesn't mean that you'll never be plagued by such intense grief again. It's not at all uncommon to feel pretty okay with the loss (or at least not devastated by it) and then suddenly relapse into sorrow as intense as when you first grieved the loss. Grief professionals even have a term for this relapse: Sudden Temporary Upsurge of Grief, or STUG.

It's exactly what the name says — a sudden and *temporary* upsurge of grief. A STUG is often triggered by a stimulus (such as a special scent, sound, environment, an anniversary date, or even something that you're not even aware of) that reminds you of your lost loved one or the relationship you shared. The nice thing about a STUG is that it reconnects you to your lost loved one, and the pain that it brings, although intense, doesn't last.

The most important thing to remember when a STUG tugs at your heart is that it's not a signal that you're about to fall back into your original grief and have to do all your grieving work again. Grieving definitely isn't a game of Chutes and Ladders where, when you fall down, you have to start all over again to climb back up.

Never felt so alone

Grieving can be a tremendously isolating experience, one in which you feel totally alone and abandoned. This is true even when you're surrounded by family and friends who you know are there to support you every step of the way. Of course the feeling of being alone is stronger when you don't have this kind of support system to help you.

Facing the isolation

Grieving feels isolating in large part because you've just had a loved one taken from you, and all you want is the impossible — to have him back again. In these circumstances, you may understandably feel totally bereft (ripped off) and quite forsaken. This can be the case regardless of whether your loved one's death was anticipated or sudden and completely unexpected.

Being separated by death from someone you love is nothing like being separated in any other way. Not matter how much you may believe that you'll be reunited with your loved one in the world to come, you know (or are coming to realize) that you'll never see him again in this world. For all the rest of your days on this earth, however many or few they be, you'll be forever without that loved one.

Turning isolation into a positive

Isolation is an integral part of the grieving process for most bereaved people. A certain amount of seclusion and privacy can enable you to express your grief more freely and gives you an opportunity to contemplate the meaning of the relationship and consequently the meaning of the loss.

This contemplation is a part of the process of fully acknowledging the loss (the first task in the grieving process, as I explain in Chapter 1). This task doesn't simply entail finally giving up on the denial stage in which your mind refuses to accept that the death is real and that your loved one won't ever be coming through that door again. Rather, acknowledging the loss also involves formulating a response to this hard reality, what some people refer to as making meaning of the death. At first, this response can be no more than expressing all the grief that this loss brings you. But in time, this response can grow to embrace new ways of staying connected to your lost loved one and incorporating the love you shared with him in your new life (see Chapter 18 for more on incorporating the loss).

Dr. Phil (McGraw) never tires of telling his guests on his popular TV show: "You can't fix what you don't own." In this instance, owning or acknowledging the death is more than a precondition to healing the grief — it's part and parcel of the healing process itself.

Never got a chance to say goodbye

One of the most prevalent regrets that bereaved people have is not having had an adequate chance to say goodbye to their loved ones before they died. This regret plagues both those whose loved ones die sudden and unexpected deaths and many whose loved ones die long-anticipated deaths.

You can feel this regret even if you were at the bedside of your loved one until the moment of his death, profusely proclaiming your love and how much the relationship has meant to you. No matter how much opportunity you have to actually say goodbye to your loved one, you may never feel as though you had enough time to express yourself.

I think that the principal reason for this feeling is that saying goodbye isn't so much a part of attending to dying loved ones as it is part of grieving the loss of them. Therefore, having all the chance in the world to declare your devotion before your loved one passes away will never be a real substitute for saying goodbye to him after the death.

You can still say goodbye

You may not have to live in utter regret about not having the chance to say goodbye to your loved one if you were suddenly parted from him. You may be able to come to terms with this regret as part of figuring out how you're going to say goodbye as part of grieving this loss.

My process for saying goodbye as part of your grieving includes the following tasks:

- ✔ Create a list of all the things that you're already missing with your loved one gone.
- ✔ Add any things that you're pretty sure you're going start missing about him over time.

✔ Add all the things that you don't and won't miss.

✔ List everything that you learned from your loved one.

✔ List all the ways you're a better person because your loved one was in your life.

✔ Express your gratitude for all you've learned and all he's given before you say your farewell (as in "till we meet again").

That's a good start toward saying goodbye and one that you'll undoubtedly add to and improve upon as you move through the rest of your grieving and uncover ways to express your grief (see the later section "Expressing Your Grief" for suggestions).

Being a little late doesn't matter

If you're concerned that saying your goodbyes after the death of a loved one just isn't the same as saying them before he dies, I invite you to approach the matter in a slightly different way. Even if you did get the chance to say something at the bedside, you were probably much too upset to express even a fraction of how much the person means to you and how much you'll miss him. This means that you still have to go through this important little exercise by which you come to understand all that your loved one meant to you and therefore all that you've lost in his passing. This understanding turns out to be not only your goodbye to your loved one but also your admission of all the grief you carry and have to express as part of grieving the loss.

Expressing Your Grief

Finding appropriate ways to express your grief is one of the most important tasks in grieving a profound loss. In giving fitting expression to all the feelings you have regarding the loss, you can gradually let go of the pain.

Note that I prefer to use the phrase "express your grief" rather than "experience or feel your grief." Express has plenty of meanings, all of which have some relevance to this topic; they include:

✔ **Depict or delineate,** as in finding ways to describe your grief

✔ **State, utter, or vent,** as in finding ways to release your grief

✔ **Show or signify,** as in finding ways to display your grief

✔ **Recount or describe,** as in finding ways to share your grief

✔ **Symbolize, reflect, or embody,** as in finding ways to understand what this grief means to the rest of your life

As you can see from this list, when it comes to expressing grief, I'm not simply talking about getting in touch with feelings such as anger or sadness and finding efficient ways to release them. Although getting in touch and releasing feelings are definitely ways of expressing the grief you feel (and important things to do), I'm talking about doing more. Use the expression of your grief not only as a means of letting go of some of the sadness but also as a means of telling the story of the relationship you shared with your loved one.

Using expression in this way lets you relieve some of the physical and emotional stress you're under and helps you gain some insight into what the loss means to the bigger picture of your life. Most important, as your sadness naturally diminishes through the expression of your grief over time, your understanding of how you'll reconcile the loss to the rest of your life increases.

There are probably as many different ways to express your grief as there are individual bereaved people. That said, I invite you to consider these general approaches to expressing grief:

- ✔ **Expression through ritual:** Ritual can open channels through which you release your sorrow and become able to share it with others.

- ✔ **Expression through creative activities:** Creative activities can open channels through which you can describe your sorrow and explore its depths.

- ✔ **Expression through sharing your feelings and stories with trusted people:** Talking with others who understand and empathize with your situation can be most beneficial and very healing.

Expressing grief through your own rituals

A ritual is any ceremony that progresses in established steps. Although people generally think of ritual in the context of formalized religion, it need not be. You can (and probably do) make a ritual out of the smallest and most mundane acts in your everyday life, such as getting ready for work in the morning, preparing the evening meal, or getting ready for bed at night.

To develop your own grief ritual, all you have to do is figure out the following three things:

- ✔ **Place:** Select a clear, clean space in a room where you can erect some sort of grief memorial or shrine. If possible, choose a room where any noise you make won't disturb the neighbors.

- ✔ **Time:** Select a time when you can devote yourself totally to remembrance of your loved one.

> ✔ **Activities:** Select a prayer, inspirational reading, piece of music, or poem that you can recite or play when opening and closing the ritual, and then fill the middle of the ritual with whatever it is you need to articulate and convey at the moment you conduct the ritual.

Creating a shrine

When setting up the grief memorial or shrine, adopt an attitude of loving care and great awareness as you select and arrange each element.

You may want to add pictures of your loved one along with some personal or natural objects that remind you of him. Personal objects can include effects such as jewelry; awards and trophies; caps, hats, and other clothing; and even favorite books (especially a loved one's Bible or missal). Natural objects can include anything you have at hand, such as rocks (which you can decorate), shells and sand if you live near a beach, and bird nests (abandoned, of course) and branches from the back yard. And if it feels right, you also can add candles, incense, and flowers to the memorial.

Choosing activities

When selecting activities for your grief ritual, I suggest that you pick one inspirational verse, poem, or song that you use each time you open the ritual and another that you use each time you close the ritual. That way, you have two established steps that you can rely on to mark both the beginning of the ritual and its end.

Even if you're not particularly musically inclined, you may want to release some energy by making your own sound for the ritual. If you don't have a musical instrument, you can use anything that makes noise — from an empty cereal box for percussion and an empty bottle as a wind instrument. And if you can't find something to use as an instrument, don't forget your voice. You can always recite words as a chant even if you can't carry a tune.

Performing a ceremony

Before starting the ceremony, take a few deep breaths to center yourself. Don't worry if you break down in tears at this point or any other during the ritual. After all, this ceremony is all about expressing your grief as openly and freely as possible, whenever you need to.

After opening the ritual, play the middle activities completely by ear. Sometimes you may need to communicate something to your loved one, and other times you may have nothing particular to say but have a great need to release pent-up emotions.

When you need to communicate, speak the words out loud or meditate on the thoughts silently. When you need to release your emotions, don't hold back. Yell, scream, whine, and cry as much as you need to. If you're feeling a great deal of anger as part of your grief, keep pillows nearby that you can pummel as you rail against whomever or whatever you hold responsible for your woeful situation.

You don't have to conduct your grief rituals all alone (unless you want or need to). This is a perfect time to share your grief with others, especially other friends and family members who are also grieving the same loss. If you share your ritual with others, they may find it a great comfort if you allow each person to relate something about your lost loved one, such as a description, story, or vignette (and yes, it's okay to include a funny story and have a laugh amid your tears).

Conduct your grief rituals and keep your memorial up as long as you need to use it. At some point when you're ready and your grief is finally subsiding, you will want to conclude your grief rituals. At that time, you may or may not want to dismantle the memorial as well. If you do decide to dismantle it, after concluding the final ritual, take down the memorial or shrine with the same loving care with which you erected it.

Expressing your grief creatively

Everyone's an artist in their own way. Some are good with words. Others have really vivid imaginations and are particularly gifted with visual images. Still others have an excellent sense of rhythm and stand out musically.

It doesn't matter in what area your gift lies or even whether you've let it lie idle for quite some time. You can draw upon anything in your artistic side to help you express your grief and, in the process, hopefully end up not only furthering your artistic sensibility but maybe even your artistic abilities.

Three major creative areas have great potential for the expression of grief: writing, the visual arts, and music. Within each of these areas, you can find dozens of ways to express your sorrow, tell your story, and begin to heal your grief.

Note: I purposely don't include primarily somatic activities such as drama, dance, athletics, and other disciplines for exercising and developing the body in this section. They're certainly creative activities, but I cover some of them in Chapter 15 in my discussion of the physical aspects of grief.

By their very nature, creative activities are both intuitive and experiential. This means that you need to let yourself go and let the creative process take over. Doing this makes it a great deal easier to get in touch with and then convey your feelings and also to discover how it is that you can exist outside the sorrow that has gripped your heart.

Using writing and words

Most of the writing you and I do aims to convey messages in the most clear and unambiguous way possible. When you're writing as a means for expressing your grief, however, you may want to forgo this very analytic approach in favor of adopting a more open, nonlinear, and poetic style.

Favor expressiveness in your writing at the expense of the content. In other words, it doesn't matter so much *what* you write as that you write from your heart. Obviously, your writings may center on your loved one and the relationship you shared, but your grief will also show through even if you're writing about something completely unrelated.

When thinking about topics to write about (either in prose or poetry), consider the following prompts:

- ✔ One of the best times I shared with you is . . .
- ✔ The first time I ever laid eyes on you, I . . .
- ✔ Your love is like . . .
- ✔ Life without you is like . . .
- ✔ The place where I want to you meet next is . . .
- ✔ Here's what I'll miss most: . . .
- ✔ Here's what's going on with me now: . . .

Explore your own topic ideas and add them to this list. At times, you may be too vulnerable emotionally to tackle some of these topics, but that doesn't really matter. In time, as your sorrow subsides, I guarantee that you'll tackle all these topics and more — either on paper or just in your head.

If you're not into poetry and writing essays reminds you just a tad too much of being back in school, try keeping a journal instead. Daily or even weekly journaling (or whenever you can manage it) is great because it captures your feelings on a regular basis and therefore enables you to chart your ups and downs over time. Journaling is also great because you can write as much or as little in each entry as your time and energy allow.

Using visual art and imagination

You've probably heard that old Chinese saying "A picture's worth 10,000 words." (Interestingly, this comes from a culture in which written words are all just little pictures!) If this adage is true and you have a knack for any kind of visual art (and there are plenty of them), you may find art to be one of the most efficient and satisfying ways to express your grief.

Visual art works so well for bereaved people of all ages (despite the fact that many grief professionals think of art only as a tool for grieving children). Visual arts enable you to convey emotions for which you have no words and sometimes reveal areas of pain and strength that you didn't know were there.

The other great thing is that some visual arts, such as watercolor painting and brush painting (and finger painting too, for that matter), require a great deal of spontaneity. You don't have the chance to overwork or overthink the execution of the piece, so you may be able to more easily reach and release submerged feelings.

Even visual arts such as photography that can require a lot of manual settings as well as a goodly amount of specialized skill in the end rely upon pure intuition in knowing what shot to go for and exactly when to take it.

Whatever visual art you practice, pursue it with as open a mind and heart as you can muster. Forgive all your mistakes and don't bother to judge the end results (it really doesn't matter if all your artwork ultimately gets consigned to the garbage heap). Concentrate solely on the process, and welcome all the stumbling blocks and impediments you encounter. You'll undoubtedly open yourself to many of the feelings of frustration and helplessness that your grief has brought to your life. By facing down these demons as they arise in the creative process, you may have half a chance of exorcising them from the rest of your life.

Using music and sound

Music is an extremely effective way of getting in touch with and giving voice to your grief. This goes for both the making of music, which includes playing instruments, singing, chanting, and listening to music as well.

You've probably had the experience of being transported to another place when listening to a particularly beautiful piece of music as well as being deeply moved emotionally during the experience. Music's ability to transport and move is what makes it such an effective grieving tool.

When selecting the music you want to make or listen to, choose music that uplifts you and transports you to some place out of time and space.

When selecting music that moves you, you have a choice between musical pieces that literally move you (in other words, inspire you to move rhythmically or to sing or dance along) and those that move you emotionally (most often to tears, especially when grieving). Of course, some music may move you both literally and emotionally.

Releasing Your Grief

The emotion most commonly associated with grief is sorrow — a profound and almost unending sadness over the loss. Although sorrow is the most common grief emotion, it's by no means the only one that bereaved people feel. They often have strong feelings of guilt, anger, and helplessness, too.

Sometimes these other dark emotions overshadow the sorrow in your grieving. When this is the case, I think it wise to deal with these emotions first so that they can't taint or derail the feelings of sadness that are at the heart of the grief.

In time, as your grieving comes to its end, your sense of deep sorrow dissipates, becoming a kind of sadness that's not so bad that you can't live with it. You need to understand, however, that this residual sadness may never go away, and you may have to live with it for the rest of your life. I like to think of this sadness as a kind of badge of courage (like the one the Lion got from the Wizard of Oz) that you wear always. It serves as a reminder that, although you do survive your grief over the loss, you never overcome missing the love you shared.

Dealing with feelings of anger and helplessness

I think of the relationship between helplessness, fear, and anger in this way: Fear's the mastermind of anger and helplessness is the mastermind of fear, and experiencing the death of a loved one is the quintessence of human helplessness. You first stand powerless to save your loved one from death, and then you're equally powerless to avoid the sorrow that comes from that loss.

You don't have to be what people offhandedly refer to as a "control freak" to be shaken to your very core by this degree of vulnerability. This is probably why so many bereaved people are as angry about the death as they are sad.

Naturally, because people like to think of themselves as "reasonable" beings, they spend lots of time finding good reasons for their anger. Instead of spending time on that, I think they'd probably be a lot better off simply admitting that the helplessness they feel as a result of the loss threatens them as nothing has before and that in the face of this threat, they're really angry.

Given the tight little bond between anger, fear, and helplessness, there are a couple of good and effective ways to deal with the anger that may come up when grieving:

✔ Find safe ways to vent and release your anger.

✔ Find ways to feel less helpless and more in control while grieving.

Venting anger safely

Anger is the epitome of a volatile or explosive emotion. As such, you need to find a safe and appropriate way to vent and release this emotion.

If you don't vent your anger properly, you run the risk of striking out blindly, hurting and alienating friends and family who are not in any way responsible and who you really need on your side in this time of sorrow. If you don't vent the anger at all, it has this nasty little habit of turning on you and eating you up inside.

Venting anger without hurting yourself or anybody else is relatively easy. Here are some suggestions of ways to release anger both when you're all on your own and when you're with other people:

✔ Gather together old pillows or string up a punching bag and have at it.

✔ Drive out to an isolated but safe part of the countryside or a vacant part of town, get out of your car, and yell your head off until you're hoarse.

✔ Participate in a martial arts class such as karate or tae kwon do and empower the movements with the energy from your anger.

✔ Take a particularly strenuous exercise class at your local gym and use all your anger to tough it out and make it through.

✔ Take a brisk walk to the park or around the block.

Feeling more in control when grieving

The best way I know to feel less helpless in the face of grief is to exercise some personal control over the grieving process. Decide that although you weren't given any choice in being bereaved, you're going to have a choice in how you grieve the death.

Anything you can do that enables you to fully express the emotions you feel without constantly being overwhelmed by them is bound to make you feel more on top of the grieving process (instead of the other way around). The goal here is ultimately to develop skills that allow you to remain buoyant as you express grief so that the emotions don't always take you under. You also need to remember to be gentle with yourself and cut yourself plenty of slack.

Ways to gain and retain a certain amount of control over your grieving include:

✔ Creating your own grief rituals that enable you to frame your grief by expressing it ceremoniously (refer to the section "Expressing grief through your own rituals," earlier in this chapter).

✔ Finding creative activities you can do that give full range to the expression of your grief (refer to the section "Expressing your grief creatively," earlier in this chapter).

✔ Sharing your grief with others, both one on one and in a group setting (see the section "Getting Help Expressing Your Grief," later in this chapter).

✔ Acquiring new physical skills that make you feel empowered (see Chapter 15).

For more suggestions of how to control your grief, check out Chapter 15.

Using forgiveness as a way to deal with guilt

Guilt related to the loss of a loved one comes in two rather insidious forms:

✔ Blaming someone else in whole or in part for the death of your loved one (as in the doctor, the hospital, the medical insurer, God, the weather, and on and on)

✔ Blaming yourself in whole or in part for the death of your loved one — including things that you did and didn't do for him

Neither one of these forms of guilt, however justified you feel it to be, is really conducive to helping the grieving process along. In fact, guilt more often than not staves off grieving and sometimes stops the process cold in its tracks.

Removing the poison arrow of guilt

Finding the reason for your pain isn't the same as dealing with the pain. In this way, although assigning blame for the loss may have its place, it in no way alleviates your need to grieve the loss.

I'm reminded of a parable that the Buddha told his disciples about a nobleman who was shot in the leg with a poison arrow. When his attendants were about to remove the arrow so they could staunch the poison and save his life, the nobleman stopped them cold. He told them that they could not remove the poison arrow until after they had identified exactly who shot the arrow and conveyed the reason for the shot to the nobleman. Of course, before his attendants could give their master the lowdown on who did the dirty deed and why, the nobleman died from the poison.

In terms of grieving, guilt is the poison arrow that some people refuse to remove. In my modest version of Buddha's parable, a bereaved person says that he must know exactly who's responsible for his terrible loss and why it occurred before he'll remove the arrow of guilt. And, of course, until he removes this arrow, he can't possibly staunch the poison of the grief, thereby saving himself by giving him back his life.

Finding your way to forgiveness

The only way I know to remove the guilt you feel about a profound loss is to exercise forgiveness. This is a really tough remedy for a lot of people to accept because they equate forgiveness with being weak (like a victim) and with exonerating those who really are responsible for their pain.

We've all become so used to wanting to exact justice (or even better, revenge) for any wrong done to us that sometimes I think that we've forgotten the damage that this need does to us. It isn't as it says in the Lord's Prayer — that we simply forgive others their debts just so that ours are forgiven in return. We need to forgive so that we don't have to be saddled with the weight of the emotional baggage that almost always accompanies the need for retribution.

When you're bereaved, you're already suffering under the weight of the sorrow you feel. Having to spend what little energy you have left playing pin the blame on the donkey seems like such a shame. Forgoing this game, if you can, leaves you much more power to deal with the real work of grieving: personalizing the loss and letting the grief it brings transform you.

Because forgiveness for yourself as well as others you hold responsible can be so difficult, this is often the time when you need to seek out the help of someone who is both impartial and trusted such as a grief counselor or other mental health professional. Sessions with such a professional can enable you to freely express all your feelings of guilt and blame (both toward yourself and others) as well as explore specific strategies for letting these feelings go.

Getting Help Expressing Your Grief

Grieving the loss of a loved one is a very personal experience and something only you can do yourself. Despite this fact, I don't think that you have to go it totally alone. Although it's a journey that only you can make, you can make the journey quite a bit easier by seeking out the help of others.

In seeking out help, you need to look principally for someone who can really listen to you and with whom you can freely share your feelings about the loss. This person can be a friend or acquaintance, but more likely than not it will be a professional grief counselor.

In addition to finding someone with whom you can share your feelings one on one, you may also want to attend a grief support group. A support group gives you the chance to share your feelings with others who are grieving their own losses (often of the same type as yours).

A support group affords you a good opportunity to share your struggles with grief and the story of your relationship with other empathetic and understanding people. It also enables you to learn from other bereaved people as they share their own stories and ups and downs in dealing with grief.

Finding someone who can really listen

When looking for a person who can really listen as you express your grief, ideally you want to find someone who fits all the following criteria:

- ✔ Someone not currently grieving his own loss, especially not the same loss as yours
- ✔ Someone neither uncomfortable with the subject of death nor uncomfortable with your displaying your feelings
- ✔ Someone with no agenda regarding your feelings or your grieving process

Usually these criteria rule out close friends because they're normally the ones who, although they may be willing to listen to your feelings, can't refrain from commenting on them and telling you honestly what they think of what you're saying and doing. Moreover, good friends have a definite agenda when it comes to your feelings and your grief: They all want you to be over the grief and happy again as soon as possible.

You may be wondering what's so bad about relying on a close friend who'll readily tell you his honest opinion. It's simply because you're not really seeking feedback on what you're saying so much as encouragement to keep expressing your feelings.

The primary purpose for finding someone to listen is so that you're able to speak about and vent all the feelings you have concerning your loss without reservation *and* without having to engage in a discussion about them. Ideally, your listener will validate your feelings when he can without evaluating them in any way. Getting the opportunity to express yourself in this manner lets you begin doing the hard work of piecing together what the loss really means to your life and, in so doing, begin releasing some of the sorrow and easing the pain.

If you have to rely upon friends as your listening post, be sure that you don't overburden them with your grief and burn them out on listening to you. Don't always call upon the same person to listen to your feelings, and seriously consider relying upon a grief counselor and/or a grief support group to give your friends a rest from providing this kind of support.

Seeking out professional help

Professional help with grieving is usually available to you in one of two forms:

- ✔ Specially trained grief counselors (most of whom are marriage and family therapists, psychologists, or licensed clinical social workers) who offer one on one counseling sessions
- ✔ Bereavement support group facilitators with training and experience in conducting different types of grief support groups

Both formats are designed to fully support you in grieving your loss as well as to offer you an opportunity to freely express your grief.

In deciding between one on one counseling and a support group, you first need to assess your comfort level in expressing your grief. If you don't think you'll be comfortable expressing your grief in a group situation, you probably should opt for one on one counseling.

Finding a grief counselor or support group in your local area

Probably the easiest way to find a qualified grief counselor or grief support group in your vicinity is to contact a hospice organization that operates in your local area. If your deceased loved one wasn't on hospice when he died, you can still make use of a hospice's grief support services (although you'll probably have to pay a nominal fee for the services).

To locate a hospice in your area on the Internet, enter "hospice near [your city and state]" (as in "hospice near Saint Louis, MO") into your favorite search engine. If you don't have Internet access, contact your physician. Most doctors are familiar with the hospices that they recommend for their terminal patients. (And if you find out that your doctor isn't familiar with any of the hospice organizations in your local area, you may want to seriously consider changing doctors!)

If your loved one was on hospice before he died, you and your immediate family members may have free access to the hospice's grief counseling and support group services. Some hospices offer up to a year of grief support to families of the people that have been on service.

If you don't have any luck finding grief support services through a local hospice (or you don't have a local hospice), then contact your local church, synagogue, mosque, or temple or the senior services that operate in your community. Sometimes these institutions offer their own grief support services (often in the form of bereavement support groups).

If you're looking for grief support services to help you with grieving the loss of a pet, you don't want to hook up with any human grief support services offered by your local hospice, religious institution, or senior service organization. Instead, you need to contact your local SPCA or animal control service to find out who in your local area offers one on one counseling or grief support for bereaved pet parents. People grieving a pet loss who try to use human grief support services (especially those who inadvertently get into bereavement support groups) are usually poorly received by the other members. Believe me, rather than face this kind of resentment, you definitely want to opt for the acceptance and understanding offered by local pet bereavement services.

Selecting the right grief support group for you

Bereavement support groups generally fall into one of the three following categories:

- ✔ **Open:** These groups are ongoing and often offer general bereavement support. They accept drop-in attendance and usually aren't restricted to a particular number of members.

- ✔ **Closed:** These groups run for a preset number of weekly sessions (generally between 6 and 12) and often are tailored to a particular type of loss. They require preregistration and usually are restricted to a set number of members (generally between 8 and 12).

- ✔ **Special:** These groups run for just a set number of sessions (sometimes as few as one or two) and are tailored to special topics such as Anticipatory Grief and Creativity and Grief. They require preregistration and usually are restricted to a set number of members (generally between 8 to 12).

Depending upon where you live, you may have the opportunity to choose between joining a general bereavement support group and a special loss group designed just for people suffering a particular type of loss. The most common types of special loss bereavement support groups are

- ✔ Parental loss group (for people who've lost a parent)
- ✔ Spousal/partner loss group (for people who have lost spouses, significant others, or life partners)
- ✔ Children loss group (for parents who have lost a child of any age)
- ✔ Children's group (for children who have lost parents or siblings)

The $64,000 question in terms of bereavement support groups is whether or not, given the chance, you should select a special loss support group that matches the type of loss you've suffered over a general bereavement group. If you select a special loss bereavement support group, you know that you'll be among people who understand firsthand the type of loss you've suffered. On the other hand, if you select a general bereavement support group, you'll probably be among people suffering a real variety of profound losses. The answer all comes down to your comfort level.

To join a general bereavement group, you need to be open to listening to people talk about a number of different types of losses. If you think you'd be more comfortable with people talking about a loss similar to your own, join the special loss bereavement group instead of the general one.

What to expect and not to expect from your grief support group

The facilitator or leader of your bereavement support group not only sets the tone of the group but also determines what, if any, agenda it follows. Many groups, especially open general bereavement support groups, have a cofacilitator in addition to the leader or main facilitator.

Because so much of the group's success depends upon the group leaders, it's very important that you be comfortable with their personalities and leadership style. Some group leaders are more organized and fastidious, while others are much more laissez-faire and easygoing. Each style, of course, has its own pros and cons. The important things are that you're comfortable with the style and that it doesn't interfere with your ability to express your feelings at the meetings.

At the first meeting of a closed support group, you can generally expect the group facilitator to do the following:

- ✔ **Review the purpose and goals of the group:** These can include sharing and giving support as well as providing educational information about grieving.

✔ **Explain the leader's role in the group:** This can include facilitating discussions and seeing that each member has an adequate opportunity to share.

✔ **Establish the group's ground rules by which it operates:** These generally include ensuring complete confidentiality for all that's said within the group and the equality and safety of each member. There also may be rules about being able to pass during a discussion and expected attendance.

✔ **Encourage discussion and answer all questions:** This generally includes making sure that all the members are clear on the group's ground rules and comfortable with its goals.

✔ **Introduce each of the members in the group:** This generally includes having each member tell why he or she is at the meeting, what they expect from the group, and what they have to offer other members.

✔ **Close the group:** This generally includes calling upon members to identify what they found significant during the meeting as well as a brief discussion of topics for future meetings.

In subsequent group sessions, the facilitator usually opens the session by revisiting the previous session to make sure that all loose ends are tied up from previous discussions before opening the present session to new discussions.

You can expect your bereavement support group facilitator to do the following:

✔ Fully listen to each member and provide appropriate direction to the group

✔ Apply knowledge and expertise in group processes and dynamics

✔ Model the behaviors that are desired in the group and openly share himself or herself with the group's members

✔ Apply and share knowledge and expertise about the process of grieving

In turn, as a member of the bereavement support group, you're usually expected to be willing to commit to do the following:

✔ Talk about yourself and share your feelings with others

✔ Listen to other group members as openly as possible

✔ Take responsibility for your own feelings

✔ Give and receive feedback

✔ Be constructive and work for the benefit of the group

Chapter 15

Exploring the Physical Side of Grief

I'd be willing to wager that you usually think of grieving as a mental or emotional process without stopping to consider its physical manifestations. People tend to forget that the feelings most commonly associated with grief are definitely demonstrated physically. Sadness is evident in weeping and the sounds of wailing or even yelling. Anger shows in tightened muscles, a red face, and even shortness of breath. Even grief-related emotions, such as helplessness, not normally associated with particular physical manifestations, can show in the body through a rather downcast and retiring demeanor.

This chapter takes a look at the physical aspects of grieving with an eye toward understanding how you can help your grieving process along through the use of various physical therapies and disciplines.

I begin the chapter with an examination of the physical effects that grieving typically has on bereaved people. Then I look at various soothing therapies, types of bodywork, and exercise that you can pursue to help reduce stress associated with grieving as well as to ameliorate the entire grieving process. I conclude with a look at a couple of the nontraditional body-related therapies that may bring you some good grief relief as well.

The Relationship between the Mental and Physical Aspects of Grief

After centuries of Western shortsightedness regarding the intimate relationship between body and mind, it seems as if we're finally rediscovering what our ancestors knew so well: namely, that body and mind are tightly integrated with one another. Thus, something that strongly affects the mind is ultimately bound to affect the body, and vice versa.

In light of this renewed understanding of the body/mind connection, the idea of a psychosomatic illness takes on a new dimension. Instead of referring to an imaginary illness, you can see it clearly as a process with discernible physical symptoms resulting directly from emotional stress or conflict. In this sense, you can regard grieving as the quintessence of a psychosomatic process (not necessarily a psychosomatic illness, however, because many people don't count grief as a type of injury or illness).

Typically, during grieving, a bereaved person's normal mental processes are disrupted at times by the following emotions:

- ✔ Sadness
- ✔ Anger
- ✔ Anxiety and guilt
- ✔ Apathy or depression

During the grieving process, a bereaved person often displays the following physical problems:

- ✔ Loss of appetite
- ✔ Difficulty concentrating and remembering
- ✔ Sleeplessness
- ✔ Fatigue
- ✔ Listlessness

While no one can establish an exact one-to-one cause and effect relationship between a bereaved person's typical emotions and typical physical problems, you can see how these kinds of emotions, especially when they're as overpowering as they often are at the outset of the loss, may induce these kinds of standard physical conditions. And if you're someone who suffers from some other physical weakness or ailment (such as diabetes, heart problems, or high blood pressure), you need to very mindful of ways in which this added stress can impact your condition.

In addition to the outright physical conditions that mental stress can induce sometimes during grieving, you also may have to contend with temporary, anxiety-related physical conditions that suddenly come over you while grieving. These can range from simple chest pains and shortness of breath all the way to full-blown panic attacks, when you feel like you can't get any breath and your heartbeat races uncontrollably.

Soothing Therapies

As regards grieving, soothing therapies are any therapies that either alleviate the grief emotions or help you to release them. They include meditative or deep-breathing exercises that can help you reduce grief-related stress (and are often the only way to counteract anxiety-induced physical conditions).

Getting a massage is another great soothing therapy. This massage can be one that you give yourself, a simple backrub you get from a friend or family member, or a professional massage.

Doing meditative deep-breathing exercises

Breathing is such a fundamental physical process that it's often considered synonymous with life itself. Breathing is also one of these few bodily functions that, although normally regulated automatically, your mind can consciously take over and direct as well.

Each breath you take consists of two distinct phases:

- ✔ **Inhaling,** when you take new air into the lungs (so that your body can take needed oxygen into your bloodstream)
- ✔ **Exhaling,** when you expel used air (so that your body can force out unneeded and harmful carbon dioxide along with a little water moisture)

To help reduce anxiety-induced stress that may crop up from time to time when grieving a profound loss, you may want to start practicing meditative breathing. This is breathing in which you exert conscious control over both the inhaling and exhaling phases, calming and slowing them down in order to breathe as deeply and as thoroughly as possible. Here are some tips for meditative breathing:

- ✔ To help you slow down your breathing, count silently to yourself as you inhale and exhale during each breath. Begin with a count of five for each phase, and slowly work up to a count of ten. At the end of each phase, be sure to pause for at least one count before beginning the alternate phase.

✔ When inhaling a new breath, be aware of filling the lungs from the bottom to top by releasing your diaphragm muscle above your belly and allowing your chest to naturally expand upward and outward with air.

✔ When exhaling used air, be aware of emptying the lungs from bottom to top, this time by contracting the diaphragm muscle to push the air out as your chest shrinks and falls a bit.

As you slow down your breathing in this manner, you should also feel a release of tension first in your chest and then in the rest of your upper body. If you do this breathing long enough, this release of tension will spread to the rest of your body, and your mind will definitely relax. Just make sure that your shoulders don't start rising and falling as you inhale and exhale — you want to keep the shoulders down and relaxed at all times during deep breathing.

Deep, meditative breathing can be quite effective after only a few minutes' time. I suggest that you start out breathing in this manner for no more than two to five minutes. As you feel comfortable with the practice, extend the period to ten minutes. If you create your own grief ritual, consider making meditative deep breathing part of the opening and closing of the ritual (see Chapter 14 for details).

When you count as you inhale and exhale, stray thoughts (maybe some even having to do with your grief) may come into your mind, interfering with and throwing off your count. When you lose count, just start over again from one and don't follow the thought any further. In this way, you start training yourself to stay focused on the task at hand (breathing, in this case) and release thoughts that you don't want to pursue at the time.

Massaging away the tension

There's nothing like a good massage to melt those awful tensions away. (Just thinking about it while I'm banging away at this keyboard has me wanting one real bad.) In the hands of a talented and qualified masseur, you can get rid of plenty of unwanted stress in your body, whether it's there because of grief, your job, or just the busy pace of life in general.

The only problems with professional massage are that it's by appointment only and can be pretty expensive. If you can't wait for a scheduled time when a masseur can work on you, or if you simply can't afford his services, then you'll have to make do with either self-massage or nonprofessional rubs you can cajole out of your friends and loved ones.

Check out *Massage For Dummies* by Steve Capellini and Michel Van Welden (Wiley) for how-to information on both giving and receiving massage.

Professional massage

If you've never had a professional massage before, you need to let the masseur know that, and be sure to communicate well with him or her about how deep to go as well as any really sensitive areas or physical injuries you've sustained.

The only thing you need to be acutely aware of when getting a professional massage during the time you're grieving a profound loss is that massage can release not only pent-up physical tensions in the body but emotions as well. Because this is a time when you're probably exceptionally vulnerable emotionally, you may find that various types of deep-tissue massage are more than you can handle at this time; such therapies often trigger deeply held emotions and cause them to surface.

Self-massage

You don't have to think of self-massage as a poor-man's massage so much as one where you both give and get immediate feedback. After all, because you're both pressing the flesh and simultaneously receiving the touch, you immediately know when you're applying too much or too little pressure to any area.

You can do effective self-massage to any of three following areas of the body:

- **Face and head** (part of Shiatsu self-massage): For tension, place your two thumbs on your temples at the side of your face and your other fingers on the top of your head. With very gentle pressure rotate your thumbs to massage your temples. You can also relieve tension by using the knuckles of both hands to gently drum on the head with very light and rhythmic movements.

  To relieve eye fatigue, place your palms over your eyes with the fingers outstretched and your thumbs on your temples, and then press the hands gently on the face and hold.

- **Hands** (hand reflexology): For relaxation, hold one hand with the other, placing the thumb of one hand in the center of the other palm and the other fingers on the back of the hand. Use the thumb to gently massage the entire palm area.

  To increase energy flow in the body, use your hands to gently massage the pads and the areas between each finger, giving special attention to the area between the thumb and the forefinger.

- **Feet** (foot reflexology): For relaxation, hold one foot in both of your hands with your thumbs pressing the sole of the foot, and then rub the bottom of your foot rigorously.

  To increase energy flow in the body, use your hands to separate and carefully massage the area between each toe.

Some folks think it's possible to do effective self-massage to your own shoulders (using opposite hands, of course). I have to disagree because I think it's really difficult to get sufficient leverage to do a really good job. I recommend that you stick to massaging the body parts listed here and turn to a professional for massage in other areas.

Pursuing Transformative Bodywork

There are more physical techniques designed to reduce tension and advance better functioning than you can shake a stick at (there's probably one that even uses sticks!). These include such diverse bodywork and movement techniques as Rolfing, the Rosen Method, the Feldenkrais Method, and Alexander Technique.

Transformative body techniques such as these generally promote body awareness in the performance of each movement. Some such as Rolfing and the Rosen Method consist primarily of touch therapies designed to release long-held tension and stress as well as help release chronic pain.

Others such as the Feldenkrais Method and Alexander Technique consist primarily of movement therapies designed again to release long-held tensions as well promote more-efficient physical functioning in the form of increased flexibility and more-fluid, less-strenuous movement, as well as a greater range of movement.

All these various bodywork and movement methods are designed to transform your awareness of your body as well as promote a release of tension and the lessening of any pain. When you're grieving, these therapies also can be very helpful in releasing pent-up grief emotions.

Releasing stress and pain with Rolfing and the Rosen Method

Created by Dr. Ida P. Rolf (1896–1979), Rolfing is officially known by the much loftier name of Structural Integration of the Human Body. Rolfing takes into account how gravity affects the body and deals primarily with restriction of movement caused by the connective tissue (rather than the muscles). Rolfing can include a number of sessions in which a trained rolfer seeks to unlock stress and pain throughout the body.

The tissue work in Rolfing can be quite intense, and this type of bodywork has earned a reputation for sometimes being pretty painful. This is especially true in particularly tense areas of the body or areas where you've sustained an old injury.

In contrast, the Rosen Method is known for its use of gentle direct touch rather than intense muscle or tissue manipulation. Despite that difference, the goal of the Rosen Method is very similar to that of Rolfing: namely, the release of muscle tension, the increase of flexibility and body awareness, and the lessening of chronic pain. The Rosen Method operates on the basic theory that muscle tension often has psychological roots and therefore emotions are often released along with pent-up muscular tension.

Augmented functioning thanks to the Feldenkrais Method and Alexander Technique

Created by Moshe Feldenkrais (1904–1984), the Feldenkrais Method primarily is a learning process intended to promote increased awareness in body movement; it's based on the assumption that improving one's movement improves one's overall well-being and attitude toward life. The Feldenkrais Method is renowned for its understanding of the relationship between intending a movement, imagining the movement, and actually making the movement.

The Feldenkrais Method isn't a therapeutic technique like Rolfing or the Rosen Method but rather is a learning system dedicated to teaching you how to be aware of the integration of body and mind and through this to simultaneously improve your physical functioning and your mental outlook. As such, it's comprised of a great number of experience-oriented lessons. (Some Feldenkrais students spend hundreds of hours in training!)

Alexander Technique was created by Frederick Matthias Alexander (1869–1955), a Shakespearean actor who developed his system of body awareness and movement based on his own experience correcting his problems with chronic laryngitis. Like the Feldenkrais Method, Alexander Technique is a way of learning to increase body awareness and simultaneously reduce unnecessary tension.

Alexander Technique is normally taught through private lessons with a trained facilitator. These lessons teach the student to observe how his habitual ways of sitting, moving, and standing can be expanded or modified to release tension and pain. Note that you can apply the benefits taught by this technique to a whole array of activities — from creative endeavors including athletics, acting, dancing, singing, and playing a musical instrument to more mundane undertakings such as recovering from a physical injury and working long hours at a computer.

To get more information about any of these body techniques and to find a local class or instructor, check out the following Web sites:

- **Feldenkrais Movement Institute** at www.feldenkraisinstitute.org
- **The Rosen Institute** at www.rosenmethod.org
- **American Society for Alexander Technique (AmSat)** at www.alexandertech.org

Practicing Meditative Body Movement

Eastern body movements systems such as yoga and Taijiquan (t'ai chi chuan) and martial arts such as karate, judo, and tae kwon do attempt to integrate body movement with breath and awareness. Taking classes in any of these meditative body movements systems is a good activity for someone grieving the profound loss of a loved one.

The best thing about these kinds of body-development systems is that they challenge and develop you mentally as well as physically. The mental portion of these disciplines, while it may initially prove a challenge if you're having trouble concentrating in your grief, ultimately can be just as helpful as the physical exercise in supporting the grieving process and keeping it moving along.

Doing yoga

Yoga is one of the most well-known and popular forms of Indian philosophical/spiritual practices pursued in the West. Even if you've never attended a yoga class in your life, I'll bet you have a mental picture of the human-pretzel-type postures (called *asanas*) that are part of the practice.

Yoga, however, is so much more than eccentric, rather painful-looking poses. It also includes a whole diet system and full-blown meditation with lots of concentration on deep breathing similar to the exercise outlined in the earlier section "Doing meditative deep-breathing exercises."

The great thing about yoga is that it's for people of all ages and physical skill levels. Moreover, given its popularity, you're bound to find a teacher or a class that suits your particular needs (just check with your local YMCA, community center, or junior college). Keep in mind that yoga has many schools, each of which has its own slightly different way of teaching the basic postures and integrating them with other aspects of yoga including breathing and meditation. One school, iyengar yoga, even lets students use props (including belts and chairs) to help them attain some of the physical postures; the assists can be very helpful if you're at a stage in your life when you're not particularly flexible. Take the time to find a class that's right for you.

Even if you only dabble with the physical part of it (generally referred to as *hatha yoga*), yoga has many benefits for you as a grieving person. The most important benefits are increased flexibility and better circulation, which can help you release stress and tension as well as increase your overall energy level.

Perhaps the most important thing about hatha yoga is the way it can help improve your self-image. Mastering the postures and breathing can definitely help you focus and enhance your powers of concentration, which, in turn, can't help but make you feel a little bit more in control of your life.

Learning Taiji

Although technically a martial art, most people think of Taiji (which you may be more familiar with as t'ai chi chuan or simply t'ai chi) as an exercise discipline whose movements are performed in a synchronized group in very slow motion. Perhaps the most common mental image of Taiji is that of a bunch of senior citizens all doing the forms very slowly together outside in a park.

Like yoga, Taiji helps you maintain mental agility as well as physical flexibility. Because its forms are normally performed very slowly and methodically, it's a perfect discipline for older people who aren't able to keep up with some of the faster paced and more demanding exercise and martial art forms.

Ideally, you assume a stance with a low center of gravity and let all the movements come from the body's center or core (the area immediately beneath the belly). This stance not only promotes the psychological feeling of being centered and balanced both in stillness and motion but also is said to improve circulation and increase flexibility in all the body's joints.

The main drawback to Taijiquan is that it's quite complex, with many distinct movements to learn (usually between 88 and 108). This can represent quite a commitment in terms of class time and concentration. If you don't have time to commit to learning the full Taiji, you may want to look into taking a qigong (ch'i kung) class or seminar. This Chinese discipline also combines breathing, concentration, and movements to promote better health, but its movement sequences are normally much less complex than in Taiji.

T'ai Chi For Dummies, by Therese Iknoian with Manny Fuentes (Wiley), is an excellent beginner's guide to Taiji; it also contains some instruction on qigong and combining the two forms.

Doing other martial arts

Taiji appeals to folks of all ages because of the relaxed and slow nature of its movements, but by no means is it the only martial art that you can pursue to obtain some relief when grieving.

In fact, if you're experiencing a lot of anger along with the sadness or you just have a lot of unharnessed energy (the opposite of the listlessness often experienced as a part of grief), consider a more energetic martial art. You may get more benefit from an activity that not only makes use of more energetic movements but also enables you to test your mental and physical agility directly against an opponent.

Here's a short list of some other popular martial art forms whose movements tend to be a bit more energetic than Taiji and which are known more for their hand-to-hand (or even hand-to-foot) contests:

- **Karate:** Japanese martial art known for quick strikes that can include a whole bunch of punches and kicks
- **Judo:** Japanese martial art known for throws, pins, and locks (punches and kicks aren't allowed)
- **Tae kwon do:** Korean martial art known for fast and powerful kicks and punches

Note that all three of these martial arts burn up a lot of energy, offer you a safe way to release some pent-up frustration, and instill a new level of self-confidence and feeling of control over your destiny. For this reason, these kinds of martial arts can be particularly well-suited for grieving folks of both genders who need to release pent-up emotions but also need a little boost in their self-confidence.

Physical Exercise

If none of the fancy-Dan bodywork and movement systems described earlier in this chapter appeal to you, there's always good old-fashioned physical exercise. This can be anything from taking a walk around the block or jogging in the park to doing calisthenics or participating in some sort of team sport. Although calisthenics and traditional sports aren't normally thought of as being particularly meditative, you need not approach them this way. Indeed, you can bring a new level of awareness both in terms of breathing and body movement to any exercise routine you do or physical game you play (note that playing Xbox or Playstation doesn't count).

The problem you may run into is that, if you're the type of person who has trouble motivating yourself to do routine exercise when you're not grieving, you may find it nigh unto impossible to get yourself motivated to do it when you're suffering the emotional imbalances that come with grief (especially the listlessness).

If this is your case, you may need to get take a class that offers a favored physical activity or join a team sport so that you get outside encouragement and reinforcement (from the class instructor or coach and fellow classmates or teammates) to help keep you motivated.

Doing cardio and strength training

When I think of getting physical exercise, I usually think of going to the gym to get a good cardiovascular (also known as *aerobic,* meaning "with oxygen") workout on a treadmill as well as to strength train by lifting weights or using one of the many resistance-type weight machines.

As you're probably well aware, a cardiovascular workout is great for the health of the old ticker because it gets more oxygen into the blood and more blood to the heart. Some kind of aerobic exercise is considered essential to physical fitness — although there are tons of ways to get this kind of exercise without walking or running like a gerbil on a treadmill (such as bicycling, running, and swimming, to name a few).

Strength training, which is considered an *anaerobic* (without oxygen) exercise, is used to strengthen and shape different muscle groups. You can do this type of exercise by lifting weights or by using some sort of resistance mechanism, which can be anything from a sophisticated weight machine to a simple elastic band.

Note that strength training is good not only for building up particular muscles but also for increasing bone density, both of which can help improve your overall posture. The only downside to strength training is that while it goes about increasing the bulk and density of particular muscles, it does nothing to enhance their flexibility. Therefore, if you get serious about strength training, you may also want to do stretching exercises to maintain flexibility.

If you're not at all interested in bulking up your muscles but want to increase your strength and maintain flexibility, consider a Pilates exercise program. Pilates is said to strengthen the muscles without adding undue bulk to them. It's also known for its emphasis on maintaining body awareness and breath control during all phases of movement, both of which are especially beneficial for folks dealing with grief.

Playing sports

Sports are great forms of exercise if you're grieving because you participate with other people either in teams or as individual competitors and because sports normally challenge you both mentally as well as physically.

It doesn't really matter which sport you select; it can be something as tame as pee-wee golf, as artistic as ballroom dancing, or as thrilling as skateboarding and whitewater rafting. The biggest reward for a bereaved person participating in the sport comes from the pure enjoyment of doing the activity. It gives you both a needed respite from the grief and a chance to release some pent-up frustration.

The competitive aspect of many sports, whether played in teams (like soccer and baseball) or against a sole competitor (like handball and tennis), also may be beneficial for a person who's grieving. Whether you win or lose, competition can help you release emotions surrounding grief, help improve your self-confidence, and help you regain the sense of being in control of your fate again.

Doing activities that get you back to nature

Sometimes the best form of physical therapy is one that's also good for the spirit. Here, I'm thinking of any physical activity that gets you back into nature. Depending upon where you live, this can mean taking a simple walk in a local park, horseback riding out in the country, or doing something as challenging as backpacking and rock climbing in the mountains.

Combining much needed physical exercise with the opportunity to re-experience the beauty and wonder of nature can do you a world of good when you're grieving a profound loss. Being back in nature presents you with a new, more open perspective from which to process your grief. It also can help reconnect you with the bigger process of life, of which you're still a vital part.

Going with Nontraditional Body Therapies

Twenty years ago, Eastern physical disciplines such as yoga and Taiji might have been considered really "out there." Yet, nowadays they're looked at as no more exotic than learning to golf or going swimming.

So too, alternative body therapies such as aromatherapy and acupressure (also known as Shiatsu), which today are often seen as being either pseudo-scientific or, in some cases, downright nonscientific, may be regarded tomorrow as no more controversial than taking aspirin for a headache. This section covers using aromatherapy and acupressure in case you have the desire to try something less traditional to help you with grieving.

Calming your senses with aromatherapy

Aromatherapy is the name given to the use of essential oils from various plants to relieve pain and increase your sense of well-being. Sometimes these oils are applied to the skin in hopes of attaining pain relief; other times, they're heated (often in diffusers or dishes warmed by candles) to release scents into the air.

Although most of the evidence for the effectiveness of aromatherapy is anecdotal and many doctors attribute any benefit to the placebo effect (or psychosomatic, to get technical), none of that really matters when you're dealing with grief. The bottom line is if these aromas soothe your physical or psychological pain in grieving, it's not so terribly relevant whether the benefit actually comes from the fragrances themselves or from your faith in their ability to provide this relief.

Here are some of the more popular essential oils that you may want to try out, along with the purported benefits that they bestow:

- ✔ **Basil:** Considered good for nervous exhaustion and depression

- ✔ **Lavender:** Considered good for calming strong emotions such as anger, panic, and insomnia

- ✔ **Rose:** Considered to be an aid in healing emotional wounds and good at relieving sorrow and depression

- ✔ **Rosemary:** Considered to be an aid to confidence and creativity as well as good in calming nightmares and helping you remember good dreams

- ✔ **Sandalwood:** Considered to be an aid to meditation and concentration as well as good for calming nervousness

Don't ever take any essential oils internally (not even ones like basil that you would normally use in your spaghetti sauce in abundance). Also, many essential oils are irritating to the skin, so you should never put them directly on your skin. Instead, add a drop or two to your bath water or use a diffuser to release their aromas.

For information about aromatherapy and how you can use scents to help you relax, check out *Aromatherapy For Dummies* by Kathi Keville (Wiley).

Getting holistic help from acupressure

Acupressure is derived from traditional Chinese medicine. The purpose of acupressure is to stimulate particular pressure points in order to correct certain energy imbalances in the body, thereby relieving pain and restoring health. Although it utilizes the same meridians and pressure points as acupuncture, it uses either hand or elbow pressure instead of needles to stimulate the energy.

Although many Western scientists and physicians remain skeptical of the effectiveness of both acupuncture and acupressure, both therapies are gaining more and more converts as purely anecdotal evidence gives way to medical studies.

Also known in the Japanese form of Shiatsu (meaning "finger pressure"), acupressure is reported not only to relieve tension but also to promote overall health and well-being by increasing the circulation of vital energy throughout the body. To get a taste for what Shiatsu can do for you, try my face and head self-massage techniques that appear in the section "Massaging away the tension," earlier in this chapter. For more information on acupressure and referrals to practitioners, check out the Acupressure Institute Web site at www.acupressure.com.

Chapter 16

Coping with Holidays and Anniversaries

. . . .

In This Chapter

▶ Getting through major and minor holidays without your loved one

▶ Observing birthdays and anniversaries

▶ Creating your own anniversary celebrations after a loss

. . . .

Getting through holidays is often a tough enough job on its own without adding the extra burden of grieving a profound loss. When you're grieving a loss, especially a new one, the entire annual cycle of holidays, birthdays, and other anniversaries can be very trying and painful and a real challenge to get through.

Normally, holidays, birthdays, and anniversaries are days of celebration, in the sense of both merriment and remembrance. When you're grieving the loss of a loved one with whom or for whom you celebrated these days, however, such days are completely devoid of festivity but remain full of memories. Many of these memories are extremely painful because they remind you how alone you are on a day you would otherwise spend with your loved one.

This chapter looks at some of the typical challenges that arise when special days roll around, particularly in the first year of the loss. I guide you through some strategies you can employ to deal with the concerted grief that these days bring and, hopefully, also convert them from particularly miserable days into special celebratory days. If you can't turn a holiday or anniversary into an honest-to-goodness festivity, then you can at least aim for a constructive kind of commemoration (although it's perfectly okay if you can manage nothing more than simply getting through the day).

Why Holidays Can Be Difficult

Under the best circumstances, holidays are festive times when family and friends gather together to enjoy each other's company and love as they commemorate some special event. Secular or religious, this special event just has to be an occasion deemed worthy of observance in the senses of remembrance and making merry.

Holidays are particularly awkward times for people grieving a profound loss because someone with whom you generally celebrate the day is not present. This absence makes it difficult to enjoy the day and almost impossible not to be reminded of the loss. And because so many holidays are public celebrations where you interact with other people (sometimes lots of other people), it may be difficult when all you want to do is hide and grieve.

When talking about holidays, most people make a pretty big distinction between the string of holidays that occur in the last few months of the year (which are often just referred to as "the holidays") and all the other holidays spread out over the rest of the year. When you're grieving, these end-of-year holidays can be particularly grueling, especially in the first few years immediately following the loss.

In surviving holidays after the loss of a loved one, you may find it works better for you to try and meet each one head-on with a touch of grace and grit rather than trying to avoid it. (Of course, if you find yourself too exhausted from the grieving one year to do anything more than lie low, then by all means cut yourself the necessary slack and realize that you may well be able to manage this approach next year.) If you're able to face holidays head-on, I suggest that you celebrate them with the loved one in mind. Use the celebration to remember and honor your loved one, keeping in mind that, for the time being, you're under absolutely no obligation to enjoy these special days; you just have to get through them.

Dealing with the End-of-the-Year Holidays

For the folks living in the Northern Hemisphere, the holidays celebrated in fast succession in the last three months of the year are winter holidays. These holidays are celebrated in times when the hours of darkness, storms, and cold are increasing and when vegetation is dying back and nature is going into hibernation.

As such, these holidays have a certain amount of solemnity built into them. This may be part of the reason that they sometimes involve rather intense and expressive celebrations that most people find very important. If you're grieving the loss of a loved one during this time, you have to deal with the general gloominess of the season as well as with a certain amount of garishness built into the celebrations.

Halloween and the Day of the Dead

The first end-of-the year holiday you encounter is Halloween, a holiday that could be a particularly appropriate celebration for bereaved people. But in the United States, at least, Halloween has become primarily a children's holiday associated as much with begging for sweets and the more macabre aspects of death as with honoring and remembering the dead.

Because children commonly dress up in costume and go trick-or-treating to neighborhood houses for Halloween, if you're grieving the loss of a young child, you may have a particularly difficult time with this aspect of the celebration. Make sure that you're away from home that night so that you don't have to deal with all the children who visit or feel that you have to hide out and not answer the door.

In Mexico and other South American countries, Halloween is intimately tied to the celebration of the Day of the Dead on November 1 (All Saints' Day in the Catholic Church), a day when people honor deceased ancestors by visiting their graves and making offerings of food, drink, flowers, and candles (see Chapter 17 for more on this celebration).

Consider borrowing a page from the Day of the Dead and making Halloween a celebration that honors all your loved ones who have passed on. If the weather's too harsh to actually visit their graves, or if you don't live anywhere near them, create an altar by decorating a spot in your house with candles and flowers and maybe even pictures of your loved ones.

Thanksgiving

Next up on the end-of-the-year holiday calendar is Thanksgiving (at least in the U.S., as Canadian Thanksgiving comes earlier in October). This is the first of the holidays in which family traditions may play a part in making the day especially difficult to get through without your lost loved one.

Family members traditionally travel to gather together for Thanksgiving, and traditions usually include hosting or helping to prepare a special dinner. Not having your loved one may make this holiday tremendously difficult or even impossible to get through if he acted as the traditional host of the celebration.

Bereaved people often struggle with this holiday in part because many families routinely set aside time at the table to reflect upon and recount the blessings they've enjoyed during the preceding year. The loss of a loved one makes for a year that comes up short in the blessings department. If this is your family tradition, you may want to alter it slightly: Have each person at the table recount the blessings that they received as a result of having the lost loved one in their lives.

For the first Thanksgiving after the loss, you may find more comfort in keeping in place the established family tradition for the meal (assuming that's still possible). If you do, you may want to set a place for your loved one at the table and have the family talk about and toast your loved one before eating. For the second Thanksgiving, I suggest that you intentionally modify the traditional meal either in terms of the menu or where you gather while still remembering and toasting your lost loved one.

Christmas, Hanukkah, and Kwanzaa

The major holidays celebrated in December include Christmas in the Christian tradition, Hanukkah in the Jewish tradition, and Kwanzaa in the African American tradition. In addition, a few people still celebrate the winter solstice (the shortest day of the year) in the form of some sort of yule celebration.

These are often the hardest holidays to get through because they carry the most pressure to make merry and have a good time. Especially in industrialized countries, Christmas is a particularly glitzy affair that's impossible to avoid — signs literally appear everywhere and throughout all the media as merchandisers try to sell, sell, sell.

Because gift giving is such a big part of Christmas (and is becoming more and more important in some Hanukkah celebrations), you need to be especially careful not to give into the temptation to overspend in hopes of shopping your way out of your sorrow. If you have children, keep in mind that you can't buy bereaved children out of their grief anymore than you can shop your way out of it.

For the first Christmas, Hanukkah, or Kwanzaa after the loss, you may find it more comforting to continue your established holiday traditions with your immediate family, even if you need to cut back on or cut out entirely other parties and social gatherings. If you put up stockings for Christmas, be sure to have a stocking for your lost loved one that you can fill with things that remind you of him or messages containing anecdotes and stories of favorite Christmases you spent together. If you light candles on a menorah, be sure to remember your loved one on each of the eight days. If you light candles or pass around a chalice during the celebration of the seven days of Kwanzaa, be sure to remember your lost loved one before lighting them or taking a sip from the *kikombe cha umoja.*

New Year's Day

New Year's completes the string of year-end holidays. In the first year after the loss, this is the one celebration when you may want to forgo all previously established traditions because it's the one holiday normally celebrated with public parties and other types of get-togethers that will probably be too much to manage at this time. For example, if you normally host a New Year's Eve party, consider canceling it, and if you usually go out to a party or fancy restaurant, consider staying home.

Instead of exuberant celebration, make this a time of quiet reflection. New Year's Day is usually the time for making resolutions for the year ahead, so you may benefit from remembering a particular quality that your loved one embodied that you would like to possess in such abundance. Make it your New Year's resolution to work hard on cultivating that quality in yourself during the forthcoming year.

Dealing with the Rest of the Holidays

After contemplating the difficulties of getting through the slew of holidays all bunched together at the end of the year, you may think that holding up through the remainder of the holidays that are spread out over the rest of the year would be a piece of cake. But that's not quite the case.

Although it helps that these other holidays are celebrated during times of extended daylight hours and often much milder temperatures, depending upon the particular loss and the nature of the relationship, the remaining holidays may not pass by any smoother than those at the end of the year.

Valentine's Day

Valentine's Day is a celebration of love. Although ostensibly a holiday set aside specifically for romantic lovers, Valentine's Day has come to include all types of love. You can see the pervasiveness of the spirit of Valentine's Day in the exchange of Valentine's messages, candies, and even stuffed animals between children, friends, parents and their children, and lovers.

Given the holiday's theme of love, February 14 is especially painful for those suffering the loss of a spouse or partner as a result of divorce or death. However, Valentine's Day can be equally difficult if you're suffering any other kind of profound loss because love is part of your relationship and one of the things you miss and mourn for in your grief.

View Valentine's Day as an occasion for reflecting upon all the love you received from your lost loved one and giving thanks for that love. Also, contemplate this love as being the one thing that lives on beyond the death and one thing that will sustain you through your grief.

Easter and Pesach

The spring season brings with it two religiously inspired holidays: Easter in the Christian faith and Pesach (Passover) in the Jewish religion. For believers, these holidays represent renewal of God's power in history; for Easter, it's God's power to free His people from slavery, and for Pesach, it's God's power to free them from death. Because of the spring timing of these celebrations, the underlying renewal theme is reinforced in nature by the regeneration of vegetation (at least in the Northern Hemisphere).

Bereaved people of faith can find comfort in celebrating these holidays even if their sorrow doesn't allow them to celebrate as fully as they might otherwise. Christian believers may be reassured by Christ's deliverance from the grave and may find hope in being reunited in due time with their loved ones in the Kingdom of Heaven. Jewish believers may be reassured by God's deliverance of their ancestors from bondage and may find hope in being reunited with their loved ones in the World to Come.

Mother's Day and Father's Day

Mother's Day and Father's Day are opportunities to honor the love and sacrifice that mothers and fathers routinely make for their children. As such, they're traditionally occasions when children show their affection for their parents with cards, gifts, dinners out, or all of the above.

As you can imagine, these two holidays are particularly difficult both for children or adults grieving the recent loss of a parent and for mothers and fathers grieving the loss of a child.

Children who have recently lost their mothers or fathers feel the loss intensely on the respective days because they're reminded that they no longer have a living parent to fete. Parents grieving the losses of children can also feel the loss intensely on their special days; they're reminded of their losses on the days when their children would have honored them.

If you're a son or daughter grieving the loss of a parent on Mother's or Father's Day, use the day to remember your parent and reflect on all the love and support you received from her or him. If you're a parent grieving the loss of a son or daughter, reflect on all the love your child engendered in you as well as all the qualities that made your child so special.

U.S. national holidays

Major U.S. national holidays honor the birth of the nation as well as the men and women who have sacrificed their lives in military service. These national holidays include:

- **Independence Day** on July 4 to mark the birth of the nation
- **Veteran's Day** on November 11 to mark the end of World War I and to commemorate those who died in that war
- **Memorial Day** on the last Monday in May to honor all servicemen and servicewomen who have given their lives serving their country

These national holidays can be particularly stressful if your loved one died in military service. When this is the case, it's inevitable that the observances of these holidays remind you of your loss.

Note that Independence Day also can be a source of difficulty for those grieving losses unrelated to military service because it's a time when family and friends routinely get together to celebrate the day and focus on having fun (which may be the last thing you want to do).

People who have lost loved ones in military service can take some comfort from the fact that their fellow countrymen overwhelmingly support them in their time of grief and deeply appreciate the sacrifices that their loved ones (children, parents, siblings, or friends) made on behalf of their country.

Surviving Anniversaries

Anniversaries in the form of birthdays, death days, wedding days, graduation days, and other days marking milestones in a life can be even more difficult to deal with than holidays when you're grieving. After all, anniversaries usually mark much more private events that, without the loved one's presence, are difficult or even impossible to continue observing.

The best way to approach the anniversaries you routinely celebrated with your lost loved one is to continue to mark these days as special occasions for remembrance and reflection. Instead of celebrating these days, use them as opportunities to think carefully about all the things you miss as well as all the things you shared.

Birthdays and anniversaries of the death

During a loved one's lifetime, his birthday is one of the most important anniversaries that you mark and celebrate together. After his passing, especially in the first few years, this particular day is very sad because it reminds you of the death and often heightens the grief you suffer.

The anniversary of a loved one's death also marks an important milestone in mourning his passing. In various religious traditions (see Chapter 17), this anniversary date is meticulously commemorated with a grave-site ceremony, especially on the first-year anniversary (known as the Jahrzeit in Judaism).

I strongly suggest that you be quite proactive about observing both the birthday of a lost loved one and the anniversary of his death. If the idea of performing your own grief ritual (as I outline in Chapter 14) is something that appeals to you, these days are perfect occasions on which to do so. If rituals aren't your cup of tea, you can still mark these days in your own way. As part of these observances, you may want to reflect upon the significance that your loved one had in your life and the way in which you intend to keep those qualities alive in the rest of your life.

Other anniversaries

Depending upon the relationship you shared with your lost loved one, you may have other special days (in addition to birthdays and death anniversaries) that bring his absence to the forefront of your consciousness.

These anniversary days can mark big events in your shared lives.

> ✔ **If you're mourning the passing of a spouse or partner,** you may need to face the anniversaries of the day you met your loved one and the day you wed. You also can mark smaller, even more intimate anniversaries such as the day you moved in together, bought your first house, or took your first overseas vacation.

> ✔ **If you're a parent mourning the loss of a child,** personal anniversaries can include the day the child took his first step, graduated high school or college, or got his first apartment.

Be aware that personal anniversary days, especially the smaller and more intimate ones, can trigger a STUG (Sudden Temporary Upsurge of Grief) long after you feel as though you've finished grieving the loss. When this occurs, remember that the intense feelings of grief are only temporary, and try to use them as a catalyst for honoring the memory of your loved one and the love you continue to share.

Creating Your Own Holiday and Anniversary Celebrations

I'm all for taking as much control over your grieving process as you possibly can. I take this stance because I believe that although the process is essentially self-propelled and forward-moving, it can get stuck in places. Therefore, anything you can do to feel as though you're participating in the grieving (and maybe even taking some control of it) is beneficial to you because it assists the process you're undergoing.

The overriding problem with holidays and anniversaries is that even under the best circumstances, you can feel as though the tradition and mood of the observance is in control, so your emotional response to the event is forced and not genuine. When you're grieving and the last thing on your mind is having a good time, feeling not in control and not in the spirit of the event can be greatly exaggerated.

Instead of trying to ignore the celebration altogether and pretend it isn't happening (which usually doesn't prevent you from feeling even worse about your grief and loss), I suggest that you concentrate on creating your own celebration for the event, remembering that a celebration isn't just a time of merriment but also a time of commemoration. Although your loss may prevent you from making merry, it in no way prevents you from making the day into one of remembrance. All you need to do to take some control over the holiday or anniversary is come up with ways you can honor the spirit of the day as well as the memory of your lost loved one.

Depending upon the particular event being celebrated, you can find ways not only to specifically recall your loved one and all that you shared but also to share the love he gave you by serving others and dedicating your service to his memory. Here are a few examples:

- ✔ Instead of making an elaborate Thanksgiving meal at home, you and your other family members can volunteer to prepare and/or serve meals to those in need.

- ✔ For Christmas or Hanukkah, instead of spending a great deal of time and money on presents for family, get the family involved in providing toys, food, and much needed clothing for those who would otherwise do without.

- ✔ Raise money for your favorite charities and make donations in your loved one's name.

For birthdays and other anniversaries, come up with inventive and personal ways to share the love that you used to celebrate with your lost loved one. By holding your own celebrations instead of only staying home and feeling your sorrow, you communicate your love to others and ensure that it remains vibrant and very much alive.

Part IV
Appreciating Grief

The 5th Wave
By Rich Tennant

@RICHTENNANT

POET'S RESPONSE TO DEATH OF A LOVED ONE

Denial

Anger

Acceptance

Elegy

In this part . . .

*B*efore you can assign any value to the grief you suffer, you must complete it. To help you in this endeavor, this part opens with an investigation of the spiritual meaning that various religious and cultural traditions ascribe to grief. This part concludes with an examination of the process of reconciling yourself to your loss by incorporating it into your life and finding appropriate and significant ways of remembering and memorializing the loss.

Chapter 17

Exploring Grief in the Spiritual Traditions

• •

In This Chapter

▶ Confirming death and grieving as vital parts of all religious traditions

▶ Exploring death and grieving in secular society

▶ Contemplating death and grieving in various religious and spiritual traditions

▶ Continuing the relationship with the dead in Hispanic and Chinese cultures

▶ Cultivating a new attitude toward death

• •

*F*or most people, grieving the loss of a loved one is an intense spiritual journey. It's one that tests your beliefs and calls upon your inner strength. For some people, the journey is made all the more difficult when they lack a vigorous spiritual life at the time of the loss or have lapsed in the exercise of their childhood religious tradition and cultural practices.

This chapter looks at the spiritual aspect of grieving by examining the impact of the death and loss in a variety of different spiritual traditions and cultures. It begins by examining the universal importance of death in every one of these various traditions. Then I move on to investigate death's impact in individual traditions and cultures.

As a point of comparison, the chapter begins with an overview of the place of death and grief in the secular society that was traditionally associated with the Western culture but that's more and more becoming a global phenomenon often linked with the spread of international consumerism. I walk you through the impact of death and grief in the three Abrahamic religious traditions — Judaism, Christianity, and Islam — before exploring the viewpoints of the traditionally Eastern religions of Hinduism and Buddhism. Then I explain the veneration and celebration of the dead in the Hispanic and Chinese cultures.

The chapter concludes with a bid for a new secular attitude toward death and the dead based on a combination of modern ecological thinking and traditional

Daoist (Taoist) philosophy. I believe that combining ecology's interest in honoring and preserving the environment with Daoism's ideas on death as a natural transformation offers the best hope for developing a spiritual view of death in today's secular society.

Death's Vital Role in Spiritual Traditions

That death plays a crucial role in all major religions and spiritual traditions almost goes without saying. In large part this is because, by definition, divine beings are immortal and therefore stand in stark contrast to the human condition. A good part of the function of religion is to explain and reconcile this dichotomy.

For the most part, religions do this in their belief in some sort of life after death. In the Abrahamic religions of Judaism, Christianity, and Islam, this life after death mirrors that of the divine in that it's eternal and bestowed as a reward for a mortal life well lived in the service of God. In the case of Hinduism and Buddhism, this life after death comes in the form of a new mortal life whose state is a direct result of the type of life one led prior to death (karma).

Although the promise of renewed or continued life is most often the focus of the practitioners of various religious traditions, the fact remains that all these promises depend on the quality of the life that you lead before death. The crux of the spiritual tradition, then, is to explain the purpose of life (and consequently, death) and how to live a life that achieves that purpose. That's where the various religions differ significantly, offering different rationales for life and death and different ways in which to fulfill life's divine purpose.

The upcoming sections investigate the attitudes particular spiritual and cultural traditions have toward death and dying. My goal is to delineate the purpose of life (and consequently, death) within the tradition or culture and help you understand how this stance influences the customs and practices of its members toward death, dying, and, in the final analysis, grieving.

I start this survey, however, not with an analysis of a particular spiritual tradition but rather with an examination of modern secular society's attitude toward death, dying, and grieving. I do this because, like it or not, the strong death-denying outlook of this basically materialistic worldview permeates most of our lives, even for those engaged in strong spiritual practices. In addition, this analysis provides a perfect contrast to the attitudes of all the various spiritual traditions and cultures included in this survey.

Secular Society and Death

Given that secular society is geared toward gain, especially in the materialistic sense, it comes as no surprise that death has little or no place in its worldview. What is surprising is the depth to which secular society is both death-denying and, at times, downright hostile toward grieving. This may be due in part to the cult of youth that seems to figure more and more prominently in modern consumerism all around the world. In a society where looking good is equated with looking young and aging is no longer just a concern for women, it's not hard to understand why death has become so thoroughly taboo.

Fundamentally, in secular society death is equated with defeat. I believe that this view stems from the fact that death flies directly in the face of all that secular society holds dear. After all, according to the gospel of secular society, the purpose of life is to accumulate everything you can: power, education, and, above all, material goods.

Death, however, repudiates all these accomplishments. At death, you have to leave all your influence, knowledge, and stuff behind. Even worse, not only do you not get to take it with you, you don't have any real say in who benefits from and gets all that you're forced to leave behind!

In a worldview that can find no good use for death, it comes as no surprise to find that secular society's highest aspiration is the eventual elimination of the aging process and therefore death from natural causes. In secular society, aging and the death that results from it are relegated to the place of a fatal disease that, like AIDS or cancer, is at the top of science's checklist for eradication.

As I point out in Chapter 1, tolerance for grieving the death of a loved one in modern secular society is very low. To begin with, grieving can't help but be seen as counterproductive because it takes you away from the main goal of life (to get ahead and accumulate more). Moreover, being around someone who's actively grieving the death of a loved one is a not-so-subtle reminder of one's own mortality. In keeping with the maxim "out of sight, out of mind," the fewer reminders you have of your own mortality, the better you're able to sustain the illusion that all your endeavors to get more don't come to naught in the face of your inevitable demise. Turn to the section "Melding Deep Ecology and Daoism to Create a New Spiritual Approach to Death," at the end of this chapter for some ideas on how to counter these beliefs.

Death in Judaism

Judaism is the oldest of the three Abrahamic faiths as well as the ancestor of the two younger world religions, Christianity and Islam. Unlike most other world religions, Judaism doesn't actively seek converts. The religion is considered the direct result of a unique relationship (referred to as a *covenant* or *contract*) formed between God and the Hebrew (Jewish) people in particular.

As such, the sacred writings of Judaism (many of which are incorporated into the Christian Bible) chronicle the development of this exceptional relationship from the inception of the world's creation until the building of the Second Temple in Jerusalem (around 350 BCE). This chronicle represents a vivid portrait of a how a people's search for God shapes not only their identity but their destiny as well.

The purpose of life in Judaism

According to Judaism, soon after creating the world, God created humanity — in his own image — in the form of Adam, the original man, and Eve, his helpmate. God created this pair for the purpose of overseeing all the other creatures in His creation and, conversely, tending to His creation.

Because God created the first human, Adam, from the very "dust of the earth" and then breathed the spirit of life into him, the idea of one day returning to the dust of the earth at death is not at all a foreign idea. Indeed, the question that Judaism has wrestled with most in its long history is just what happens to the living spirit God instills in us upon our death.

Views of an afterlife in Judaism

The idea of a life after death remains somewhat vague in Judaism despite suggestions by some of the scriptures of an afterlife in the World to Come *(olam ha-ba)* — either to the world of the Law's restoration initiated by the coming of God's Messiah ("anointed one") or to the judgment of mankind at the End of Days. Rabbinic teachings speak of a resurrection of the dead that will occur as part of one or the other of these eras.

Here are three of the more prevalent Jewish views of what happens to a soul after death:

✔ The soul awaits the appearance of the Messiah, at which time the body and soul are resurrected if the person's judged to have lived a righteous life (otherwise the soul perishes with the body).

✔ The soul stays near the body until after the funeral, at which time it undergoes a period of purification (at the end of which it returns to the earth, according to some Jews).

✔ The soul perishes with the body, and immortality comes through one's descendants on earth.

While beliefs of an afterlife are a little fuzzy in Judaism, beliefs regarding duties, obligations, and goals in the current life are quite clear. In short, adherents are required to live a righteous life, which leads to the healing or mending of the world *(tikkun ha-olam)* and consequently the healing of their own souls in relationship to God.

Formal mourning in the Jewish tradition

In Judaism, both the treatment of the dead and the process of grieving the death are highly ritualized. Indeed, to honor the dead and comfort the mourner are two of the most important commandments in Judaism.

Traditionally, no formal mourning is done if the loved one is a baby less than 30 days old, is someone who has converted from Judaism to another religion, or is a person who has committed suicide. (In the case of suicide, mourning may be permitted if it's determined that the person wasn't fully aware of his actions. The decision to mourn is at the rabbi's discretion.) In addition, no mourning is carried out if the body of the loved one is missing (until the body is found or until the body's been deemed unrecoverable) or has been cremated or interred in a crypt or mausoleum (rather than buried directly in the earth).

The major phases of formal mourning in all sects of Judaism are divided into the following periods:

✔ **Aninut:** This is the period between the death of a loved one and his burial, which is to take place as soon after death as possible except on the Sabbath, High Holidays, or Festivals. After death, the body is ritually cleansed and watched over by members of a special burial society called the *Chevra Kadisha*. The funeral service is normally simple, consisting of prayers, psalms, and a eulogy with no flowers (donations are given instead to charity in memory of the deceased). Gentiles are welcome at the funeral (but take no part in the interment of the body), and all men should wear a head covering. During this period, the religious participation of the members of the immediate grieving family is limited, and they aren't comforted. Also, they don't socialize during this period, and it's a ritual that their outer garments be torn to indicate their state of mourning.

✔ **Shiva:** This is the seven-day period following the burial of the loved one. During this period, all mirrors in the home are covered; the family remains quiet and performs only rudimentary hygiene (no shaving or cutting of hair). For the first three days, the members of the immediate family mourn in private and receive no visitors. For the next four days, the family *sits shiva,* which refers to the practice of sitting on low stools when receiving condolence calls from the extended family, friends, and co-workers. Visitors normally bring food and don't greet the mourners but rather wait until the bereaved speak first. During these visits, the prayer of the Kaddish (see the sidebar "A little about the Kaddish") is recited if a minyan (a group of ten adult people — men in the Orthodox tradition) is present. Sometimes, the end of shiva is marked by an act forbidden during the period, such as cutting one's hair, studying the Torah (the first five books of the Bible), or making loud noise (sometimes by driving a nail into a board).

✔ **Sheloshim:** This is the 30-day period following the burial of the loved one. It marks the end of formal mourning for all loved ones other than the deceased's parents (for whom the mourning period is extended another 10 months, making a total of 11 months including sheloshim). During this time, weekly recitation of the Kaddish in memory of the loved one takes place at the local synagogue.

✔ **Yahrzeit:** This is the first anniversary of the death of the loved one according to the Jewish calendar. To mark this anniversary, a candle is lit, the Kaddish prayer is recited at the synagogue, and acts of charity (usually in the form of donating money) are performed in memory of the lost loved one.

At the end of the first year after the loved one's passing, the family normally meets at the grave site for the *unveiling;* they unveil a tombstone with the person's Hebrew name inscribed on it along with the date of death and often words of praise and remembrance. The tombstone clearly marks the deceased's grave site, and visitors to the grave often place small pebbles on it (assuming it's not upright) to mark their visits.

What makes an Abrahamic faith?

Judaism, Christianity, and Islam are all known as Abrahamic faiths because each regards Abraham as a patriarch of the faith and traces its monotheistic beliefs to Abraham's vision and experience of God as described in various scriptures.

In addition, both the Hebrew and Arabian peoples count Abraham as their ancestor (that is, their literal father). The Arabian people trace their lineage through Abraham's firstborn son, Ishmael, and the Hebrew people trace their ancestry through his second-born son, Isaac. For Christians, Abraham is more of a spiritual father, foreshadowing God's sacrifice of His son, Jesus, in Abraham's binding of Isaac for sacrifice as a burnt offering at God's command (see Genesis 22:1–18).

A little about the Kaddish

The Kaddish is a prayer in Aramaic (the commonly spoken tongue derived from classic Hebrew) inspired by a passage in Ezekiel (Ezekiel 38:28). The passage looks to the day in which all nations exalt the name of God. Even though the text makes no mention of death or the afterlife, this prayer is commonly associated with death because one version is recited at burial and another during the traditional mourning period.

Death in Christian Traditions

Christianity is a unique blend of monotheism and eschatology (from the Greek meaning "last" or "farthest teachings" that describes beliefs concerning the end times and final events in human history). The faith inherited both these traits from the practices of Judaism, the religion of Christianity's founder, Jesus of Nazareth. The adherents of Christianity consider Jesus to be God's Messiah (thus his title, *Christ,* Greek for "anointed," describing the anointing of a king), which was described by earlier Jewish prophets. As such, Jesus's appearance on earth and teachings are believed to have initiated the end times, although the world to come (*olam ha-ba,* what Jesus called the Kingdom of God) with the resurrection of the dead and the final judgment will only be initiated when Jesus returns to earth in glory.

Unlike Judaism, Christianity actively seeks converts based on the idea that it offers the only true way to worship God. As such, Christianity maintains that it constitutes a new covenant with God — one that supersedes God's original agreement with the Hebrew people. This new convenant (testament) isn't based on ethnicity but rather on faith in Jesus as God's Messiah as well as his resurrection and assumption into heaven after death by Roman crucifixion.

The purpose of life and death in Christianity

Christians believe that they're saved by means of their faith in Jesus Christ and are rewarded by eternal life in the form of a resurrected, incorruptible body. The only fuzzy part of the afterlife equation comes in the question of whether or not this eternal life is rewarded individually to the faithful at the time of their deaths or collectively only at the time when Jesus initiates the Kingdom of God with his return to earth in glory. (The former view has gained much more popularity than the latter among both clergy and faithful as the time between Jesus's first appearance on earth and his second coming increases.)

The purpose of a Christian life is to emulate Christ's life and the Kingdom of God (as described by Jesus's teachings in Christian scripture) until he returns and actually brings this kingdom into being on earth. Primary among these teachings is the instruction to love one another as God loves us (a virtue called *caritas* in Latin that became more widely known as Christian charity).

When it comes to the treatment and burying of the dead, Christianity is much less ritualized than Judaism. Following Judaism's customs, Christians generally prefer to bury their dead (although cremation isn't strictly forbidden as in Judaism). This burial is to take place as soon as practical after the death and may be done on Sunday, the Christian day of rest and worship.

Typical Christian grieving rituals

Christian rituals for grieving the dead aren't nearly as strict as in the parent religion of Judaism. For the most part, Christians restrict their formal mourning to the following two events:

- ✔ **Wake:** The public viewing of the body in the casket, usually at the funeral parlor shortly before burial. The casket is normally open unless the body has suffered irreparable harm or the deceased expressed wishes for a closed casket. In the case of cremation of the body, the wake either does not take place or, if it does, a picture of the deceased is used in place of a casket.

- ✔ **Funeral:** This may include a religious ceremony in a church before burial or a ceremony at the grave site immediately prior to interment of the body. In the case of cremation of the body, the funeral is restricted to a church service.

Condolences for the grieving family are relayed either at the wake in the funeral home, after the funeral ceremony at the grave site, or at a gathering at the family home immediately following the funeral.

In addition, the following formal rites are given to the Christian dead in the Roman Catholic and Eastern Orthodox traditions:

- ✔ **Requiem Mass in the Roman Catholic Church:** A commemorative service is held in memory of the deceased following the formal liturgy of the Requiem Mass that prays that God grant eternal peace to the dead.

- ✔ *Panikhidi* **in the Eastern Orthodox Church:** Commemorative services for the deceased are held 3, 8, and 40 days after the funeral. These services, which include the recitation of psalms and short anthems, mark the passage of the soul, which is said to spend its first three days grieving its own death and roaming the earth. After three days, the soul's Guardian Angel brings it into the presence of God, after which the soul spends the next five days viewing the souls of the elect in heaven and the next month viewing the tormented souls of the damned before the day of its own judgment.

Death in Islam

Although Islam (which means "submission" and "peace") is the youngest Abrahamic faith, this world religion actually claims to represent the original and therefore purest form of all three monotheistic faiths. Islam was founded by Muhammad (peace be upon him — abbreviated after this as *pbuh*) in the mid–sixth century CE. Muhammad (pbuh) is considered to be the last of God's prophets in the long line of divine messengers stretching back to Abraham and including Moses and Jesus. He's also considered to be the recipient of God's word dictated in Arabic by the Angel Gabriel, which Muhammad (pbuh) then transcribed in a series of 114 chapters *(surahs)* known collectively as the *Qur'an*.

Like Christianity, Islam actively seeks converts to what it considers to be the one true form of monotheism (considering both Judaism and Christianity as having fallen short of the original monotheistic vision of Abraham, Moses, and Jesus).

Tenets of Islam and the purpose of life and death

According to the *Sunni* ("tradition") denomination of Islam, in order for a person to be a *Muslim* (an adherent of Islam), he or she must adhere to the following so-called Five Pillars of Islam:

- ✔ **Shahada (two testimonies):** This is the profession of faith in God (*Allah* in Arabic) and Muhammad (pbuh) as His messenger. Shahada is often recited as part of prayer and must be recited publicly before an Imam (leader) in order for a non-Muslim to convert to Islam.

- ✔ **Salat (prayer):** This is the requirement to pray five times a day at fixed times facing the direction of the *Kaaba* located inside the Sacred Mosque (*Al-Masjid al-Haram* in Arabic) in the city of Mecca in modern-day Saudi Arabia (this direction is known as the *qibla*).

The Kaaba (which means "cube" in Arabic) refers to the masonry structure roughly in the form of a cube that's said to have been built originally by Adam and then later rebuilt by Abraham with the help of his firstborn son, Ishmael, who's considered to be the original ancestor of the Arabian people.

- **Zakat (almsgiving):** This is the requirement for able Muslims to give charity to the poor and needy.

- **Sawm (fasting):** This is the requirement for able-bodied Muslims to fast during the month of *Ramadan* (the ninth month of the Islamic lunar calendar). During this period, they abstain from eating, drinking, smoking, and sexual intercourse between dawn and sunset, and they're also supposed to put more effort into the practice of Islam's teachings.

- **Hajj (pilgrimage):** This is the requirement for Muslims who are able to do so to make a pilgrimage to Mecca at least once during their lifetimes. The greater Hajj occurs during the month of *Dhu al-Hijjah* (the 12th month of the Islamic lunar calendar), whereas the minor Hajj (*Umrah* in Arabic) can take place in any month.

The *Shi'a* (short for *Shi'at 'Ali* or "party of Ali," the name of the Prophet's son-in-law) denomination of Islam adds to this list *Jihad* (which means "exert utmost effort," "struggle," or "strive") and four other commandments to make up what it refers to as the ten Branches of Religion.

To some Muslims, Jihad refers to the inward spiritual struggle to be closer to God and better follow His will; to others it refers to the mobilization of outward energies to serve the needs of the collective nations of Islam. Still other Muslims interpret Jihad as participation in the military struggle to expand the influence of the nations of Islam (the so-called *fatah* or "opening").

According to Islam, the purpose of human life is to enter into a direct relationship with God through the practices outlined in the Five Pillars of Islam and the ten Branches of Religion. Death, then, is seen as the culmination of this ongoing relationship with God; it's the point in which the devotee is united with the object of his devotion.

Islamic burial customs

Islam follows Judaism in the following burial practices:

- The person's body is always buried. (Cremation is against Islamic law.)
- The burial takes place as quickly as possible after death (the same day whenever feasible).
- The person's body is ritually cleansed prior to burial.

Ritual cleansing of the body before burial is performed by a family member or by specialized washers who are the same gender as the deceased (it can't be performed by a non-Muslim). After it's washed, the body is shrouded in white linen that's free of knots (as these might interfere with the soul's escape from the body). The body is then buried only in these shrouds without any type of coffin.

Conducting the appropriate ceremony

Before the burial, a short ceremony takes place in which a congregation of friends and family assemble to say their private farewells to the deceased. This ceremony can take place in any number of settings ranging from the local mosque to the grave site or funeral home. At the start of the ceremony, the cloth covering the deceased's head is folded to one side, allowing the people assembled to see the deceased's face one final time while making their farewells. When making their farewells, it's important that no one touches the body or allows any of their tears to fall upon it and thus undo its purity. During this ceremony, prayers are said for the deceased and he is forgiven his sins by the entire congregation.

At the end of the ceremony, the Imam asks the congregation whether the deceased is a good man and the congregation responds "good" in unison (no matter how they actually feel about the deceased). The ceremony concludes with the recitation of the Prayer for the Dead, in which the four praises of God are punctuated by the congregation's *Allahu Akbar* ("God is Great"). Then the body is ready for burial.

Undertaking the burial

An Islamic burial is handled by a group of men who often are kin of the deceased. These men convey the body to the grave site, lower it into the ground, position it (turned slightly to the right with the eyes pointing toward Mecca and the feet pointing south), and cover the grave with earth. During this activity, the Imam recites verses from the Qur'an, and he remains at the head of the grave after the men have finished the burial and leave the grave site.

According to popular belief, the moment that the last man involved in the burial (other than the Imam) leaves the grave site, the deceased awakens in his grave and is visited by two angels who ask him the following five final questions (this is known as the *anguish by the grave*):

- ✔ "Who is your God?" to which the deceased answers "Allah."

- ✔ "Who is your prophet?" to which the deceased answers "Muhammad" (pbuh).

- ✔ "Which is your book?" to which the deceased answers "The Qur'an."

- ✔ "Who is your Imam?" to which the deceased gives the name of his Imam.

- ✔ "Which is your qibla (prayer direction)?" to which the deceased answers "Mecca."

Because the dead has only recently awakened, he may have trouble answering these questions even when he knows all the answers. That's why the Imam remains at the grave site after the other men leave; the Imam aids the deceased. Those who are able to successfully answer the five questions are said to lie in their graves in bliss until the final days of judgment.

According to the official teachings of Islam, the dead remain in their graves until the Day of Resurrection (*Al-Qiyamah* in Arabic), which is equivalent to the Last Judgment or Judgment Day in Christianity. On this day, all of mankind is gathered together and each is judged according to his or her deeds and consigned either to one of the seven levels of *Jannah* (paradise) or *Jahannam* (hell).

Typical mourning rituals in Islamic cultures

Because Islam, like Christianity, is embraced by many people in very different cultures around the world, its mourning rituals aren't nearly as uniform as those in Judaism. On the whole, however, the traditional outward expression of grief in Islamic countries falls more on the women of the family than the men. This tradition holds true when saying farewell to the deceased as well as when he is buried.

Women's formal mourning rituals may include a change of clothing (black is the mourning color in the Middle East, whereas white is the mourning color in North Africa). Younger women may wear this mourning color for three months following the death; older women may wear it for an entire year.

In addition, Islamic women often prepare sweet foods for special days, especially the 3rd, 7th, and 40th days after the burial. These treats are distributed to people in the community who then are supposed to offer up sweet thoughts for the deceased.

For those who mark these three days, the 40th day is by far the most significant. It's marked by a recitation of the story of the Prophet's birth during which many shed tears and for which many believe the spirit of the deceased returns to listen.

In some Islamic cultures, it's also customary to hold a ceremony on the one-year anniversary of the death and to mark a visit to the grave site by leaving a pebble on the grave. Both of these traditions are similar to practices in Judaism.

Death in Hinduism

Hinduism (*sanatana dharma* or "eternal duty or order" in Sanskrit) is an ancient and heterogeneous religious tradition of India. Despite claiming that its followers worship more gods and goddesses than in any other religion, Hinduism sees itself as essentially a monotheistic faith. This apparent contradiction is resolved by the belief that all the various deities are simply forms of the one reality called Brahman (from the root *brh* meaning "to expand").

However, unlike God of the monotheistic faiths of Judaism, Christianity, and Islam who is always conceived of as a masculine personal deity, Brahman is considered beyond all personality and gender. As such, it's looked on as the ultimate repository of all consciousness and the unchanging source from which everything springs and to which everything eventually returns.

Hinduism is like Judaism in that it seeks no converts to its faith. This is because the religion regards itself as the unique spiritual heritage of the Hindu people. As such, Hinduism doesn't consider its teachings and practices as the only sanctioned way to achieve unity with the divine but rather as the particularly Hindu experience of this spiritual journey.

The purpose of life and death in Hinduism

Hindus believe that the goals of human life encompass the following four broad categories:

- **Kama (pleasure):** Includes the pursuit of sensual and sexual desires as well as artistic and aesthetic pleasure

- **Artha (goals):** Includes the pursuit of material well-being, skills, and personal and familial goals

- **Dharma (religious and moral duties):** Includes the pursuit of righteousness, virtue, and religious obligations

- **Moksha (liberation):** Includes the pursuit of freedom from all worldly obligations and desires (as expressed by *kama, artha,* and *dharma*) as well as from the cycle of birth and death *(samsara)*

It is through moksha, the final goal of life, that a Hindu achieves unity with the ultimate underlying reality, Brahman. As part of this union, he realizes the unity of the essential self (*atman* in Sanskrit) with Brahman and is released from all worldly desires. In so doing, the individual also is freed from a chain of ignorance and karma that causes his soul to be reincarnated in various human and nonhuman states in this world.

In order to achieve this type of liberation, the Hindu pursues a spiritual practice or path (*yoga,* meaning "yoke" or "union"). There are several popular paths in Hinduism:

- **Bhakti Yoga:** The devotional path on which one attempts to gain liberation by worshiping Brahman in the form of a particular deity (such as Brahma, the creator; Vishnu, the preserver; or Shiva, the destroyer) or an avatar (such as Rama or Krishna, both said to be incarnations of Vishnu).

- **Karma Yoga:** The path of service on which one attempts to gain liberation through the offering of his talents, skills, and resources to others without any thought of recognition or personal gain.

- **Hatha Yoga:** The path of steadfastness on which one attempts to gain liberation through a combination of physical yoga postures (*asanas*), breath control (*pranayama*), meditation, and body postures that reflect a spiritual state (*mudras*).

- **Jñana Yoga:** The path of knowledge on which one attempts to gain liberation through the study of self and scripture and by direct inquiry.

- **Raja Yoga:** The path of meditation on which one attempts to gain liberation by quieting the mind and body through the practice of meditation (*dhyana*) and the recitation of mantras (chanting sacred sound symbols).

The function of reincarnation in Hinduism

According to Hindu teachings about the law of karma (cause and effect), a follower's current station in life is the result of his actions and willful decisions made in his past lives. So too, his deeds in this lifetime will determine his station in the next life.

Due to this strong belief in the reincarnation of the soul (*atman*), physical death represents nothing more than a brief break between one life and the next. This continuous cycle of life and death (*samsara*) continues until the time that one achieves moksha through the pursuit of one or more of the paths to liberation, thereby completely terminating the process of rebirth.

Death, then, is often seen merely as a prelude to another lifetime that may or may not be better than the one just ended depending upon the quality of the life that a loved one led. The purpose of mourning the death of a loved one is to help him achieve the best possible rebirth rather than to help him find everlasting peace.

Mourning rituals in Hinduism

As in Judaism, the treatment of the dead and mourning are highly ritualized in Hinduism. Indeed, the treatment of the deceased is considered to be a sacred duty (*dharma* in Sanskrit) within the family.

When a loved one is dying, the family members remain at the bedside. When it's determined that the loved one is about to die, he's lifted out of bed and placed on the floor. The family members surround him singing holy songs, and he's offered water from the sacred River Ganges on a basil leaf. At the time of death, it's customary for the family members, especially the women, to cry out loudly or even shriek at the top of their lungs.

After death, the body is ritually washed and shrouded in white linen that covers every part of the body but the head until the time of its cremation. Traditionally, widows remove their wedding marks (the *sindoor*) and close female relatives dress in white mourning saris for a complete year. Sons of the deceased often have their heads shaved completely except for a small tuft of hair.

The rituals associated with the funeral extend for 12 days during which the family members sleep on the floor and eat only vegetarian food. They also undergo formal ablutions at both sunrise and sunset, sing their prayers, and visit the shrouded body of the deceased until the time of the cremation (which is determined by the priest through various astrological calculations).

On the day of the funeral, the body is anointed and garlanded with flowers and led by procession to the burning ghat, where the funeral pyre is ignited by the priest (or the eldest son in the case of the death of a parent). After the cremation, the ashes are collected so that they can be scattered in the sacred River Ganges during another ceremony.

After the cremation, in the case of more well-to-do Hindu families, the family will pay to have local beggars in the area fed to benefit the deceased and, after further ablutions, will meet with extended family and the community to receive their condolences and to grieve with them. (Sometimes, a professional mourner is employed to encourage the public display of grief, especially the shedding of tears.)

Death in the Various Buddhist Traditions

Buddhism (*Buddha Dharma* or "teachings of the Awakened One" in Sanskrit) is like Christianity in that it came out of a long-established religious tradition —

Hinduism in the case of Buddhism and Judaism in the case of Christianity. They're also alike in that each of the newer religions is attributed to a single founder — Siddartha Gautama, known as the Buddha, in the case of Buddhism and Jesus of Nazareth, known as the Christ, in the case of Christianity.

As a prince of a small Hindu kingdom in the sixth century BCE, Siddartha renounced his royal and familial duties at the relatively young age of 29 in search of *moksha* (liberation that he called "Nirvana"). After a six-year period of rather strenuous ascetic yoga practice, Gautama renounced asceticism and realized his goal of complete liberation in an event known as the Great Enlightenment, after which he was known as the Buddha (which translates to "Awakened One").

As the Buddha, Gautama spent the next 45 years or so of his life teaching a growing community of monks and laymen in northern India his particular method of attaining liberation. According to the Buddha, the sole purpose of his dharma (religious teachings) is to eliminate suffering *(dukkha),* thereby attaining Nirvana.

Buddha outlined his fundamental assumptions about human suffering and its elimination in the following so-called Four Noble Truths:

1. **The Truth of Suffering:** Suffering prevails in human life in such diverse forms as birth, aging, sickness, death, not getting what one desires, and being separated from what one desires.

2. **The Cause of Suffering:** The cause of suffering is a deep craving for satisfaction and continued existence.

3. **The Cessation of Suffering:** Suffering can end through the abandonment of this craving.

4. **The Path to the Cessation of Suffering:** The Noble Eightfold Path is the way that leads to the abandonment of this craving and the cessation of suffering. The path consists of the following steps:

    1. **Right Understanding:** Comprehending and accepting Buddha's truths about the nature of suffering and its cessation

    2. **Right Thought:** Renouncing suffering and all ill will toward oneself and other beings

    3. **Right Speech:** Engaging only in speech that isn't hurtful, untrue, or exaggerated

    4. **Right Action:** Engaging in wholesome actions that do no harm to oneself or other beings, including not taking life, not taking what isn't given to you, and not engaging in unwholesome sexual activities

    5. **Right Livelihood:** Engaging only in occupations that do no harm to oneself or other beings

6. **Right Effort:** Rousing the will to cultivate wholesome mental states and overcome negative mental states

7. **Right Mindfulness:** Cultivating self-awareness and the ability to see things as they are rather than how you want them to be

8. **Right Concentration:** Cultivating meditative states of mind in which the boundary between self and others disappears

Unlike its parent religion, Hinduism, Buddhism actively seeks converts as it considers the Buddha's truths about suffering and path to liberation to be open to all humans. As a result, Buddhism originally spread throughout its native India and from there to all parts of Asia. Today, it's practiced in many modern Asian countries and has recently spread to the West, finding new converts in Europe as well as the Americas.

The purpose of life and death in Buddhism

Like Hindus, Buddhists believe that beings are reborn again and again according to the fruits of their karma (moral actions) until they're enlightened. However, unlike the Hindu belief in an indestructible soul *(atman)* that's incarnated in each succeeding lifetime, Buddhists believe that only one's tendencies and the fruits of one's karma survive and are carried over to the new life.

Therefore Buddhists see death as a break in the connection between one's present life and the next. This cycle of death and rebirth *(samsara* in Sanskrit) continues until one is fortunate enough (through the merit of his good karma) to hear the teachings of the Buddha and actually have a chance to practice them and become enlightened.

Human life is a highly revered state of rebirth in Buddhism because it's considered a very rare state of being and, more importantly, because it's a state of being that offers some of the very best opportunities for becoming enlightened.

In many Buddhist cultures, the lay people who are householders and must work for a living support the community of Buddhist monks *(sangha)*. They do so in hopes of gaining sufficient good karma that, in a future life, they'll be reborn as humans in a condition that enables them sufficient leisure to practice Buddha's teachings and therefore achieve enlightenment.

Mourning rituals in Buddhism

Mourning rituals in Buddhism aren't nearly as uniform and formal as in Hinduism. They differ not only because of practitioners' cultural differences but also because of doctrinal differences of the particular schools of Buddhism that have developed over time.

The two major schools of Buddhism are the *Theravada* ("the Way of the Elders," also called Hinayana, "the Small Vehicle") and the *Mahayana* ("the Great Vehicle"). These two schools differ primarily in the Buddhist ideal they emphasize:

- ✔ **Arahant** ("worthy one") in the Theravada school: This is a disciple who attains final enlightenment in a single lifetime, following Gautama Buddha's example. As you may expect, the Theravada stresses personal self-reliance.

- ✔ **Bodhisattva** ("enlightenment being") in the Mahayana school: This is a disciple who achieves awakening but, out of compassion, puts off final enlightenment until he has helped all other beings achieve enlightenment. The Mahayana is much more comfortable with the idea of relying on other powers in the forms of specialized bodhisattvas (the Bodhisattva of Compassion being one of the favorites) and more cosmic, primordial Buddhas.

Although early Buddhists tended to follow Hindus in preferring cremation of the deceased's body over burial, this custom wasn't followed uniformly in all the Asian countries to which Buddhism spread. For example, because many parts of Tibet lacked sufficient wood for cremation, the practice of "sky burial" arose, in which the body of the deceased was fed to vultures and carrion birds. And in China, most people continued to bury their dead in accordance with Confucian views even after the widespread adoption of a form of Mahayana Buddhism.

In both Theravada and the Mahayana teachings, a person's state of consciousness at the moment of death is considered a crucial factor in determining the quality of his next life. In keeping with this notion, some Mahayana traditions created rituals for helping the deceased achieve the best possible rebirth or, in the case of those with advanced spiritual training, enter Nirvana directly and avoid being reborn altogether.

This type of ritual is most developed in the *Bardo Thodol* teachings of the Vajrayana school of Mahayana Buddhism. As part of this ritual, the Bardo scripture is recited to the body of the deceased (or to a picture if the body is not available) on the weekday of the death for a period of seven weeks or a total of 49 days (considered to be the maximum period that one exists in between lives). This recitation guides whatever consciousness survives death either to enter directly into an enlightened state or into seeking out the most fortuitous condition for rebirth.

Other schools of Theravada and Mahayana Buddhism mark a special ceremony on just the 49th day after the person's death. During this ceremony, friends and family of the deceased join together in chanting and listen to a specially selected Buddhist scripture before commemorating the lost loved one.

Venerating the Dead in Chinese Culture

In traditional Chinese culture, the veneration of one's ancestors (commonly referred to as *ancestor worship*) played a significant role in forming the society's attitudes toward death in general and the dead in particular. The basic idea behind ancestor worship is that one's family members survive death as spirits that continue to take an interest in the family and have the power to influence the affairs of the living. However, in order for the ancestors to intervene positively in the fortunes of their descendants, those descendants must keep their ancestors happy through a combination of rites.

In a traditional Chinese family, these rites include keeping an ancestor tablet that marks the name and dates of the ancestor either in the family's home shrine or the clan's ancestral temple. Daily rites of veneration are performed in front of the ancestor tablet in which incense and *spirit money* (paper painted with silver or gold that the dead can use as currency) are burned and food offerings are made.

In modern Chinese culture, ancestor worship survives in the celebration of the Qingming Festival (often translated as the Tomb Sweeping Festival in English.) During this festival in April, the family members honor their ancestor by going to the grave site where they clean the grave, repaint the inscriptions on the headstone or grave tablet, make food offerings, replace all wilted flowers, and burn incense and spirit money. In addition, they place a set of chopsticks and three wine cups above the food and closest to the headstone. After pouring wine libations in front of the headstone, each member of the family shows respect to the ancestor usually by bowing in front of the headstone. In some families, the members partake of the food they've offered the ancestor (considered to be very good luck), making the affair into some sort of graveside picnic. Families also may set off firecrackers to scare off evil spirits and to let the ancestor know that the family has come to show its respect.

Celebrating the Dead in Hispanic Culture

Although we normally associate ancestor worship with traditional cultures of the Old World such as the Chinese and African cultures, it also has influence in the cultures of the New World. Nowhere is this clearer than in the celebration of the Day of the Dead (*El Dia de los Muertos* in Spanish). This remembrance of deceased ancestors is celebrated on November 1 (All Saints Day in Catholicism) in countries in Central and South America (it's particularly popular in Mexico) as well as in parts of Spain and the Philippines.

The day of remembrance is thought to have roots in rituals for the dead celebrated by indigenous American cultures including the Aztec and Mayan. (In the Aztec culture, the celebration of the dead spanned an entire month in late summer or early fall.) After the adoption of Roman Catholicism, the celebration moved to All Saints Day (November 1) and therefore became naturally enmeshed with the New World celebration of Halloween (October 31).

Hispanic Day of the Dead celebrations are similar in some respects to Chinese Qingming celebrations (refer to the preceding section). They include visits to the grave sites of deceased ancestors; graves are cleaned and decorated with flowers (especially the orange marigold referred to as the *flor de muertos* or "flower of the dead"). Surviving family members make offerings (*ofrendas*) in the form of food, drink, candles, and toys for dead children. Ofrendas also are left out in the home as a means of attracting the spirits of the dead. Celebrants also may wear necklaces of shells so that they make noise and attract the ancestors' spirits when they dance.

On the whole, Dia de Muertos celebrations are quite joyous. They're a way for people to honor the lives of their ancestors as well as continue this vital relationship after their passing. These celebrations also emphasize the belief that death isn't the end of life but rather a new beginning.

Melding Deep Ecology and Daoism to Create a New Spiritual Approach to Death

I begin this chapter's survey of spiritual attitudes toward death with the rather somber assessment of death as being seen by modern secular society as little more than an impediment. In this section, I conclude the chapter with a suggestion (a modest proposal, if you will) for a more accepting and appreciative attitude of death, a new spiritual attitude built upon a blend of modern ecological consciousness and some of the insights of the ancient Chinese philosophy of Daoism (originally transliterated as Taoism).

✔ *Deep ecology* is a philosophy developed out of the modern science of ecology. The basic supposition is that mankind isn't endowed with any special rights within the ecosystem. A corollary of this idea is that all beings within the ecosystem are considered "aspects of a single unfolding reality."

✔ *Daoist philosophy,* as expounded in traditional writings, concerns itself with how mankind can best be in accord with the natural order (which is named *Dao,* Chinese for "the Way"). The basic tenet of this philosophy is that mankind should emulate the Dao by decreasing desires and artifice. In so doing, mankind can nurture the world without attempting to possess it and can accomplish things without interfering with the process *(wei wuwei).*

To me, Daoism and deep ecology seem to be natural partners. They share a fundamental concern for nature and strong misgivings about how human interference in the natural process can upset the natural balance. They also both hold the natural process in great reverence and consider mankind to be an integral part of the natural process without endowing humanity with some kind of inherently special or superior status in the system.

In both systems, death is considered a completely natural phenomenon. In ecology, death plays a crucial role in enabling the continued richness and diversity within the ecosystem, thus ensuring its overall health. In Daoism, death is equated with transformation and returning to unity with the natural order.

Once you regard death as a vital agency of transformation, death regains a kind of dignity and necessity that it normally lacks in the view of the typical modern consumer. In concentrating on the well-being of the whole system, you automatically anchor and integrate yourself within a greater framework and context that both sustains and guides you.

I suggest that deep ecology tinged with a little Daoist wisdom can stand as a positive alternative to the cynicism of secularism and the superficiality of consumerism. It can do this by providing the traditionally nonreligious person with the following comprehensive beliefs:

✔ Human beings are an integral part of the natural system that creates, supports, and sustains them.

✔ The purposes of human life are to appreciate and to nourish the natural world.

✔ All beings in the ecosystem are precious to it and of intrinsic value within it.

✔ The diversity of life in the ecosystem should be celebrated as a sign of its underlying unity.

✔ Each human being has the moral duty to do as little damage to the environment as possible and to sustain the diversity of its life-forms whenever possible.

✔ Life and death are essential processes of the ecosystem that aid in sustaining the system by fostering its unfolding and furthering its diversity.

As part of seeing death as a fully natural process, one can look to the Daoist idea that death is just another transformation of life. Death just happens to be a great transformation that's shrouded in the same kind of unknowing that precedes birth.

On the death of a loved one, you can counter your grief over the loss with a deep appreciation of the unique life you were privileged to share as well as appreciation of the Dao that brought forth and sustained such an exceptional and irreplaceable individual. And in returning to the Dao, you can take comfort in knowing that your loved one's spirit is once again reunited with its source, as in the words of the modern Daoist sage, Tu Weiming, "like the flowing stream returning to ocean."

Chapter 18

Integrating the Loss

· ·

In This Chapter

▶ Making peace with your loss

▶ Findings ways to stay connected to your lost loved one

▶ Dealing with the life changes that death brings

▶ Using grieving as compassion training

· ·

I have to admit that I cheated a bit in Chapter 1 when I purposely introduced grieving as a process entailing three distinct tasks:

1. **Acknowledge the loss.**

2. **Experience the grief that the loss produces.**

3. **Incorporate the loss into the rest of your life.**

Another way to see it is that these aren't three separate tasks at all. According to this view, grieving actually consists of this single, very large task with its own phasing and timing: namely, that of finding ways to successfully integrate the loss into your life. This makes the first two steps of acknowledging the loss and experiencing the grief simply part of the process known as *integrating the loss.*

You may never entirely finish the job of integrating the loss into your life. And although this fact may seem shocking at first and even a little daunting, you need not take it that way.

It doesn't mean anything dire — like you'll never be happy again or you'll never love again. Rather, it means that you're one of those lucky people who enjoyed a relationship of such complexity and depth that it defies a quick and easy reconciliation. (It may also mean that continually working on integrating the loss is one of the ways that you keep your love alive.)

This chapter looks specifically at strategies and techniques you can adopt for integrating your profound loss into the rest of your life. This process offers you the opportunity to both renew and transform your life. It also initiates you into a brand new club — the select group of people who know firsthand that although death has the awesome power to separate you from a loved one, it's completely powerless to disband the relationship you created and end the love you have. And at the culmination of this process lies an equally great opportunity: the chance for you to transform your personal grief into great compassion and understanding for others.

Incorporating the Loss into Your Life

Initially, the very idea of incorporating something as traumatic as the loss of a loved one into your life may seem downright inconceivable. In time, however, as you go through your grieving process, hopefully you'll come to see this as both feasible and desirable.

In terms of profound loss, *incorporate* means to unite with something already in existence to form an indistinguishable whole that can't be restored to its previously separate elements. In other words, this is integration par excellence.

Therefore, for you to successfully incorporate the loss of a loved one into your life, you have to be able to live with the loss as though it were your customary state of affairs (something akin to that "new normal" that grief counselors sometimes speak of). To accomplish this task, you have to fully accept the loss not only in the sense of acknowledging its reality but also in becoming reconciled to it. And as part of this reconciliation, you need to find ways to maintain some sort of connection to your lost loved one.

Reconciling with your loss

In order to be reconciled with the loss of a loved one, you have to restore the harmony that was disrupted by the grief and be at peace with the loss.

Being at peace with the loss doesn't mean that you're finally okay with the death in the sense of no longer regretting that it ever happened. (You'll likely wish that your loved one were with you and that the death didn't have to occur to your dying day.) This peace also doesn't necessarily include ever accepting the reason for the death and understanding exactly how it fits into the grand scheme of things.

Being at peace does mean that you've come to a place in your life where the grief no longer rubs you raw and its emotions don't sit at the top of your consciousness, making it all but impossible to think of or feel anything else. It also means that you're ready to fully reengage in your life — in all its mundane as well as more creative aspects (what some grief counselors refer to as "moving on").

Giving meaning to the loss

One way to restore the harmony interrupted by your intense grief is to give meaning to the loss. Finding meaning in the loss indicates that you're looking at its repercussions in your life, which means that you're beginning to look toward your own future.

An effective method for giving meaning to your loss is to employ a little technique known as *reframing*. Reframing is the process of finding new ways to interpret and understand an event without altering or ignoring any of its essential facts. When you reframe an event, especially a traumatic one, you restructure the event's meaning and therefore its consequences without altering its underlying reality. The classic example of reframing is encapsulated in the old tale in which a father tells his neighbor about his son being thrown from his horse and subsequently breaking his leg. The neighbor replies, "Oh, that's terrible!" to which the father replies, "Oh no, that's good because when the king's men came to induct my son into the army, they left him alone because of his broken leg!"

To discover the meaning of your loss, you may need to be in a mental space where you're able to shift your focus away from the present pain of the grief and the struggle with the reasons why this grief was laid at your doorstep. If you're not yet in this place, you may not be able to attempt this task. It may be like trying to push the river when you just really need to go with its flow. You simply may need to concentrate more on acknowledging the loss and finding ways to vent and express the pain you're feeling, as I outline in Chapter 14.

In the process of reframing your loss, answer the following questions:

- What kind of person do I want and need to be in the wake of this loss?
- What kinds of personal changes do I have to make in order to live with this loss and move on from this point?
- What lessons can I take away from this grieving experience?
- In what ways has my life been changed forever as a result of this loss?
- How can I remain in some way connected to my lost loved one and still live the rest of my life?

Finding meaning in the loss is essentially a creative task. It requires you to be resourceful, inventive, and, above all, imaginative when it comes to your own personal growth in the face of your loss and your understanding of its lasting effects on your life.

In reframing the loss, you begin to replace the grieving process with the process of restoring harmony in your life — a harmony that may have been missing for some time. You slowly but surely replace the chaos of emotional upheaval with a new order (that good ol' new normal). Most important of all, you finally recognize that you'll be okay: You start to understand that you'll not only survive this loss but also have the possibility of thriving in the face of it.

Looking at grieving as an act of love

A vital element of reconciling with your loss is to finally be at peace with it, and one way to make peace with the loss of your loved one is to recognize the grieving you're undergoing as a supreme act of love.

Normally, people see grief as an entirely negative process, as the ultimate downer (and in very many senses, grief fully fits this bill). However, when you look a little harder, you realize that you grieve a person only because you love him. You never grieve the loss of a person you don't really know or deeply care about, even if you feel a little badly or express some token of grief at the passing.

So you should understand grieving as a way of honoring the love you shared with the one you've lost. You also can see grieving as the first step in learning how to keep this love alive beyond the loss.

When you come to see grieving as an indispensable process of loving, it no longer feels like some sort of punishment. Rather, grieving reveals itself as an initiation into the true appreciation of the love you shared. And that appreciation enables you to make your peace with grief as you learn how to keep that love alive in your life long after the grieving is over and done with.

Maintaining a connection with your lost loved one

Although death may mark the end of a loved one's life, it certainly doesn't mark the end of your love for that person, nor does it necessarily mark the end of your relationship with that person. After the loss, the supreme challenge becomes how to maintain a connection with your loved one that enables you to feel as though your relationship endures.

Many newly bereaved people find that they maintain the connection with their lost loved ones through dreams. Later on, these grief dreams give way to other more-psychic or spiritual connections that enable them not only to feel the presence of their loved ones but also to sustain some sort of communication with them.

Connecting via grief dreams

Grief dreams are very common among newly bereaved people (although there's nothing wrong with you if you never dream about your loved one). Having vivid dreams about a loved one who's recently died is so common among newly bereaved people that grief professionals have separated the dreams into categories that include:

- **Visitation dream:** Your lost loved one simply appears to you, usually in a very familiar setting. He may or may not speak to you, but you recognize him and are reassured by his appearance.

  The visitation-type grief dream is the most common, and both visitation- and reassurance-type dreams are the most comforting to the dreamer.

- **Message dream:** Your lost loved one actually delivers some sort of message to you. This message may be in the form of pure information, some type of instruction, or even a warning. In some cases, the message may not be intended for you but for someone else that both you and the deceased know.

  The message-type dream can be comforting, but it also can be confusing if the message that you're given is cryptic and frustrating. This type of dream is particularly frustrating when you awaken and remember the dream but forget the actual message you received.

- **Reassurance dream:** Your loved one appears to you to give you some sort of encouragement. This can be in the form of praise for the way you're handling yourself or in the form of letting you know that there's no need to worry because your loved one is at peace and doing just fine.

- **Trauma dream:** You relive a traumatic event associated with your loved one. Often this flashback concerns the death of your loved one, especially if his death was sudden and violent.

  The trauma-type grief dream is the least common and, without a doubt, the most upsetting. This type of dream may be an indication that you have serious issues that you need to address before you actually can grieve the loss (see Chapter 12 for more information on troubled grieving).

As you can see, with the exception of the fairly rare trauma dream, grief dreams are generally positive experiences. They reassure you that your loved one is okay and still able to find a way to communicate with you.

The major drawback to grief dreams is that, for most folks, they don't continue much beyond the period of acute grief immediately or shortly after the loss of their loved ones. As such, these dreams are much better at providing you with reassurances that your loved one is both okay and not actually lost to you than they are at providing you with a means of remaining in contact with him. Another frequent problem with grief dreams is that many folks don't remember them after awakening. They can recall distinctly having just had an important and vivid dream, but they can't recall the details. This can be really frustrating especially when you've had a message-type dream and can't recall the message your loved one wanted so desperately to impart to you!

The best way to avoid forgetting the contents of any visitation-, message-, or reassurance-type grief dream is to write them down immediately upon awakening. Be prepared by placing a pen and a pad of paper on your bedside table before you retire for the night. Then immediately after you wake up, write down all that you can remember about the encounter. When jotting down the contents of the dream, remember that no detail is too small to include. (Trauma-type dreams are often all too vivid to forget and are better off forgotten as soon as possible.)

For much more on grief dreams, how to go about interpreting them, and how they can help you with your grieving, I recommend *Grief Dreams: How They Help Heal Us After the Death of a Loved One,* an excellent book by T.J. Wray and Ann Back Price (Jossey-Bass).

Maintaining a spiritual connection

When you first think of maintaining a spiritual connection with a lost loved one, TV psychic mediums Sylvia Brown, John Edward, or James Van Praagh may come to mind. However, I'm not talking at all about using another person's psychic abilities to contact and continue communication with your lost loved one. Rather, maintaining a spiritual connection means using only your own abilities to find ways to make and maintain some sort of contact with your loved one.

If you want to refer to such abilities as "psychic," that's fine. Just understand that in this context, psychic abilities indicate nothing more out there than finding and using your own subjective means of staying in touch — means that are completely internalized and therefore can be verified only by you. Naturally, these subjective means of staying in touch have to be spiritual in nature, if only in the sense that, because the loved one's no longer physically available to you, he's reachable only through unconventional, nonphysical means.

In modern societies where individuality is emphasized over community, you'll probably address your lost loved one in prayers, meditations, and rituals separately as an individual. In more-traditional societies where community is emphasized over individuality, you may feel more comfortable addressing your lost loved one as part of the clan composed of all your deceased fore-bears and ancestors.

However you feel most comfortable addressing your lost loved one, the main thing is to find a means of address that enables you to state your current situation freely and openly (including all your feelings about your grief and being without him). Here, it's crucial that you feel as though you're being heard and listened to regardless of whether your loved one or ancestors make any kind of reply. Feeling that you can state your feelings to your lost loved one and that you're being heard will go a long way in helping you make peace with the loss.

If you create your own grief rituals (see Chapter 14), your rituals offer perfect opportunities for you to address and communicate with your lost loved one. You can address the loved one out loud (even when other friends and family members are in attendance) without fearing that men with butterfly nets are coming to haul you away to the loony bin.

Being Transformed by Grief

Like it or not (and most people hate it), grieving is essentially a transformative process. This is one way in which grieving doesn't resemble a physical injury in the least bit. For example, when you break your leg and that break eventually heals, your leg is essentially the same as before (although it may be a little bit weaker). However, when you experience the loss of a loved one and your grief eventually runs its course, your life is never quite the same as before the loss.

As Sobonfu Somé reminds us at the end of her great and wise little book on loss called *Falling Out of Grace: Meditations on Loss, Healing, and Wisdom*, (North Bay Books), losing a loved one is essentially an "initiation" that changes our lives forever.

In looking on grieving as a type of initiation, you're essentially admitting that the grieving process constitutes both a rite of passage full of its own observances and ordeals and also an induction into a new level of knowledge or wisdom. At the end of this initiation, this wisdom transforms you and gives you a new lease on life.

Growing as a result of your loss

Here's one thing I've learned firsthand from my own grieving: Whenever you lose a loved one, you grieve the loss of that person as well as the relationship you shared. And in grieving the loss of the relationship, you're essentially grieving over the changes forced on you by the unfortunate circumstances with which you're faced. Despite the fact that you probably weren't ready for your life to change in such a drastic manner, in the end, you have no choice but to submit and adjust to the new situation.

Here's another thing I've learned directly from grieving: Death forces far-reaching changes in your life, but you still control how you make those changes and how far you take them. For example, you can choose between merely surviving the loss and getting through its pain, growing from the loss, and using it to become a more complete person. In my own case, the deaths of my life partner of 16 years and my mother in the very same year eventually inspired me to complete my postgraduate education and get my doctorate as well as to become a hospice volunteer.

Renewing your spirit

One way to grow from a profound loss is to use that loss as your reason for renewing your spiritual connection to life. Surely anyone who's suffered the loss of a loved one is vividly reminded how short and precious human life is and how empty and hollow so many dearly cherished goals of gain and material success are in the face of death.

Instead of becoming embittered by the fact that life is short and many cherished goals are momentary, I suggest you use your grief as a stimulus for replenishing your spirit. Seek out every opportunity you can find to revive your connection to those very things in life (such as love and compassion) that are impervious to death.

Here are some suggestions of ways to replenish your spirit as the pain and hard work of grieving starts to ease:

- ✔ Volunteer for a favorite community project or a project run by your local church, synagogue, mosque, or temple.

- ✔ Take long walks in the country or a local park, during which you expressly note the beauty and unity of the natural world.

- ✔ Take time to listen to music that you specifically find uplifts your spirit.

- ✔ Reflect regularly on the goals you have in light of the loss you've suffered.

- ✔ Get in touch with all those things that nurture you and find ways to bring more of them into your life.

Reconnecting with family and community

Death is the great divider. It separates you from your loved one, and it doesn't stop there! All too often, the stress and grief it brings put people at odds with friends and family. Grieving the death of a loved one also can isolate you from the rest of your community and even make you question your trust in the integrity of the world and your faith in the goodness of life.

Finding ways to reconnect with your friends, extended family members, and your community is an important step in reconciling with your loss and integrating it into your life. It's a sign not only that your pain is finally easing but also that you're getting set to take the lessons learned from your experience with grief and apply them in your day-to-day life.

Here are some suggestions of ways to reconnect with living loved ones and the community of which you're still a part:

- ✔ Begin or continue research on your family tree, eliciting input and help from all your family members.

- ✔ Plan a family reunion to honor the accomplishments and contributions of the elders in your extended family.

- ✔ Write thank-you cards to all the family members and close friends who supported you and your immediate family after your loss and during your grieving.

- ✔ Get involved in tutoring or mentoring young people at a local school or community center.

- ✔ Invite close friends and family members to gather and help you erect some sort of memorial to your lost loved one (see Chapter 19 for ideas on memorials).

Grieving as training in compassion

No one who has the opportunity to love another is spared the pain of grief. Only those who die so young that they never know the loss of other loved ones manage to escape grief's bitter embrace. So grieving is a great equalizer — the one experience besides birth and death that all people have in common. The fact that grief is such a shared human experience can make it a great basis for developing and practicing compassion in your life.

You can't be truly compassionate of the suffering of others if you haven't known that suffering yourself. Having experienced and survived the pain of grief, you're in a unique position to help others who are grieving.

The best ways you can help others who are grieving are by letting them know about your experience and how you managed to survive your own pain and by listening openly and without judgment to their feelings and doubts. Your presence as someone who survived your own grief and who now wishes to help others can be a mighty reassurance.

The biggest potential problem in extending compassion to others, especially others who are grieving their own losses, lies with your own reason for helping. If you help others with their grief as a way of making yourself feel better about your own grief, you're likely to get in the way of their grieving. Make sure that your intentions are truly altruistic so that you can maintain the distance necessary to avoid interfering with their grieving processes and actually help them work through everything.

Chapter 19

Commemorating Those You've Lost

In This Chapter

▶ Keeping your loved one alive in your heart

▶ Exploring memorial options

▶ Gathering for memorial services

▶ Honoring your loved one through community service

*C*ommemorating is a process of memorializing your loved ones. You do this by finding ways to remember, honor, and celebrate their lives as well as the relationships that you shared with them. By remembering the loved ones you've lost, you keep the love you shared alive and a vibrant part of your life.

I begin this chapter with an overview of the ways you can remember lost loved ones and keep their love flourishing in your heart. I explain the role of memorials and memorial services in commemorating your loved ones, looking at both traditional memorials (monuments and markers) and nontraditional ones (butterfly releases and virtual memorials on the Internet). I explain that memorial services can be anything from a formal traditional ceremony conducted at the grave site to an informal get-together with friends and family at your home or at a loved one's favorite hangout.

The chapter concludes with an examination of how you can honor your loved one's memory by creating a living legacy for him through various types of community service. This service can include volunteer work that you do to support your loved one's favorite cause as well as donations made to your loved one's favorite charity in his name.

Remembering Your Loved One

Strangely enough, lots of people view grieving the loss of a loved one as essentially a selfish process. This process is self-centered because, as a bereaved person, you indulge in your sorrowful feelings mostly because you're newly deprived of the love and comfort that your loved one provided you.

I, on the other hand, see this same grieving process as basically *unselfish*. According to my view, it's altruistic work because the sorrowful feelings you have over being deprived of this love ultimately serve the greater purpose of helping you realize just what this love meant to your life and how you'll go about keeping this love alive.

 As grieving reaches its conclusion, you may also reach the understanding that your deceased loved one could be truly lost to you only if he were no longer remembered. As long as you remember him however it feels right to do so, you keep the love you shared alive.

"Remember" is really a wonderful word. It breaks down into "re-" and "member," which together literally mean "to get back an appendage" or "to become associated anew." When remembering a deceased loved one, hopefully you're doing both these things: once again incorporating your loved one into your life as well as getting acquainted with your lost loved one all over again.

If you can do both these things successfully, I'd say you've found the secret to keeping the love you shared alive and well in your heart. To help you in this endeavor, you can create remembrances that reflect your loved one's qualities, skills, and interests. You can also construct remembrances that display and chronicle the unique relationship you shared together.

Here's a short list of remembrances you can create to help you recollect and celebrate your loved one's life:

- ✔ Create a picture album or book that chronicles the milestones in your loved one's life, including major accomplishments and relationships.
- ✔ Create a collage or montage that uses images, tokens, keepsakes, and mementos that represent your loved one's best qualities and highest interests.
- ✔ Write a series of anecdotal stories that chronicle your loved one's goals, major accomplishments, and interests.
- ✔ Paint a series of pictures that epitomize all that your loved one valued most about life.

Check out Chapter 22 for a list of more-detailed suggestions of ways you can honor and memorialize your loved one.

Love lives on beyond goodbye

Shortly after beginning work on this book on grieving, my beloved Sheltie dog of 12 years had a massive heart attack and died in my arms. One day a couple of weeks later, as I was taking a walk and feeling particularly down about his death, out of the blue, Foreigner's pop tune from the '80s "I Don't Want To Live Without You" started playing in my head. I started singing the chorus line to myself: "I don't want to live without you. I don't want to live without you. I could never live without you — live without your love."

In that moment, I realized not only that I didn't want to live without my dog's love but also that

I didn't have to. I made my mind up right then and there to take his love with me by remembering him, all he meant to me, and all we shared together.

Strangely enough, this realization made me feel quite a bit better and made me understand that this is exactly what I do with all the loved ones whom I've lost. Every time I stop to remember them, the love they gave me, and the lessons that they taught me, I feel as though I'm no longer living without them. Rather, I'm keeping them alive in my heart and using their love to help me be all that I can be.

Memorializing Your Loved One

The main purpose of a memorial is to preserve the memory or knowledge of someone or some event. When you think of memorializing a loved one, you probably think of erecting some sort of monument or marker at his grave site or place of rest. This type of traditional memorial usually also contains a short inscription that identifies the deceased and very often his relationship to the person or people erecting the marker.

In addition to or in place of these kinds of traditional memorials, you can create more-innovative memorials for your loved ones. These nontraditional memorials, which are gaining in popularity, can include anything from living memorials and keepsake jewelry to online virtual memorials.

Erecting traditional grave monuments and markers

Most people are familiar with the traditional cemetery monuments and markers. Typically, these types of memorials are created and set in place at the grave within the first year after the death and interment of a loved one.

Grave markers or headstones are usually made of granite or some other hard stone. Most often it's a single block that either lies flat or is erected vertically at the head of the grave. It's inscribed or etched with the loved one's name, birth and death years, and usually a short dedication or memorial passage.

A monument is typically higher and much more ornate than a simple vertical headstone. Often, it's intricately carved with religious or natural symbols (crosses and trees are big favorites) and may include raised or even free-standing statuary (usually in the form of the Virgin Mary or an angel).

If money's no object and you have enough cemetery real estate and the cemetery rules allow it, you can have a mausoleum erected as a grand memorial for your loved one. A mausoleum is a stone structure that actually houses your loved one's tomb (or tombs, as the case may be, as mausoleums traditionally accommodate more than one crypt).

If your loved one was cremated instead of buried, you can still create a memorial by having a special urn made for his cremated remains. Personalize the urn by attaching a medallion or nameplate containing your loved one's name, dates, and a short memorial message. You can have this urn stored in a niche in an indoor or outdoor columbarium at your local cemetery. Or if your cemetery has an urn garden, you can have the urn buried and then have a plaque erected on the site instead.

Creating more-nontraditional memorials

Nontraditional memorials run the gamut from ecological living memorials and memorial gardens to virtual memorials that you place on the Internet. If your loved one was cremated and didn't specifically ask to have his ashes scattered, innovative memorials can include lockets in which you store some of your loved one's ashes to using the ashes to create a synthetic diamond that you can have set in a necklace or ring!

Establishing a living memorial

The most popular form of living memorial is the living tree memorial. For this kind of memorial, you arrange to have a tree planted in honor of your loved one in a nature preserve or on some public land. Some living tree memorials enable you to select the type of tree that you want planted, and all provide you with a certificate of planting. Some tree memorials also mark the tree so that you can go and visit it, perhaps as part of a memorial ceremony. For specific information on agencies that offer living tree memorials, type "living tree memorials" or "living memorials" into your favorite Internet search engine.

If your loved one was cremated and was ecologically minded as well, you can use his cremated remains to create a memorial reef. A *memorial reef* is a cast-concrete reef in which your loved one's remains are mixed. This cast reef is then lowered into a particular location on the seabed off the coast of Fort Lauderdale, Florida. The reef provides shelter for marine life and is estimated to last for many hundreds of years. For more information on memorial reefs, visit the Eternal Reefs Web site at www.eternalreefs.com.

Wearing memorial jewelry

Many people find wearing memorial jewelry, most often in the form of pendants, bracelets, and pins, a very comforting way to honor and remember their lost loved ones. Several jewelry companies specialize in designing memorial jewelry specifically for the bereaved. Some of their designs incorporate inspirational poetry, and others can be customized with photos and other mementos of your loved one.

You can also wear memorial jewelry that either contains a small portion of the cremated remains of your loved one in some sort of pendant or whose gemstone is actually made from your loved one's carbon. (These options definitely aren't my cup of tea, but to each his own.)

Cremation jewelry usually comes in the form of a strung pendant that opens to store a small portion of your loved one's cremated remains. The pendants are available in a number of different designs, including crystals and those that look like tiny funeral urns.

Gemstones containing your loved one's carbon can be created either from the cremated remains or, if the loved one was buried, from a lock of his hair. Called LifeGems, these gemstones are synthetic diamonds made from some of the graphite of your loved one's carbon. They're available in a variety of hues (including blue, red, green, yellow, and colorless) and faceted cuts. You can have these diamonds set in a ring, pendant, or bracelet of your own design. For more information on LifeGem memorials, visit the LifeGem Created Diamonds Web site at www.lifegem.com.

Designing and planting memorial gardens

If you have a yard, you can design and plant your own memorial garden for your deceased loved one. This garden should definitely include the types of flowers and other plant life that were special to your loved one. If you have the space, consider planting a tree to be the focus and the heart of the garden.

In addition to the flora in your loved one's memorial garden, you can add other personal touches to the garden, including:

- ✔ Statuary or fountains placed at strategic places in the garden to enhance its features. The statues can be anything from likenesses of Jesus, the

Virgin Mary, Buddha, or your loved one's favorite animal to abstract designs that mean something to you.

✔ Benches to sit on as you and others enjoy the garden and remember and commune with your loved one.

✔ Commemorative plaques containing your loved one's name and dates or favorite inspirational sayings and symbols of good fortune.

✔ Flagstones used to create pathways through the garden. You can make personalized flagstones with stepping-stone kits available in most home improvement or garden stores. You also can use specially designed flagstones with inspirational sayings or special symbols.

✔ Stones that you arrange to mark off certain areas of the garden. These can be left natural or decorated with sayings, symbols, and dedications for your loved one.

Posting a virtual memorial

Virtual memorials are memorials that you place online within special memorial Web sites. Typically, a virtual memorial contains vital information about your loved one as well as your dedication and remembrances. You also may include a photo of your loved one and images or artwork that you think appropriate or that bring you comfort.

The wonderful thing about virtual memorials is that they're so easy to share with friends and family (assuming that they have computers and Internet access). Most memorial Web sites make it really easy to send a link to your virtual memorial to anyone who has an e-mail address. The accessibility is really convenient if your family is spread out geographically, making it impossible to get them together for any other kind of memorial unveiling.

For more information on virtual memorials and to visit some sites to see first-hand the kind of memorials you can create for your loved one, type "online memorials" into your favorite Internet search engine.

Performing Memorial Ceremonies

A memorial ceremony can be as simple as gathering a group of friends and family members for a dinner honoring your lost loved one (featuring, of course, all his favorite foods) or as formal as a ceremony at the grave site marking the anniversary of the death.

The most formal memorial service, after the funeral itself, is one in which your commissioned grave-site monument or marker is set up and dedicated at the graveside. For some people, this is definitely a religious ceremony that officially marks the end of the formal mourning of a loved one (which often has little or nothing to do with the period of personal grieving). For others, the monument dedication simply offers an opportunity to pay your respects to the deceased loved one and visit the location chosen as his final resting place.

Memorial ceremonies are often timed to coincide with other holidays and celebrations (see Chapter 16), but they need not be. If you've established a grief shrine or a memorial garden for your loved one, you can conduct a memorial service anytime the spirit moves you. Long after you finish conducting your own grief rituals (see Chapter 14), you can still conduct your own informal memorial ceremonies that honor your loved one and enable you to recall his great qualities and contributions to your life.

Undertaking a Living Legacy of Service

Beyond the remembrances, memorials, and ceremonies that you can create for your deceased loved one, you also can keep his memory alive by creating a living legacy of service. Here are two easy ways to create a legacy of service that honors the memory of your loved one:

- ✔ Volunteer at a nonprofit organization or in a community service that you believe in or your loved one supported in life.
- ✔ Donate to the causes and charities that your loved one supported (always make your donations in his name).

Giving back not only enables you to reconnect with your local community but also enables you to continue supporting the organizations and causes that your loved one championed.

In supporting the organizations and continuing to advance the causes dear to your loved one's heart, you honor his choices in life. Best of all, you get to give something back to others in your community in his name, thus reminding both you and them of his best qualities.

Part V
The Part of Tens

In this part . . .

Traditionally, the Part of Tens contains various and sundry pieces of useful information related to the main theme of the book, and this Part of Tens is no exception. I give you tons of practical advice in the form of the top ten clichés about grieving that you should avoid at all costs, the top ten ways to help someone you care about who's grieving, as well as the top ten online resources to consult for even more information and support. Finally, this part concludes with ten meditations related to grief that you, as someone grieving the loss of a loved one, can do both to give meaning to the loss and mitigate its effects.

Chapter 20

Top Ten Clichés about Grieving

I wish the number of useless and often hurtful platitudes that bereaved people have to contend with were limited to just ten. Unfortunately, in the name of helping (and often simultaneously deflecting their own discomfort with death), well-meaning clergy, counselors, friends, and other family members have many more than just my top ten dreadful clichés about grieving up their sleeves.

So, if you're grieving the profound loss of a loved one, you need to prepare yourself to hear the following top ten horrible clichés (or variations on their themes) and more. And if you're trying to support a grieving friend or family member, you need to think twice about giving such simple, trite advice.

What makes these platitudes so hurtful is that they're usually delivered by caring people with the best intentions. Ironically, some of these little beauties actually may be true, but I think that the biggest problem with them is that their timing is all wrong. To be supported in grief, bereaved people really only need to hear two simple messages over and over again, delivered in as many different ways as possible:

✔ You're not going crazy — grief just hurts that much.

✔ You will be okay. This agony is going to end someday.

No matter how true and well-intentioned, any other message you deliver to a bereaved person soon after a loss is actually pretty counterproductive. Someday, when the grieving person has had adequate time to process and integrate the loss, hearing some of these platitudes may be helpful (well, at the very least, not hurtful), but now just isn't the right time.

One last thing about these clichés: Most are intended to turn the grieving person away from his feelings of sorrow rather than help him give voice to and fully express them. If you truly want to help, be really open to this expression and be able to listen to it. (See Chapter 21 for more suggestions on how to help someone who's grieving.)

I Know How You Feel

My gut-level response to the first cliché, "I know how you feel," is "Oh no you don't. How can you possibly think you know how I'm feeling when most of the time I don't even know how I'm feeling?"

I guess this platitude is meant to bring comfort by having the speaker identify with the grieving person he's addressing. Unfortunately, it's not really empathetic or compassionate in the best sense. For one thing, it turns the spotlight on the speaker and away from the griever, which is just the opposite of where the focus needs to be if you really want to support your bereaved friend.

The sentiment behind this cliché is essentially a good one. However, its delivery needs some work. I suggest that rather than state what you know, you question the grieving person about his feelings in this manner: "I can only imagine what you're going through. I'm here to find out how you're doing if you want to tell me."

You're Never Given Anything That You Can't Deal With

This is a pious platitude that many people — not only clergy — use to try to comfort you when you're grieving. But as Rabbi Harold Kushner so eloquently explains in his little gem of a book, *When Bad Things Happen to Good People* (Avon Books), this expression is actually one that can be hurtful to a bereaved person's faith in God.

It's intended to help a bereaved person of faith feel better by telling him (in a theologically inept way) that he's strong enough to pull through this terrible grief. However, instead of comforting him, hearing this platitude is more likely to make him wish that he weren't so strong on the faulty assumption that if he were too weak to bear the grief, then God wouldn't have taken his loved one away.

This cliché is especially dangerous because newly bereaved people often try to find ways to blame themselves for the death of their loved ones. Unfortunately, the misguided logic of this platitude can play right into a bereaved person's sense of responsibility, and that only delays his grieving the loss and makes his grief work a lot harder.

If your aim is to let a bereaved friend know that he'll ultimately get through this terrible grief even if that notion seems ludicrous now, you can accomplish it in a better way. Simply let your friend know that it's your understanding (from your reading, if not from your own personal experience) that the loss of a loved one almost always feels like it's too much to bear, but in all but a very few cases, people do survive the sorrow. Further, let your friend know that you're here for him as a sounding board and a shoulder to cry on as long as he needs you.

Time Heals All Wounds

This little truism seems to be the one that gets trotted out whenever you suffer a loss of any kind, not just the death of a loved one. And like a lot of the other clichés in this chapter, it's based on a half-truth.

Time is indeed necessary for healing profound grief — in most cases, you need lots more time than people are normally willing to grant you. But (and it's a big BUT, as Pee-Wee Herman was wont to say) it's not the passage of time that heals the grief; that job, like it or not, is one that only you can do for yourself.

Grieving is your own unique journey in search of ways to make peace with the loss of your loved one. Although grieving unfolds in time, it's totally your responsibility and work to do. This process is all yours to help along or impede as you're able and best see fit.

Rather than telling a bereaved person that time heals all wounds, you would do better to let him know you understand that grieving takes time while at the same time reminding him that eventually the intensity of the sorrow will lessen as part of this process.

Don't Dwell on It

I don't know of any sillier grieving platitude than this one. After all, isn't grieving all about dwelling on it, the terrible loss you've suffered? In fact, dwelling on it may be the only thing you still feel capable of doing in the wake of the upheaval you've just endured.

Instead of hurling this kind of veiled criticism upon a bereaved friend or family member, ask if there's anything he can think of that may give him a temporary but much-needed respite from his grief. Taking some time off to recharge during this very stressful time is often quite a boon to the overall grieving process rather than a betrayal of it.

Don't Feel Bad

Well, if you're not supposed to feel bad about the loss of your loved one, how are you supposed to feel? How about enraged, distraught, or dispossessed? Just wait a little while in your grieving and I pretty much guarantee that you'll feel all these emotions as well.

This dumb cliché is just a second-rate version of "Don't dwell on it" (refer to the preceding section) and a poor relation of "It's time to move on" (see the next section).

"Don't feel bad" is one of those expressions whose motive is more than a little suspect; it says, in essence, that you shouldn't be such a downer because I find it upsetting. This sentiment is simply no way to support someone whom you care about and whom you want to support. Just don't say this or anything like it to someone who's grieving the loss of a loved one. Enough said.

It's Time for You to Move On

This second cliché about time (the first is "Time heals all wounds"; see that section earlier in the chapter for more) is a bit trickier than it may seem at first glance. There will come a time when it may actually be time for you to move on, and, at that time, it may be quite correct for someone to tell you so.

However, if you tell a grieving loved one to move on — essentially telling him to get over his grieving — before he's ready and able to do so, you aren't helping him with a thing. Instead, you run the risk of alienating your friend precisely at a time when he needs you and your support the most.

The message behind this platitude is probably best conveyed to a bereaved person by his grief counselor or psychologist (one who's well-versed in end-of-life issues) rather than by a close friend. Professional counselors have the training needed to gauge when a client's grieving is stuck and when it's high time for him to move the process along to its conclusion.

It's Probably All for the Best

This grieving cliché has my vote as the most tasteless of the top ten. It's full of a kind of sham piety, and, worse, it hints at a kind of omniscience to which few, if any, are really privy. However, the real reason this particular cliché is so tacky is that whether or not the words are true makes absolutely no difference to the bereaved.

It doesn't matter if you agree with the sentiment; for example, your loved one suffered greatly for a very long time, so his passing gives you a certain amount of relief tied in with the grief. This fact still doesn't mitigate the loss and mean that you grieve his death any less.

When someone actually meets the passing of a loved one with some sense of relief, there's always the danger that such feelings will fuel a real sense of guilt that can make grieving more difficult. For this reason, if you know the death of your friend's loved one was anticipated for some time and brought a certain sense of relief, you're playing with fire if you voice any sentiment close to this platitude's.

It's in the Natural Order of Things

Of course death is part of the natural order of things, just as love is. But if death and love are part of the natural order of things, grieving the death and missing the loved one must be as well.

Telling a bereaved person that profound loss and grief are just part of the mix (a sentiment of which I'm guilty of expressing in a few places in this book) isn't really telling him anything new. It's only the least little bit helpful if you also tell him that grieving the loss is a natural part of love (a message that I also try to get across in a number of places).

This cliché also carries an underlying implication that isn't benign: Because loss is a natural part of the world, you should basically adopt a stoic attitude whereby you suck up the pain and get on with your life. That's certainly not the message you want to give or receive about grieving. In other words, you need to stop reminding those around you that suffering this greatly is a part of everyone's fate.

He Lived a Full Life

You probably won't hear this cliché unless your loved one lived a fairly long life and, hopefully, one in which he was able to accomplish almost everything he set his sights on. Although the sentiment of this platitude isn't as grating and insensitive as some of the others in this chapter, it's still not particularly helpful.

The negative implication is that you shouldn't grieve so much because your loved one had such a long and rich life. You have to admit that, on the surface anyway, this logic seems sound. After all, it would appear as though the death of a loved one blessed with a long and productive life wouldn't be nearly as difficult to accept as the death of a loved one in the prime of his life. However, that logic doesn't hold up upon closer inspection; after all, the longer you spend with a loved one, the more you miss him and the more difficult it is to make the adjustments necessary to live without him.

I think that you can express the more-positive sentiment carried by this platitude in a way that actually helps support a grieving friend. All you have to do is say something like "Although you must miss your loved one terribly, you might take some comfort in the fact that he lived such a long and happy life. And, although they may not bring you much comfort right now, the memories of all the great times you shared together will surely one day become for you a source of great support and continued joy."

Be Grateful You Had Him with You for So Long

This cliché is one that friends usually don't burden you with unless your loved one lived to a ripe old age before he passed on. (If you hear anything like this from so-called friends when your loved one perished well before his time, then you definitely need to get yourself some new friends.)

I definitely feel as though you should be grateful for every single day you get to spend with your loved ones, so I don't have any problem with the idea of expressing gratitude for being blessed by love. However, I don't know how an outsider can judge when you've had sufficient time with your lost loved one or shared enough love with another, so I do have a problem with the idea that you ought to express thanks for the amount of time you end up getting to be together.

Hopeless romantic that I am, I feel as though love should go on forever and ever (actually, I make it clear in Chapters 18 and 19 that I think love *does* go on forever or, at the very least, lives on beyond being parted from your loved ones in this lifetime). The genuine gratitude for the time you get to spend with a loved one isn't something that can be foisted upon you by some dumb cliché. This feeling of gratefulness comes in its own time as the pain from the loss gives way to an appreciation for what you shared.

If you're the least little bit tempted to voice anything close to this sentiment to a friend grieving the loss of a loved one, do yourself and your friend a big favor and put a sock in it. Any appreciation for the duration of the relationship *has* to come from your bereaved friend in his own time and way. Any attempt to suggest that this sense of gratitude will somehow help heal the grief is simply a case of putting the cart before the horse. Fully grieving the loss leads to the sense of gratitude, not vice versa.

Chapter 21

Top Ten Ways to Help Someone Who's Grieving

. . . .

In This Chapter

▶ Being present and supportive

▶ Knowing what not to say or do

▶ Offering comfort through touch

. . . .

*T*his chapter gives you some quick and easy-to-follow ideas for what to say and do if you're trying to support a bereaved friend or family member. Many people are uncomfortable in this role, especially if they haven't had any firsthand experience with grieving themselves. But all it takes to handle the situation with poise and grace is a little preparation and sensitivity.

 The good news about trying to support someone who's grieving is that you don't have to do anything special. You just have to be available and be yourself. You aren't responsible for your friend's feelings (that's his job), and you don't have to be able to offer him helpful advice or dispense any great wisdom about life and death or the way the world should work (that's my job). All you need is genuine empathy for your friend's plight and a willingness to support him.

Just Listen

Possibly the best way to help a bereaved friend is simply to be open to listening to all he has to express. I need to warn you straight up, however, that this isn't always as easy as it sounds. Depending upon your friend's personality and the depth of his grief, just listening actually can end up being quite challenging.

In the context of grief, listening doesn't merely mean paying attention to the words that your friend is saying or the emotions he's displaying; it also means paying attention to *how* he's saying and showing them.

This kind of listening also involves responding to what your friend expresses. The only caveat I have for you is that you try not to respond with a purely abstract opinion or some ready-made response you found in some old rule or etiquette book (see the section "Dump Clichés and Worn-Out Platitudes," later in this chapter for more on this point).

Respond from your heart and from your own experience. And if you don't have any experience to draw upon, don't try to gild the lily and push yourself to say something that you *think* might be helpful or sound wise. If you don't know, say you don't know. And if you don't understand something, ask for clarification. Asking questions is sometimes one of the best ways to help someone express his feelings and work through grieving issues.

Many bereaved people have a deep need to repeat certain grief feelings or some part of their stories with their lost loved ones. Sometimes, hearing the same thing over and over again can be very trying, to say the least. If you find yourself getting fatigued and having more and more trouble actually listening to something that you've heard before, it's probably a sign that it's time to find other ways to support your friend and get other people to help. (Chapter 14 has information on getting professional grieving help.)

Don't Worry about Saying the Wrong Thing

One of the biggest concerns that people often have in supporting their bereaved friends is the uncertainty that comes from not knowing the right thing to say. The good news is that there is no right thing to say. After all, what can you say to someone who's grieving the death of a loved one other than you're so sorry that he's had this loss and has to go through this pain?

Even if you say something awkward or trite (see Chapter 20 for ten good examples), you needn't worry. As long as it's clear that your words come from a place of love, you're not sitting in judgment of your friend's feelings (see the section "Hold Any Judgments," later in this chapter), and you're not trying to influence the course of his grieving (see the later section "Don't Push an Agenda"), a few grieving faux pas on your part don't matter all that much.

Be Okay with Having Nothing to Say

Sometimes it's enough just to be with someone you care about. Sitting in silence, however, is sometimes very uncomfortable and much more challenging than trying to find the right thing to say.

There may be times when your bereaved friend doesn't really want to talk about the grief or doesn't have anything much to say. During those times, try to remember that you don't have to fill the silence.

Spending some time together quietly may be all your grieving friend needs from you. Moreover, he'll probably appreciate the fact that he isn't feeling pressured to speak when he doesn't want to, and he'll be very relieved that you're comfortable to be with him in stillness.

Be Honest

This suggestion may sound obvious, but people tend to forget. Being honest is simply the most effective way for you to keep the lines of communication open, encouraging the friend you want to support to fully express his feelings.

Remaining honest with a close friend in the midst of actively grieving a loss, however, is sometimes a lot trickier than remaining honest with him under normal, optimal conditions. Because your friend's emotions are probably more volatile than usual, you may find yourself editing your responses before you make them in an attempt to ensure that they don't aggravate or challenge him in any way.

A bit of extra sensitivity on your part is fine provided that it doesn't go so far as to impede candid communication between the two of you. If your friend starts to feel that your responses to his expressions of emotion are not genuine in any way, he unconsciously may start reining in the emotions that he feels make you uncomfortable.

Although this kind of self-checking between friends may be fine under normal conditions, it's not at all what you want to cultivate in a period of grieving. Your grieving friend really needs to be able to express any and all his emotions (the conflicting ones as well as those that seem downright contradictory). This free expression is a vital part of the process of working out what the loss means to him and figuring out how he'll eventually reconcile with it.

Hold Any Judgments

You may have one of those really tight friendships where you freely give your friend advice on every subject under the sun from general appearance to romantic relationships. But this is one time when you need to drop the usual role of an intimate counselor and hold back on giving all that free advice.

Grieving is one of the most personal and individual journeys that anyone will ever take. Advice on how to handle grief may work just fine for one person but not at all for the next person. Moreover, grieving is one of those journeys of self-discovery in which the lasting breakthroughs and changes almost always come directly out of one's own experience with his grief rather than from the knowledge and experience of others.

If you come up with a great idea of something you think your friend should definitely try or steer clear of while grieving, don't deliver this information to your bereaved friend in the form of advice. Instead, open up a dialogue on the subject by questioning your friend's feelings about the idea. By asking him if he's ever considered a particular course of action or how he feels about it rather than telling him to follow that course, you broach the subject while avoiding the risk of making him defensive and interfering with his grieving process.

Dump Clichés and Worn-Out Platitudes

If you take a quick gander at the list of crass clichés I put in Chapter 20, you see that quite a few expressions that you may have thought would cause no offense and may actually be helpful to grieving folks are, in fact, not helpful and may even be somewhat offensive.

My recommendation here is that, as much as is humanly possible, you drop all old sayings, truisms, and the like when trying to support a grieving friend. You don't need to resort to somebody else's kitchen wisdom to speak with a good friend about the hard times he's facing.

In place of other people's so-called wise sayings, I suggest that you speak from your heart and your own personal experience.

If you don't have a lot of personal experience with profound loss, don't worry about it. Instead of making up stuff, admit that you lack experience and knowledge. Then use that admission as an opportunity to ask your friend questions about his feelings and the issues he's dealing with at the moment. Doing this can show that you're genuinely interested in learning from your friend's current experience.

Don't Try to Fix It

The normal reaction to seeing anyone in pain is to want to jump in and make it all better — there's a little bit of mother in everyone. This is one time, however, when you should definitely back off and make no attempt whatsoever at setting right the situation. This means you don't have to come up with things calculated to make the person feel better by taking his mind off the grief. This also means you don't have to try to figure out what this person needs to do to get over his grief or to make the process smoother.

The pain that your bereaved friend feels over the loss is an integral part of his grieving process. If you try to get in there and fix his sorrow and take it all away, you're robbing him of his necessary feelings. It's inappropriate, especially after he's already been robbed of his loved one. So, although it may be difficult to hold back and not try to make all your friend's grief disappear, that's exactly what you need to do.

Be Mindful of the Effects of Touch

Touch, as a form of reassurance and a token of the love you feel for your bereaved friend, is really important and, in most situations, greatly appreciated. However, you need to be mindful of the effect that your touch can have on your bereaved friend, especially when he's in the midst of expressing deep sorrow.

Sometimes just lightly touching a grieving person is all it takes to make him break down in sobs. Other times, when he's just about to break down or has just started crying, lightly touching him shuts the weeping down completely. Assuming that you neither want to bring on the waterworks or stop them cold, be terribly judicious with your touch whenever your friend is in the midst of expressing deep emotion. That's not to say that there won't be times when you need to get in there and hold your friend for all you're worth. Just check with your friend first to see what he needs and feels would bring the most comfort.

On some occasions, your friend may actually need you to hold him throughout an emotional upsurge. Be aware when you do this that many people feel their grief emotions deep in their bellies. Your friend may therefore find it more comforting if you put your arms around him from the back and hold his midsection tightly (this is best done with both of you sitting on the floor). Rocking together is also often very comforting. Again, you always should check with your friend to find out whether and how he wants to be held before you touch him. Remember, he can always answer your yes or no questions with a nod of his head even if he's too choked up to respond to your questions in words.

Try Not to Change the Subject

Listening to someone you deeply care about agonize over the death of his loved one can be really quite difficult (I'm talking excruciating here). A typical reaction is to immediately try to change the subject in hopes of moving your friend away from whatever's causing him so much pain, thus making both you and him feel better.

As natural as this reaction to move your friend on to a lighter subject may be, it's not a good way to respond to this situation. Although you don't want to force any emotion, you most definitely don't ever want to shut that expression down. After all, the main way to support your friend in his grieving is to provide an open, nonjudgmental space in which he's free to express anything and everything.

If you're having a really hard time staying on track with your friend through a particular emotional upsurge, take a moment to breathe deeply and remember that you're neither responsible for his grief nor responsible for making it go away. Then, take a new look at your friend and make another attempt at staying present with the emotions he's expressing. If you find that you're overcome by his emotions, let him know that and then give in to them. Being overcome with emotion may be one of those occasions when holding each other (after checking that it's okay with your friend; see the preceding section) can do a world of good for both of you.

Don't Push an Agenda

Everyone wishes that they could just wave their magic wands and make all the pain related to their friends' grief instantly go away. But the worst thing you can do for a bereaved friend is to try to impose on him your agenda for how he should get through and over his grief.

Given that it's not possible (and not advisable) to speed a friend through his grieving process, the best thing you can do to support him is to give him all the time and space that he needs to get the grieving job done. Remember the following things about grieving the loss of a loved one:

- ✔ Grieving is a natural human process.
- ✔ Grieving is an intensely personal emotional journey.
- ✔ Grieving proceeds at its own pace.

- ✔ Grieving moves in its own course.
- ✔ Grieving advances are often nonlinear.
- ✔ Grieving eventually comes to an end.

Only the bereaved person can figure out when his grieving has come to its end. Like most other major transformational processes that people undergo, the process responds to outside pressures but isn't really guided by them. Also, grieving is such a subjective and self-directed process that it's very difficult, if not impossible, for someone other than the person grieving to decide its direction.

Chapter 22

Top Ten or So Online Bereavement Resources

In This Chapter

▶ Seeking out information on grieving

▶ Exploring message boards

▶ Checking out bereavement camps for kids

The Internet is a great source of information on grieving as well as actual support. Check out the following recommended Web sites to get an idea of what's out there in terms of suggestions on how to handle particular losses as well as assistance in grieving them.

The International Center for Attitudinal Healing

www.attitudinalhealing.org

The International Center for Attitudinal Healing is an organization with which I'm very familiar, having been a volunteer for their Home and Hospital Visiting program for a number of years. The center is where I learned firsthand the power of active listening (see Chapter 13), a tool for supporting people changing their attitudes toward their circumstances by freely telling their stories.

The center is founded on the notions that

✔ People are capable of making constructive changes by consciously modifying their approaches to their particular circumstances.

✔ People are capable of supporting one another in making those changes.

Its many service programs offered free to the public are based on a peer support model.

The center, whose main office is located in Sausalito, California, has affiliated centers all around the world. It also offers training and intern programs to help people replicate the Attitudinal Healing model in their own communities.

The Bereavement Journey

www.thebereavementjourney.com

The Bereavement Journey Web site offers online support for anyone grieving the loss of a loved one. This site includes a link to a chat room where you share your story as well as a message board where you can post an online memorial for your loved one.

Hospice Net: Bereavement

www.hospicenet.org/html/bereavement.html

The Bereavement page of the Hospice Net Web site contains all sorts of links to articles on grieving. These cover such topics as a general guide to grief, children and teen grieving, suggestions for healing after loss, and a collection of stories about death and dying.

Living with Loss Magazine and Bereavement Publications

www.bereavementmag.com

This is the Web site for *Living with Loss* magazine (previously known as *Bereavement*). The site contains links for subscribing to the magazine as well as for various online articles. You also can find links for purchasing their Seasons of Grief calendar as well as grief-related cards, books, videos, and audiotapes.

The Bereavement Group

groups.msn.com/bereavement

The Bereavement Group Web site is the place to visit if you're interested either in posting your feelings about your loss and grief or in sharing your story with others who are also mourning losses of their own. Note that you must have a valid e-mail address in order to join the Bereavement Group.

Bereavement.org

www.bereavement.org

This page contains links to a wide variety of different bereavement Web sites. They run the gamut from a site for sending same-day flowers to someone who has just experienced a profound loss and purchasing personalized sympathy cards all the way to books on grieving that you can purchase on Amazon.com.

Bereavement Camps

www.kidscamps.com/special_needs/bereavement.html

The Bereavement Camps Web page enables you to search for a bereavement camp in your local area. These camps are great places for children and adolescents who have lost parents to share their feelings and experiences with others going through similar trials. Camp also is a great opportunity for kids to reconnect with nature and get some much-needed respite from grief.

Coping with Loss: Guide to Grieving and Bereavement

www.helpguide.org/mental/grief_loss.htm

This Web page contains a really good online article on how to cope with loss in all its manifestations and stages. It also contains valuable information on dealing with loss due to suicide.

Frequently Asked Questions on Grief and Grieving

www.davidkessler.org/html/qa_grief.html

This site created by David Kessler, a noted author of several books on grieving, contains an array of links to articles and informational lists on bereavement. You'll find links to all kinds of information on grief and grieving in question-and-answer, helpful-hints, and article formats.

AARP: Grief and Loss

www.aarp.org/families/grief_loss

The Grief and Loss page of the AARP Web site contains links to all sorts of useful articles for people who have lost loved ones. These articles cover the necessary papers to have after the death, claiming your loved one's benefits, and the steps that you usually need to take in the months immediately following the loss.

GriefNet.org

www.griefnet.org

GriefNet is an Internet community with support resources for both kids and adults grieving a profound loss. This site also offers a variety of online support groups where you can share experiences and online memorials that you can create to honor your lost loved one and tell your story.

Chapter 23

Ten Meditations Related to Grief

In This Chapter

▶ Focusing on breathing

▶ Working through visualizations

▶ Re-experiencing your lost loved one

▶ Letting love fill your whole body

A *meditation,* as I use the term here, refers to a devotion in which you quietly reflect upon a particular theme for some period of time. In the case of grief, you contemplate subjects specifically linked to grieving the loss of a loved one.

All the meditations in this chapter are *guided meditations,* meaning that the text directs you through each step of the contemplation. Of course, you can deviate from the suggestions in the text at any time.

The purpose of these meditations is to help you process the pain and sorrow as you reflect upon the nature of your loss. In so doing, hopefully you come closer to understanding the wider meaning of the loss to your life and reconciling yourself with it. If you perform your own grief rituals as suggested in Chapter 14, you can easily incorporate any of these meditations into the heart of your ceremonies.

To get the most out of these meditations, undertake them in a quiet place only when you have a specific block of time (five to ten minutes should do) when you can remain undisturbed. To help your contemplation, dress comfortably, sit at ease in a comfortable chair or on a pillow, and have a picture of your loved one on display nearby. If you feel it would help, light a candle or burn incense before you begin each meditation. Finally, if you've set up some sort of grief shrine or memorial in your home, you should conduct these meditations in front of that shrine.

Breathing through Your Pain

This meditation is designed to help you remain present in light of the pain and sorrow you're feeling. It uses concentration on the breath as the primary means for remaining in the moment. The meditation is recommended for those times when you need some respite from the sorrow, and it may help you stave off an upsurge of sorrow.

1. **Visualize your loved one, and feel the love you shared.**

2. **Focus your attention on your shoulders as you settle down comfortably into your seat. Then lower your shoulders and let any tension you feel roll off them.**

3. **Close your eyes or just soften your gaze as you lower your head just a little.**

4. **Exhale slowly, letting all the air out of your lungs. Wait a moment before taking your next inhalation.**

5. **Inhale slowly and completely. As you breathe in, imagine that you're taking in the affection offered by your loved one with the fresh air.**

6. **Exhale slowly and completely. As you breathe out, imagine that you're expelling all the pain you feel with the stale air.**

7. **Repeat Steps 5 and 6 until you feel ready to stop the meditation. Then slowly open your eyes wide and look at the picture of your loved one.**

8. **To conclude the meditation, thank your loved one for all his caring, and rise slowly from your seat.**

Softening Your Aching Heart

Grieving people often feel a palpable ache around the heart as a part of their sorrow. This meditation is designed to help you release the tension you may have around the heart.

1. **Visualize your loved one, and feel the love you shared.**

2. **Relax your body as you settle down comfortably in your seat. Then breathe deeply, putting your awareness on both the inhalation and exhalation.**

3. **Focus your awareness on the tension you feel in your chest, especially around the heart.**

4. Picture the tension you feel across your chest as ice crystals that formed around your heart.

5. Fix your attention on your heartbeat as you breathe in and out, slowly and completely.

6. Imagine that each inhalation brings in warmth that radiates out from your heart and each exhalation expels coldness that appears as vapor.

7. Imagine warmth spreading out from your heart across your chest in every direction as you continue to breathe, melting all the ice crystals and dissolving the tension.

8. To conclude the meditation, thank your loved one for all his caring, and rise slowly from your seat.

Reflecting on the Universal Nature of Change

Like it or not, change is the one constant of the world. This meditation is designed to help you reflect on the all-encompassing nature of change in your own life by looking at your own transformations from childhood to adulthood.

1. Visualize your loved one, and feel the love you shared.

2. Relax your body as you settle down comfortably in your seat. Then breathe deeply, putting your awareness on both the inhalation and exhalation.

3. Picture the first place you can remember living. Reflect on the feelings that arise as you remember the layout and objects in this home. Name the predominant feeling that you associate with this memory.

4. In your mind's eye, see the first celebration of your birthday that you can recall. Reflect on the feelings that arise when you recall this event. Name the predominant feeling that you associate with this memory.

5. See yourself in your mind's eye at age 5, 10, 15, and 20. Note the predominant feeling that comes to mind as you recall each of these tender ages.

6. Recall the first day you went to work. Reflect on the feelings that arise when you remember this first day and first job. Name the predominant feeling that you associate with this memory.

7. Picture the first person with whom you fell in love. Reflect on the feelings that arise when you remember him. Name the predominant feeling that you associate with this memory.

8. Picture the place where you currently live, your last birthday celebration, your current job, and finally yourself at your current age (assuming that you're over 20). Compare your current conditions to the earlier ones, and note which feelings have changed and which ones haven't.

9. To conclude the meditation, thank your loved one for all his caring, and rise slowly from your seat.

Considering the Widespread Nature of Loss

Loss, like change, is a constant factor in life. This meditation is designed to help you see the universal nature of loss by considering losses you've suffered in your life that are completely unrelated to the one you're currently grieving. Its purpose is to remind you that you've already weathered and successfully integrated many losses before this one.

1. Visualize your loved one, and feel the love you shared.

2. Relax your body as you settle down comfortably in your seat. Then breathe deeply, putting your awareness on both the inhalation and exhalation.

3. Think back to the first time that you lost an object precious to you as a child.

4. Think back to the first time you remember finding out that something you were taught as a child wasn't true, such as the truth about Santa Claus or a myth about a family member.

5. Recall every time in your life that you moved to a new home, regardless of whether you made the move willingly or unwillingly.

6. Recall every job you've had in your life, regardless of how long you held the job.

7. Recall every time a love affair you had didn't work out, regardless of whether you broke up with your lover or vice versa.

8. Reflect upon your ability to suffer all these remembered losses and yet still survive to this point.

9. To conclude the meditation, thank your loved one for all his caring, and rise slowly from your seat.

Reflecting on the Timeless Aspect of Love

As I say elsewhere in this book, love doesn't end with the death of a loved one. This meditation is designed to help you reflect upon the aspects of love you shared with your lost loved one so that you can keep these qualities with you as you grieve.

1. **Relax your body as you settle down comfortably in your seat. Then breathe deeply, putting your awareness on both the inhalation and exhalation.**

2. **Recall the first time you saw your loved one's face.**

3. **Bask in the good feeling that the memory of this encounter brings you.**

4. **Recall an instance of a timeless moment with your loved one, that is, an occasion when you lost all track of the time you spent together.**

5. **Bask in the memory of this timeless moment with your loved one.**

6. **Recall the love and affection that your loved one gave you.**

7. **Bask in the good feeling that the memory of this love brings you.**

8. **Imagine all the good feelings of these memories combining into a warm glow that then slowly moves out from your heart to permeate and warm every part of your body.**

9. **To conclude this meditation, thank your loved one for all his caring, and rise slowly from your seat.**

Practicing Lovingkindness

The preceding meditation on the timelessness of love should fill you with the warmth of your loved one's deep affection. This meditation enables you to take that feeling of love and imagine sharing it with all others.

1. **Relax your body as you settle down comfortably in your seat. Then breathe deeply, putting your awareness on both the inhalation and exhalation.**

2. **Recall your loved one and the love you shared.**

3. **Visualize this love as a ball of warm, red light that radiates in all directions as it floats in front of you like a balloon.**

4. Imagine this ball of light growing large enough to encompass you and your entire home.

5. Imagine this ball of light growing large enough to encompass your entire community.

6. Picture all the people in your community smiling big smiles and feeling good as they're engulfed by this loving red light.

7. Imagine the ball of light growing large enough to encompass and hold the entire earth.

8. Picture all the people in the world smiling and feeling at peace as they're engulfed by this loving red light.

9. Imagine the ball of loving light contracting until it once again is the size it was when you first visualized it floating in front of you (refer to Step 3).

10. Imagine that the loving light from this ball now merges with you and settles in your heart.

11. To conclude the meditation, thank your loved one for all his caring, and rise slowly from your seat.

Holding a Lost Loved One in Your Heart

This is one of my all-time favorite meditations. In it, you visualize the loved one you've lost sitting quite comfortably in the center of an open flower that resides in the center of your heart, radiating feelings of love in all directions.

1. Relax your body as you settle down comfortably in your seat. Then breathe deeply, putting your awareness on both the inhalation and exhalation.

2. Visualize a white lotus flower or rose. Note that this flower is closed tightly; each of its petals is in an upright position.

3. Gazing on the lotus or rose, you notice the petals of the flower begin to open slowly and completely. As all the petals unfold, you notice a figure seated comfortably in the middle of the flower. This figure is encompassed by a brilliant white light that radiates in all directions from the center of the lotus.

4. Continuing to gaze on the open flower and the radiant figure in its midst, you begin to recognize the figure's features as those of your loved one. Looking more closely at the seated figure, you notice that your loved one is beaming a big smile at you and is totally at peace.

5. Visualize the open flower with the radiant figure of your loved one as entering your heart and coming to rest there.

6. Feel the white light from your radiant loved one permeate every part of your body.

7. To conclude the meditation, thank your loved one for all his caring, and rise slowly from your seat.

Extending Your Compassion to All

The preceding meditation involving a lotus flower lodges your loved one comfortably in your heart, and this meditation takes that contemplation a step further by helping you share this love by extending compassion to all other beings.

1. Relax your body as you settle down comfortably in your seat. Then breathe deeply, putting your awareness on both the inhalation and exhalation.

2. Visualize your loved one, and feel the love you shared in your heart as an intense white light that permeates your entire body.

3. Think about all the other family members and friends of your loved one who are grieving his loss. Extend the love you feel in your heart to all these people by visualizing the white light in your heart radiating out and expanding to encompass and enfold them.

4. Think about any other people you know who are currently grieving the loss of their loved ones. Extend the love you feel in your heart to all these people by visualizing the white light expanding further to encompass and enfold them.

5. Think about all the people you don't know who are currently grieving losses of loved ones. Extend the love you feel in your heart to all these people by visualizing the white light expanding even further to encompass and enfold all these folks.

6. Visualize this white light expanding to enfold all living creatures who are suffering for any reason.

7. Conclude this meditation by visualizing the white light contracting until it's condensed tightly in your heart.

8. Thank your loved one for his caring, and rise slowly from your seat.

Saying Your Goodbyes

This meditation is designed to help you if you feel as though you didn't get a chance to say goodbye to your loved one before his death. In it, you commune with your loved one to say all that you still feel needs to be said.

1. **Relax your body as you settle down comfortably in your seat. Then breathe deeply, putting your awareness on both the inhalation and exhalation.**

2. **Visualize your loved one as a radiant white figure sitting upon the open lotus in your heart (see "Holding a Lost Loved One in Your Heart," earlier for details).**

3. **Direct all the affection and caring you have for your loved one to your heart.**

4. **Speak to your heart, conveying to your loved one all the things that you wish you could have told him when he was still present in the flesh.**

5. **Commune with the loved one in your heart as long as you need to until you feel satisfied that you've conveyed all things you need to say.**

6. **Feel the white light from your heart permeate every part of your body.**

7. **To conclude the meditation, thank your loved one for his caring and rise slowly from your seat.**

Saying "Thank You" to Grief

This final meditation is intended solely for those who are near or at the end of their grieving and are very deeply involved in the process of reconciling the loss. If the very idea of being thankful for grief is repugnant to you, then you're not ready for this meditation and should definitely skip it and work on some of the other meditations in this chapter.

1. **Relax your body as you settle down comfortably in your seat. Then breathe deeply, putting your awareness on both the inhalation and exhalation.**

2. **Visualize your loved one, and feel the love you shared.**

3. In your mind's eye, review the most significant things that you learned from your relationship with your loved one. Then put your palms together and give thanks for those lessons.

4. In your mind's eye, review the important qualities that your loved one demonstrated and that you wish to emulate. Then put your palms together and give thanks for being exposed to those qualities.

5. In your mind's eye, review the positive transformations you've undergone as a result of grieving the loss of your loved one. Then put your palms together and give thanks for those changes.

6. In your mind's eye, visualize the pain of your loss as a ball of cold, impenetrable blackness that's congealed in your belly. Immediately visualize the white lotus in your heart opening and the intense white light with the love of your loved one dissipating all the darkness in your stomach as the light and its warmth spread to every part of your body.

7. Feel the warmth of the love you still share with your loved one as you conclude this meditation by thanking your loved one for all his caring, and rise slowly.

Index

• E •

BUSINESS, CAREERS & PERSONAL FINANCE

0-7645-9847-3   0-7645-2431-3

Also available:
- Business Plans Kit For Dummies
  0-7645-9794-9
- Economics For Dummies
  0-7645-5726-2
- Grant Writing For Dummies
  0-7645-8416-2
- Home Buying For Dummies
  0-7645-5331-3
- Managing For Dummies
  0-7645-1771-6
- Marketing For Dummies
  0-7645-5600-2

- Personal Finance For Dummies
  0-7645-2590-5*
- Resumes For Dummies
  0-7645-5471-9
- Selling For Dummies
  0-7645-5363-1
- Six Sigma For Dummies
  0-7645-6798-5
- Small Business Kit For Dummies
  0-7645-5984-2
- Starting an eBay Business For Dummies
  0-7645-6924-4
- Your Dream Career For Dummies
  0-7645-9795-7

HOME & BUSINESS COMPUTER BASICS

0-470-05432-8   0-471-75421-8

Also available:
- Cleaning Windows Vista For Dummies
  0-471-78293-9
- Excel 2007 For Dummies
  0-470-03737-7
- Mac OS X Tiger For Dummies
  0-7645-7675-5
- MacBook For Dummies
  0-470-04859-X
- Macs For Dummies
  0-470-04849-2
- Office 2007 For Dummies
  0-470-00923-3

- Outlook 2007 For Dummies
  0-470-03830-6
- PCs For Dummies
  0-7645-8958-X
- Salesforce.com For Dummies
  0-470-04893-X
- Upgrading & Fixing Laptops For Dummies
  0-7645-8959-8
- Word 2007 For Dummies
  0-470-03658-3
- Quicken 2007 For Dummies
  0-470-04600-7

FOOD, HOME, GARDEN, HOBBIES, MUSIC & PETS

0-7645-8404-9   0-7645-9904-6

Also available:
- Candy Making For Dummies
  0-7645-9734-5
- Card Games For Dummies
  0-7645-9910-0
- Crocheting For Dummies
  0-7645-4151-X
- Dog Training For Dummies
  0-7645-8418-9
- Healthy Carb Cookbook For Dummies
  0-7645-8476-6
- Home Maintenance For Dummies
  0-7645-5215-5

- Horses For Dummies
  0-7645-9797-3
- Jewelry Making & Beading For Dummies
  0-7645-2571-9
- Orchids For Dummies
  0-7645-6759-4
- Puppies For Dummies
  0-7645-5255-4
- Rock Guitar For Dummies
  0-7645-5356-9
- Sewing For Dummies
  0-7645-6847-7
- Singing For Dummies
  0-7645-2475-5

INTERNET & DIGITAL MEDIA

0-470-04529-9   0-470-04894-8

Also available:
- Blogging For Dummies
  0-471-77084-1
- Digital Photography For Dummies
  0-7645-9802-3
- Digital Photography All-in-One Desk Reference For Dummies
  0-470-03743-1
- Digital SLR Cameras and Photography For Dummies
  0-7645-9803-1
- eBay Business All-in-One Desk Reference For Dummies
  0-7645-8438-3
- HDTV For Dummies
  0-470-09673-X

- Home Entertainment PCs For Dummies
  0-470-05523-5
- MySpace For Dummies
  0-470-09529-6
- Search Engine Optimization For Dummies
  0-471-97998-8
- Skype For Dummies
  0-470-04891-3
- The Internet For Dummies
  0-7645-8996-2
- Wiring Your Digital Home For Dummies
  0-471-91830-X

* Separate Canadian edition also available
† Separate U.K. edition also available

Available wherever books are sold. For more information or to order direct: U.S. customers visit www.dummies.com or call 1-877-762-2974.
U.K. customers visit www.wileyeurope.com or call 0800 243407. Canadian customers visit www.wiley.ca or call 1-800-567-4797.

PORTS, FITNESS, PARENTING, RELIGION & SPIRITUALITY

0-471-76871-5

0-7645-7841-3

Also available:
- Catholicism For Dummies
  0-7645-5391-7
- Exercise Balls For Dummies
  0-7645-5623-1
- Fitness For Dummies
  0-7645-7851-0
- Football For Dummies
  0-7645-3936-1
- Judaism For Dummies
  0-7645-5299-6
- Potty Training For Dummies
  0-7645-5417-4
- Buddhism For Dummies
  0-7645-5359-3

- Pregnancy For Dummies
  0-7645-4483-7 †
- Ten Minute Tone-Ups For Dummies
  0-7645-7207-5
- NASCAR For Dummies
  0-7645-7681-X
- Religion For Dummies
  0-7645-5264-3
- Soccer For Dummies
  0-7645-5229-5
- Women in the Bible For Dummies
  0-7645-8475-8

TRAVEL

0-7645-7749-2

0-7645-6945-7

Also available:
- Alaska For Dummies
  0-7645-7746-8
- Cruise Vacations For Dummies
  0-7645-6941-4
- England For Dummies
  0-7645-4276-1
- Europe For Dummies
  0-7645-7529-5
- Germany For Dummies
  0-7645-7823-5
- Hawaii For Dummies
  0-7645-7402-7

- Italy For Dummies
  0-7645-7386-1
- Las Vegas For Dummies
  0-7645-7382-9
- London For Dummies
  0-7645-4277-X
- Paris For Dummies
  0-7645-7630-5
- RV Vacations For Dummies
  0-7645-4442-X
- Walt Disney World & Orlando
  For Dummies
  0-7645-9660-8

GRAPHICS, DESIGN & WEB DEVELOPMENT

0-7645-8815-X

0-7645-9571-7

Also available:
- 3D Game Animation For Dummies
  0-7645-8789-7
- AutoCAD 2006 For Dummies
  0-7645-8925-3
- Building a Web Site For Dummies
  0-7645-7144-3
- Creating Web Pages For Dummies
  0-470-08030-2
- Creating Web Pages All-in-One Desk
  Reference For Dummies
  0-7645-4345-8
- Dreamweaver 8 For Dummies
  0-7645-9649-7

- InDesign CS2 For Dummies
  0-7645-9572-5
- Macromedia Flash 8 For Dummies
  0-7645-9691-8
- Photoshop CS2 and Digital
  Photography For Dummies
  0-7645-9580-6
- Photoshop Elements 4 For Dummies
  0-471-77483-9
- Syndicating Web Sites with RSS Feeds
  For Dummies
  0-7645-8848-6
- Yahoo! SiteBuilder For Dummies
  0-7645-9800-7

NETWORKING, SECURITY, PROGRAMMING & DATABASES

0-7645-7728-X

0-471-74940-0

Also available:
- Access 2007 For Dummies
  0-470-04612-0
- ASP.NET 2 For Dummies
  0-7645-7907-X
- C# 2005 For Dummies
  0-7645-9704-3
- Hacking For Dummies
  0-470-05235-X
- Hacking Wireless Networks
  For Dummies
  0-7645-9730-2
- Java For Dummies
  0-470-08716-1

- Microsoft SQL Server 2005 For Dummies
  0-7645-7755-7
- Networking All-in-One Desk Reference
  For Dummies
  0-7645-9939-9
- Preventing Identity Theft For Dummies
  0-7645-7336-5
- Telecom For Dummies
  0-471-77085-X
- Visual Studio 2005 All-in-One Desk
  Reference For Dummies
  0-7645-9775-2
- XML For Dummies
  0-7645-8845-1

HEALTH & SELF-HELP

0-7645-8450-2

0-7645-4149-8

Also available:
- Bipolar Disorder For Dummies
  0-7645-8451-0
- Chemotherapy and Radiation
  For Dummies
  0-7645-7832-4
- Controlling Cholesterol For Dummies
  0-7645-5440-9
- Diabetes For Dummies
  0-7645-6820-5* †
- Divorce For Dummies
  0-7645-8417-0 †

- Fibromyalgia For Dummies
  0-7645-5441-7
- Low-Calorie Dieting For Dummies
  0-7645-9905-4
- Meditation For Dummies
  0-471-77774-9
- Osteoporosis For Dummies
  0-7645-7621-6
- Overcoming Anxiety For Dummies
  0-7645-5447-6
- Reiki For Dummies
  0-7645-9907-0
- Stress Management For Dummies
  0-7645-5144-2

EDUCATION, HISTORY, REFERENCE & TEST PREPARATION

0-7645-8381-6

0-7645-9554-7

Also available:
- The ACT For Dummies
  0-7645-9652-7
- Algebra For Dummies
  0-7645-5325-9
- Algebra Workbook For Dummies
  0-7645-8467-7
- Astronomy For Dummies
  0-7645-8465-0
- Calculus For Dummies
  0-7645-2498-4
- Chemistry For Dummies
  0-7645-5430-1
- Forensics For Dummies
  0-7645-5580-4

- Freemasons For Dummies
  0-7645-9796-5
- French For Dummies
  0-7645-5193-0
- Geometry For Dummies
  0-7645-5324-0
- Organic Chemistry I For Dummies
  0-7645-6902-3
- The SAT I For Dummies
  0-7645-7193-1
- Spanish For Dummies
  0-7645-5194-9
- Statistics For Dummies
  0-7645-5423-9

Get smart @ dummies.com®

- **Find a full list of Dummies titles**
- **Look into loads of FREE on-site articles**
- **Sign up for FREE eTips e-mailed to you weekly**
- **See what other products carry the Dummies name**
- **Shop directly from the Dummies bookstore**
- **Enter to win new prizes every month!**

* Separate Canadian edition also available
† Separate U.K. edition also available

Available wherever books are sold. For more information or to order direct: U.S. customers visit www.dummies.com or call 1-877-762-2974.
U.K. customers visit www.wileyeurope.com or call 0800 243407. Canadian customers visit www.wiley.ca or call 1-800-567-4797.